What contemporary playwrights are saying about
The Dramatists Guild Resource Directory™—

The Dramatists Guild Resource Directory™ is a valuable, useful tool for any dramatist at various stages of their careers. From submission opportunities to practical advice on securing an agent or a template for formatting your script, the *Resource Directory* is an essential guide that should be on every writer's bookshelf.

—*Doug Wright*

The most comprehensive and useful directory for playwrights. All you need to know and more. Very well organized, described and arranged. And to think, you get it free with your membership in the Guild. What a bargain!

—*Julie Jensen*

Everything a serious writer for the stage needs to know, all in one place: *The Dramatists Guild Resource Directory.*™

—*Rajiv Joseph*

Google's got nothing on this thing—it's the only search engine you'll ever need! *The Dramatists Guild Resource Directory*™ is custom-fitted for playwrights, so it's the most convenient and efficient way to find opportunities. You might even able to work on a script with all the time you save using it.

—*Chisa Hutchinson*

The Guild's annual *Resource Directory* is the premiere dramatist's handbook and an essential key to success.

—*Bobby Lopez*

A great all-in-one directory...an invaluable resource for writers!

—*Benj Pasek and Justin Paul*

The Dramatists Guild Resource Directory™ is an essential tool for any playwright, from the novice to the experienced. It is user-friendly and complete... no playwright should be without it.

—*Rebecca Gilman*

The Dramatists Guild Resource Directory™ is a fantastic, user friendly source of submission and career development opportunities for all playwrights.

—*Stephen Karam*

D1314089

THE DRAMATISTS GUILD RESOURCE DIRECTORY™

2013

The Writer's Guide to the Theatrical Marketplace™

19th Edition

 Publishing
R. Pullins Company

The Dramatists Guild Resource Directory
© 2013 The Dramatists Guild of America Inc.
The Dramatists Guild Resource Directory and The Writer's Guide to the Theatrical
Marketplace are trademarks of The Dramatists Guild.

Published by
Focus Publishing/R. Pullins Company
PO Box 369
Newburyport, MA 01950
www.pullins.com

ISBN 13: 978-1-58510-632-5

Cover image: Joey Stocks
Cartoons: Mark Krause

For more information, contact Rebecca Stump, Editor of the *Resource Directory* at
rstump@dramatistsguild.com.

10 9 8 7 6 5 4 3 2 1

1212V

Contents

Editor's Note

Welcome to the 19th printed edition of *The Dramatists Guild Resource Directory*—a springboard for every dramatist in the submission process. Each year we add features that we think our members will find important to their lives and careers as dramatists. We're continuing to include the Dramatists Bill of Rights (great for refreshing your understanding of all your rights) and our statement on submission fees. In addition to the standard submission opportunities and resources, we've added two exciting new chapters: an excerpt from the Guild's upcoming *Dramatist's Guide to Self-Production*, which will be published in 2013 and *The Road Less Traveled: Dramatists Recall Some Unconventional Paths to Production*. This year's directory features new cartoons from *The Dramatist*'s very own cartoonist, Mark Krause.

A strong word of advice about this book: by the time we go to press, a number of the opportunities listed may have new staff, updated deadlines, or may no longer exist. Such is the nature of the field; the landscape is constantly changing. It is essential that you verify the information we provide by going directly to the website of the theatre, contest, festival, etc. Please review each organization's policies carefully to ensure that all authorial rights are upheld. If you find a listing you believe is inaccurate or misleading please contact us here at the Guild. Remember, though, listings by their nature are never complete, and any listing or omission doesn't necessarily constitute approval or disapproval by the Guild, its Council, officers, employees, agents, or affiliates. Please be responsible with your submissions:

1. When submitting to a particular program within a contest, theatre, etc., cite the specific program you're submitting to. Many groups sponsor multiple programs.

2. Include a self-addressed stamped envelope (SASE) with sufficient postage. Most organizations won't return material without one and some organizations don't return material at all.

3. It's always a smart (and economically sound) choice to discover whether organizations take electronic submissions. If electronic submissions are not noted on their website, it's worth an inquiry directly to the theatre. Ask for acknowledgement of receipt.

4. Include your contact information in a query letter, since some organizations prefer blind submissions with no identification on the script itself.

Finally, many thanks to the Assistant Editor, Jennifer Bushinger as well as Melissa Aquiles, Pei-Chieh Chang, Zee Cohen, John Dietrich, Nicholas Dillihay, Ann Droppers, Emily Duncan, Lisa Huberman, Erica Knight, Polly Levi, Jason Mantell, Andres Quintero, Kiley Reid, Aryana Rodriguez, Danni Schwartz, Hallie Steiner, Joey Stocks, Tari Stratton, Roland Tec, Selin Uludogan, and Zhu Yi for their invaluable contributions to this resource.

Flip through the pages of this directory with your pencil at the ready. Take a chance on your new play or musical and send it to a theatre that has a similar artistic vision.

"What is not started today is never finished tomorrow." ~Johann Von Goethe

—*Rebecca Stump, Editor*

Bill of Rights

The Dramatists Guild is America's professional association of playwrights, librettists, lyricists and composers, with over 6,500 members around the world. The Guild is governed by our country's leading dramatists, with a fifty-five member Council that includes such dramatists as Edward Albee, Stephen Sondheim, John Patrick Shanley, Tony Kushner, Marsha Norman, Lynn Nottage, Emily Mann and Christopher Durang.

Long before playwrights or musical theatre writers join the Dramatists Guild, they often struggle professionally in small to medium-sized theatres throughout the country. It is essential, therefore, that dramatists know their rights, which the Dramatists Guild has defended for nearly one hundred years. In order to protect the dramatist's unique vision, which has always been the strength of the theatre, s/he needs to understand this fundamental principle: dramatists own and control their work.

The Guild recommends that any production involving a dramatist incorporate a written agreement in which both theatres/producers and writers acknowledge certain key rights with each other.

In Process and Production

1. ARTISTIC INTEGRITY. No one (e.g., directors, actors, dramaturgs) can make changes, alterations, and/or omissions to your script—including the text, title, and stage directions—without your consent. This is called "script approval."

2. APPROVAL OF PRODUCTION ELEMENTS. You have the right to approve the cast, director, and designers (and, for a musical, the choreographer, orchestrator, arranger, and musical director, as well), including their replacements. This is called "artistic approval."

3. RIGHT TO BE PRESENT. You always have the right to attend casting, rehearsals, previews and performances.

Compensations

4. ROYALTIES. You are generally entitled to receive a royalty. While it is possible that the amount an author receives may be minimal for a small- to medium-sized production, some compensation should always be paid if any other artistic collaborator in the production is being paid, or if any admission is being charged. If you are a member of the Guild, you can always call our business office to discuss the standard industry royalties for various levels of production.

5. BILLING CREDIT. You should receive billing (typographical credit) on all publicity, programs, and advertising distributed or authorized by the theatre. Billing is part of your compensation and the failure to provide it properly is a breach of your rights.

Ownership

6. OWNERSHIP OF INTELLECTUAL PROPERTY. You own the copyright of your dramatic work. Authors in the theatre business do not assign (i.e., give away or sell in entirety) their copyrights, nor do they ever engage in "work-for-hire." When a university, producer or theatre wants to mount a production of your play, you actually license (or lease) the public performance rights to your dramatic property to that entity for a finite period of time.

7. OWNERSHIP OF INCIDENTAL CONTRIBUTIONS. You own all approved revisions, suggestions, and contributions to the script made by other collaborators in the production, including actors, directors, and dramaturgs. You do not owe anyone any money for these contributions.

   If a theatre uses dramaturgs, you are not obligated to make use of any ideas the dramaturg might have. Even when the input of a dramaturg or director is helpful to the playwright, dramaturgs and directors are still employees of the theatre, not the author, and they are paid for their work by the theatre/producer. It has been well-established in case law, beginning with "the Rent Case" (Thompson v. Larson) that neither dramaturgs nor directors (nor any other contributors) may be considered a co-author of a play, unless (i) they've collaborated with you from the play's inception, (ii) they've made a copyrightable contribution to the play, and (iii) you have agreed in writing that they are a co-author.

8. SUBSIDIARY RIGHTS. After a small- or medium-sized production, you not only own your script, but also the rights to market and sell it to all different media (e.g., television, radio, film, internet) in any commercial market in the world. You are not obligated to sign over any portion of your project's future revenues to any third party (fellow artist, advisor, director, producer) as a result of a production, unless that production is a professional (i.e., Actor's Equity) premiere production (including sets, costumes and lighting), of no less than 21 consecutive paid public performances for which the author has received appropriate billing, compensation, and artistic approvals.

9. FUTURE OPTIONS. Rather than granting the theatre the right to share in future proceeds, you may choose to grant a non-exclusive option to present another production of your work within six months or one year of the close of the initial production. No option should be assignable without your prior written consent.

10. AUTHOR'S CONTRACT: The only way to ensure that you get the benefit of the rights listed above is through a written contract with the producer, no matter how large or small the entity. The Guild's Department of Business Affairs offers a model "production contract" and is available to review any contracts offered to you, and advise as to how those contracts compare to industry standards.

We realize that making demands of a small- to medium-sized theatres is a difficult task. However, you should feel confident in presenting this Bill of Rights to the Artistic Director, Producer, Literary Manager, or university administrator as a starting point for discussion. At the very least, any professional in the dramatic arts should realize that it is important for writers to understand the nature of their work—not just the artistic aspects, but the business side, as well—and that they stand together as a community, for their mutual benefit and survival, and for the survival of theatre as a viable art form in the 21st century.

Suggested Formatting for Plays and Musicals

Included in this document are suggested formats for plays and musicals drawn from suggestions of distinguished dramatists, literary managers, teachers of dramatic writing, producers, professional theatres and publishers. It is the Guild's belief that these formats present a standard that will work for most professional opportunities. A few additional elements to consider:

1. Formatting works towards two purposes: easy reading and the ability to approximate the performance time of the written story. For plays, we've given you a traditional and a more modern format to choose from. Admittedly, not all stories or styles of writing will work within a standard format. Therefore, use your better judgment in deciding the architecture of the page.

2. There is an industry standard (though some may say old-fashioned) of using the 12-point Courier-New font; we've also noted that Times New Roman is used in more modern formatting. With the proliferation of computers and word-processing programs, there are literally hundreds of fonts to choose from. Whatever your choice, we recommend that you maintain a font size of 12 points—thereby assuring some reliable approximation of performance time.

3. Though you wrote the story, someone has to read it before anyone sees it. Therefore, make your manuscript easy to read by employing a standard format with clearly delineated page numbers, scene citations and act citations. Headers and footers are optional.

4. If you're using a software program, such as Final Draft, to format your work, be aware that you have the ability to create your own format in these programs that can be uniquely named, saved and applied to all of your manuscripts.

5. Usually, between the title page and the first page of the story and/or dialogue, there is a page devoted to a character break-down. What's important to note on this page is the age, gender and name of each character. Some dramatists write brief character descriptions beside each name.

6. While it is cost-effective for both xeroxing and mailing, realize that some institutions prefer that you don't send double-sided documents. We recommend that you inquire about preference.

7. There is no right or wrong way to signify the end of a scene or act. Some writers do nothing but end the scene; others write "black out", "lights fade down", "End Act 1" or some other signifier that the scene or act has concluded.

8. The binding margin should be 1.5 inches from the edge. All other margins (top, bottom, right) should be 1.0 inch from the edge.

Sample Title Page

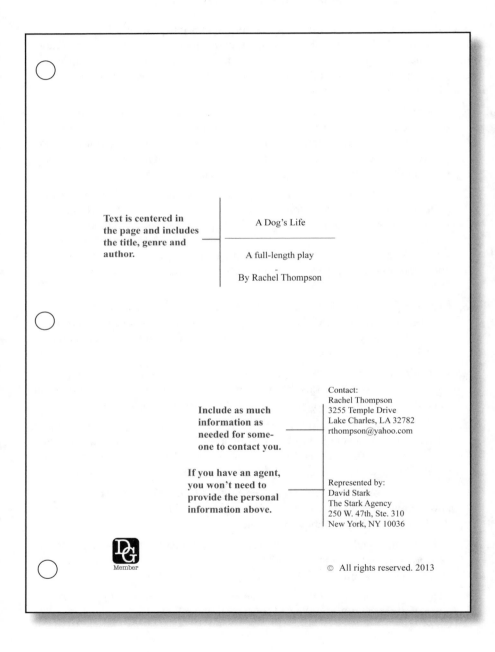

Text is centered in the page and includes the title, genre and author.

A Dog's Life

A full-length play

By Rachel Thompson

Include as much information as needed for someone to contact you.

Contact:
Rachel Thompson
3255 Temple Drive
Lake Charles, LA 32782
rthompson@yahoo.com

If you have an agent, you won't need to provide the personal information above.

Represented by:
David Stark
The Stark Agency
250 W. 47th, Ste. 310
New York, NY 10036

Modern Play Format

From Tennessee Williams' *Not About Nightingales*

Essential page
numbering
16.

BOSS

You've probably come here to question me about that ex-convicts story in that damned
yellow sheet down there in Wilkes county – That stuff about getting Pellagra in here
– Jimmy, hand me that sample menu!

Dialogue begins
1.5 inches from
left side to
account for
binding. Dialogue
is single-spaced.

JIM

She's not a reporter.

Character name
in all caps; in the
center of the page.

BOSS

Aw. – What is your business, young lady?

EVA

I understand there's a vacancy here. Mr. McBurney, my landlady's brother-in-law,
told her that you were needing a new stenographer and I'm sure that I can qualify
for the position. I'm a college graduate, Mr. Whalen, I've had three years of business
experience – references with me – but, oh – I've – I've had such abominable luck
these last six months. – the last place I worked – the business recession set in they
had to cut down on their sales-force – they gave me a wonderful letter – I've got in
with me.

Dialogue extends
to 1.0 inch from
right margin

*She opens her purse and spills contents
on floor.*

Stage action begins
in the center of the
page and scans to
the right margin. A
blank line is inserted
before and after.

BOSS

Anybody outside?

EVA

Yes. That woman.

BOSS

What woman?

Standard font for
this formatting is
12.0 point, New
Times Roman.

EVA

The one from Wisconsin. She's still waiting –

BOSS

I told you I don't want to see her.
(talking into phone)
How's the track, Bert? Fast? Okay.

Stage action reliant
on the proceeding
dialogue is indented
to the left of the
character name.

*Sailor Jack's mother, MRS. BRISTOL, has
quietly entered. She carries a blanket.*

MRS. BRISTOL

I beg your pardon, I – You see I'm Jack Bristol's mother, and I've been wanting to
have a talk with you so long about – about my boy!

Musical Format

From *APPLAUSE*, Book by Betty Comden, Adolph Green.
Music by Charles Strouse, Lyrics by Lee Adams

Essential page numbering**
56.

KAREN
(to Margo)

Margo, you've been kicking us all around long enough. Someone ought to give *you* a good swift one for a change!

Dialogue begins 1.5 inches from left side to account for binding. Dialogue is single-spaced.

(She leaves.)

Stage action is indented 3 inches from left; put in parentheses. A blank line is inserted before and after.

EVE

Miss Channing . . . if I ever dreamed that anything I did could possibly cause you any unhappiness, or come between you and your friends . . . please believe me.

Dialogue extends to 1.0 inch from right margin

Character name in all caps; in the center of the page.

MARGO
(in a low, weary voice)

Oh, I do. And I'm full of admiration for you.
(stands, approaches Eve)

If you can handle yourself on the stage with the same artistry you display off the stage . . . well, my dear, you are in the right place.

Stage action reliant on the proceeding dialogue is indented to the left of the character name.

(She speaks the following lines as the music of WELCOME TO THE THEATRE begins.)

Welcome to the theater, to the magic, to the fun!

(She sings.)

WHERE PAINTED TREES AND FLOWERS GROW
AND LAUGHTER RINGS FORTISSIMO,
AND TREACHERY'S SWEETLY DONE!

Lyric are in all CAPS, separated line to line by either musical phrasing and/or the rhyming scheme and clearly indented from the left margin.

NOW YOU'VE ENTERED THE ASYLUM,
THIS PROFESSION UNIQUE
ACTORS ARE CHILDREN
PLAYING HIDE-AND-EGO-SEEK . . .

Stanzas are separated by a blank line and distinguish themselves by dramatic thought and/or changes from verse to chorus to bridges, etc.

SO WELCOME, MISS EVE HARRINGTON,
TO THIS BUSINESS WE CALL SHOW,
YOU'RE ON YOUR WAY
TO WEALTH AND FAME,
UNSHEATH YOUR CLAWS,
ENJOY THE GAME!
YOU'LL BE A BITCH
BUT THEY'LL KNOW YOUR NAME
FROM NEW YORK . . . TO KOKOMO

For duets, or characters singing counter-point, create two columns side by side, following the same format here.

WELCOME TO THEATRE,
MY DEAR, YOU'LL LOVE IT SO!

**There are many ways to paginate your play, from the straight forward numerical sequence of 1, 2, 3 to an older format of 1-2-16, (meaning Act 1, Scene 2, Page 16).

Sample Letter of Inquiry

Though there is no right or wrong way to write a letter of introduction to your work, realize an effective submission letter should be short, professional and with just enough information so the reader knows you've submitted exactly what was called for in the solicitation. And while it's tempting to entice the reader to want to read the script with an overly expressive narrative in your submission letter, consider that this is the first exposure to your writing (of any kind) that will be read by someone in the producing organization . Be mindful, then, how you represent yourself on paper, and allow your play or musical to speak for itself.

A common question is often asked when writers construct a production resume: what do you do if you don't have a lot of readings or productions to list on your resume? Whatever you do, don't misrepresent yourself; don't say you've had a reading or a production of a play at a theatre that you haven't had. You'll eventually be found out and look worse than someone who has a thin resume. If you don't have a lot of production experience with your writing, write a brief synopsis of each of the plays you've written, cite any classes or workshops you've taken as a playwright and detail any other experience you have in the theatre (as stage manager, director, actress, dramaturg, etc.). People are more likely to be sympathetic to you being young in the theatre than they are to you being someone who misrepresents themselves.

A more accomplished playwright's resume should list the productions or readings of plays (by theatre and date), awards, grants, writers colonies attended, workshops, festivals invited to and any special recognition received as a writer. Give the reader a sense of the whole of your writing career, including memberships in theatre groups, professional organizations and related writing work. Include your address and phone number at the top or bottom of your resume, cover sheet of your play and obviously on the return envelope. Again, there are any number of variations on how to construct a writer's resume, but a template to inspire your thinking can be found on the following page.

Sample Letter of Inquiry

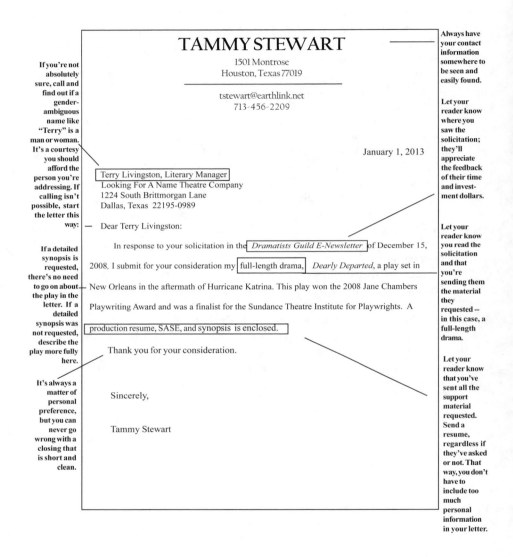

If you're not absolutely sure, call and find out if a gender-ambiguous name like "Terry" is a man or woman. It's a courtesy you should afford the person you're addressing. If calling isn't possible, start the letter this way:

If a detailed synopsis is requested, there's no need to go on about the play in the letter. If a detailed synopsis was not requested, describe the play more fully here.

It's always a matter of personal preference, but you can never go wrong with a closing that is short and clean.

TAMMY STEWART

1501 Montrose
Houston, Texas 77019

tstewart@earthlink.net
713-456-2209

January 1, 2013

Terry Livingston, Literary Manager
Looking For A Name Theatre Company
1224 South Brittmorgan Lane
Dallas, Texas 22195-0989

Dear Terry Livingston:

In response to your solicitation in the *Dramatists Guild E-Newsletter* of December 15, 2008, I submit for your consideration my full-length drama, *Dearly Departed*, a play set in New Orleans in the aftermath of Hurricane Katrina. This play won the 2008 Jane Chambers Playwriting Award and was a finalist for the Sundance Theatre Institute for Playwrights. A production resume, SASE, and synopsis is enclosed.

Thank you for your consideration.

Sincerely,

Tammy Stewart

Always have your contact information somewhere to be seen and easily found.

Let your reader know where you saw the solicitation; they'll appreciate the feedback of their time and investment dollars.

Let your reader know you read the solicitation and that you're sending them the material they requested -- in this case, a full-length drama.

Let your reader know that you've sent all the support material requested. Send a resume, regardless if they've asked or not. That way, you don't have to include too much personal information in your letter.

The DG Statement on Submission Fees

The Dramatists Guild of America denounces the practice by festivals, play contests and educational events of charging excessive fees to dramatists who submit their work. Any request for submission fees should be accompanied by a complete explanation of how those fees are to be spent. The Guild also insists that contests and festivals announce the names of all finalists and winners to all participants.

It is important that members understand that submission fees are not the norm and, when required, the festival should offer something significant in return for the writer's investment, such as a large cash prize, a residency or a production. Reading fees are in no case acceptable, as most festivals receive that money from other grant sources. In no case should playwrights have to pay to simply have their work read.

The Guild also strongly disapproves of a festival's placing any encumbrances on the work as a result of the play being chosen a finalist or a participant. Any future participation in the life of the play must be earned by the festival by producing the work, and should never be granted by the writer without consultation with the Guild. If the festival expects any subsidiary income from the plays, that information should be stated clearly in all of the organization's printed and electronic materials related to the event.

The Council of the Guild feels that its members should be made aware of all legitimate opportunities available to them, and so we have listed in this section those particular contests and festivals that charge fees and have provided explanations regarding how their submission fees are spent, as well as full disclosure of any encumbrances they place on a selected writer's work, when offered by the sponsor.

Agency, from the desk of Gary Garrison

This article originally appeared in the Dramatists Guild e-newsletter on April 18, 2008

On the average, I get three to four phone calls or emails a day that go something like this: "I need an agent. I know everyone needs an agent, but I *really need* an agent. Why can't the Guild help get me an agent or a director or anyone who can help promote my work? And why can't the Guild get more theatres to respond to playwrights and new plays? We need more opportunities!" Look, I just want to get square with you once and for all: we are a member-service and advocacy organization. And while I don't want to downplay the importance for some of you to be professionally represented by an agent (or your work placed in a theatre), it is not one of the mandates of this organization to help you secure representation or production.

It doesn't matter what anyone has to say about writers and agents, the truth is having an agent is perceived—right or wrong—as a benchmark of success that comes with certain positive opportunities and a healthy amount of validation. The desire in most of us, then, is never likely to go away. But if you really want to pursue the agent thing, I want you to take a good, honest look at simple facts and figures to help you make sense of what's ahead of you.

- The numbers: talking to my colleagues here at the Guild, and then making a few phone calls around town to some very respectable agents, to our best estimation there are approximately thirty-five agents dedicated to promoting dramatic writing for the theatre. That's thirty-five agents *total*—throughout the whole country—that represent every playwright you know by name, and then the many hundreds you don't know (yet). The simple numbers alone show the odds are against most of us having an agent.

- Most agents that I've spoken with are rarely interested in representing a single piece of work and are far more interested in representing (and helping you grow) a body of work. To approach an agent to represent a single play or musical is not likely to get you anywhere. Agents, like all theatre business people, are as interested in the present as they are the future.

- Twenty years ago, maybe even ten years ago, a hit production of a play or a musical and a good New York Times review (or any major newspaper review) would almost ensure that you'd have an agency knocking at your door. That's not true any longer; there's a glut of material and writers out there that remain unrepresented. Theatre, like most arms of the entertainment industry, is ageist.

Jeeeeeez, Gary, did you have to be so…honest? In a word, yes, because so many of us are singularly obsessed about getting an agent. Are there exceptions to any of the points above? Of course there are exceptions; that's what makes this life interesting. Can you have a productive, successful career in the theatre without professional representation? You bet, and a heck of a lot of people do.

Please understand that we provide a list of working literary agents as a convenience for you—nothing more. By listing these agents (which is not a comprehensive list), we do not intend to suggest that they are seeking new clients or that we are particularly endorsing them as agents. Unless indicated otherwise, send a query and synopsis to one agent at a time.

Excerpt from
A Dramatist's Guide to Self-Production
by Roland Tec

*With greater numbers of writers everywhere producing their own work each
year, the Guild is pleased to announce the forthcoming book:* A Dramatist's
Guide to Self-Production *by Guild Director of Membership, Roland Tec.
Drawing on his extensive experience in the field, this guide will feature many of
the key components of his popular* Self-Production Boot Camp. *The following is
a short excerpt of the book due for publication this summer.*

CASTING

As the saying goes, "90% of directing is casting." The implication is clear. Cast
properly and you're a lot closer to realizing your vision. Cast hastily or sloppily and
you've given your show a handicap that's hard to transcend. Assuming you have an
excellent director, you can relax in the knowledge that when the time comes to make
those difficult decisions about specific casting choices, you'll have a capable and
trusted partner. But, assuming the perfect cast is living somewhere in your area, waiting to be revealed to you, how on earth are you to find them?

I know one producer who will not commit to a performance schedule without at
least knowing she has her key cast members lined up. Not many of us can afford this
luxury, but the approach is worth aiming for. Casting is one of the most important
components of assembling your team, so whatever you do, don't rush it; err on the side
of seeing too many actors rather than too few.

A word about casting directors. Most independent theatre productions do not use
them, however depending on where you live, it may be possible to gain access to a pool
of casting directors, some of whom make their living primarily from casting commer-
cials or film and television. Many started out as directors or actors themselves so they
often have a keen appreciation and love for the theatre. If you know one of them it's
possible to get a reduced rate or even some sort of pro bono arrangement. This is particularly worthwhile if the person in question is very busy and sees a lot of talent every
week and if he or she loves your script. Little can compete with passion for the project
as a motivator. And it's important that whoever is organizing casting calls understands
the project, appreciates it and can speak intelligently about it to actors, managers and
agents. If you are lucky enough to have a motivated casting director on your team, you
won't have to worry about the details outlined below. Much of what follows will be
handled for you.

But most independent productions can't afford or don't have access to a casting
director per se. Nevertheless, it's a good idea to assign the role of "casting director" to
one of your producers or production assistants or possibly your stage manager. Without
one person overseeing the entire process it's too easy to make the kind of mistakes
that will reflect poorly on your production, mistakes like double-booking two actors
for the same audition time slot. This may not seem like a big deal in the grand scheme

of things but every time this occurs, two actors have been sent a message about your team. And it's not a favorable one.

The person in charge of casting will consult with the director about which sides to have actors come in and read. What are sides? Sides are merely short excerpts from the play selected by the director in order to show him or her what each actor can do. A good director will intuitively know which moments in your script might be the most challenging or the most revealing of an actor's innate gifts. Usually the sides for one lead character do not match up with the sides for another. It's a good idea to give your director a fair amount of leeway in how to organize casting. After all, it's the director who needs to work with these actors and needs to evaluate who best can embody these characters. Some directors like to see actors for 3 min. only for the first go-round and then will spend much longer on callbacks. Others prefer a more leisurely schedule. Let your director tell you how much time she needs with each actor. If a director wants to spend 5 min. with each actor, schedule actors at 10 min. intervals. If she wants 10 min. with each actor, book them in 15 min. intervals, and so on. You'll need to allow some breathing room in your schedule for people entering and leaving the room as well as much-needed bathroom breaks for all of you who are running things.

Once the sides have been selected, the next step is to select a location for your casting call. In New York City, for example, there are numerous businesses that specialize in renting out rehearsal studios by the hour for rehearsing and for auditions. If you already have an arrangement with a rehearsal space, see if you can get some additional time for auditions thrown in at a discount. Some things to consider before choosing your audition venue. Many actors work day jobs or if they're fortunate enough to be full-time working actors, will have more than one audition scheduled on a given day. Pick a venue that is easy to find and easy to get to. In New York City, this means blocks away from a subway station. In Los Angeles, this might mean a building with ample parking and good signage. Wherever you hold your casting call, be sure it's got adequate toilet facilities and, if possible, access to a copy machine and wireless internet access. While you can certainly hold a successful set of auditions without these things, they will help ease the stress of last-minute schedule changes, requests for auditions that were unexpected, last-minute ideas for new sides which then have to be copied quickly, etc. etc.

Once the venue and date have been confirmed, along with the schedule of time slots, you then have the unenviable task of filling your day. Your team should first sit down to brainstorm a list of local actors you know you hope will come in to read. Then figure out how you're going to reach them. Those that have agents are in a sense easiest. The agent's contact information should be readily available online. Those without representation are a bit trickier, although these days Facebook and Twitter make finding folks a lot easier than it once was. Another neat trick from days gone by is to leave a note with the House Manager at a theatre where an actor is currently performing outlining the scope of the production, a bit about the role and inviting them to come in to read. Once you've got that list together, you will want to put the word out by all available means.

Breakdown Services (and *Actors Access*) offers an efficient online tool for getting the word out to the community at large in major markets such as Los Angeles or

New York but there are countless tools available in other cities as well. A quick Google search with the name of your city and the word "casting" should uncover any online resources specific to your neck of the woods. Online bulletin boards, such as Craigslist.org are also increasingly proving effective not just for casting calls but for hiring in all areas of production.

In order to promote your project to the theatre community online, you'll need to prepare a casting breakdown. This is simply a list of all available roles, with a short description of type, age, gender and other important aspects of character you might be looking for. Be sure to work with your director on the breakdown carefully. The way you describe each character will have an impact on who decides to audition. For example, if you include some very specific physical characteristic such as "she's a red-head" you may be discouraging brunettes from submitting their resumes. Try to create a breakdown that gets to the essence of character rather than physical features you may have imagined when writing.

Many agents and managers will request a full script and some actors will as well. This is always a good thing for several reasons. Assuming you've come as far as casting, it ought to be safe to assume you are happy with the script in its current draft. Therefore, the more people in the theatre community have a chance to read it, the better. Second, and perhaps more important, is that the more information you make available to your talent pool, the better auditions you will see. Reading the entire play gives an actor the context necessary to do his or her best when coming in to read your sides. I can think of no good argument for saying "no" to requests for your full script during casting.

Try to fill your schedule from the start of the day working towards the end. Rather than asking an actor (or his or her agent) what time works for them, invite them to come in at a specific time. If they need a different time, they'll ask for it. But this way you'll (hopefully) avoid having a day with large gaps during which you're sitting around twiddling your thumbs. Be sure to give yourselves at least a 30 min. lunch break which will just barely allow enough time for someone to run downstairs, buy a bunch of sandwiches bring them up for you all to gulp down. Eating during an actor's audition is rude and should be avoided.

Remember, your casting call is more than a means to cast your show. It is also the beginning of your PR campaign. Nobody is more passionate about the theatre than are actors. If actors are impressed with your script, your organizational team and your vision they will tell their friends, many of whom also work in the theatre and attend the theatre. The title of your project makes an entrance into casual conversation in your community the moment casting begins. And the accompanying descriptors—positive and negative—are largely within your control. Keep actors waiting in a crowded hallway without adequate ventilation and you'll have a whole community of artists who regard you with suspicion. Make your auditions a pleasant and inspiring experience and the rewards are potentially endless.

The Road Less Traveled
Dramatists Recall Some
Unconventional Paths to Production

The truth is, you never know where a production is going to come from. I remember a few years ago, running down the subway platform at 14th Street and bumping into my friend Elyse Singer. We hadn't seen each other in months— both busy with our own projects. Suddenly we were catching up and it was wonderful! In an instant, she invited me to teach at a summer playwriting retreat her company Hourglass Group held each July at Choate Rosemary Hall in Connecticut. A few weeks later my play The Wreck Behind Us *was being read for the first time and I was teaching a screenwriting workshop to high school students in between games of ultimate frisbee. It was there that I met Darren Chilton, who upon hearing my play read, declared it ready to be produced. Those words meant the world to me and marked the start of a long and fruitful producing relationship between us that continues today.*

And so we bring you The Road Less Traveled, *stories shared by a random assortment of Dramatists Guild members with one unifying thread: expect the unexpected. It's the party you don't want to attend, the phone call you're afraid to return, the seminar you aren't sure you can afford. You never really can predict with certainty from where a production might spring. The best we can do is remain active, alert, sensitive and responsive and engaged members of an ever-expanding collection of likeminded individuals with whom we strive to cobble together something akin to an artistic home.*

Here, then, for your inspiration are a few such tales of joy.

—Roland Tec

Laurie Flanigan Hegge
Why Don't I?

I was a long-time company member and performer at American Folklore Theatre (AFT) in Door County, Wisconsin, which produces all-original work. One day, while walking down the path to AFT's outdoor theatre on the way to sound check, I chatted up my dear friend and colleague, the late Fred Alley. (Fred was one of the co-founders of American Folklore Theatre, where he was both a playwright and a beloved actor.) As we were walking, I casually asked Fred, "Why don't you write a woman's play?" and he replied, "Why don't you write one?" It had never occurred to me until that moment. My dad had given me an "E for Effort" pin that his father had been awarded for his work on the home front in a Wisconsin factory during WWII. I got to thinking—a play about women factory workers during WWII would be a great subject for an AFT show. Fast forward a few months and I'm in a hotel room in Racine, Wisconsin playing euchre with a few friends, including composer James Kaplan and my friend Jacinda Duffin, who would become my collaborators that night. Jacinda pitched the idea to move the story to the shipyards of Sturgeon Bay, about a half an hour from the theatre. With Fred's encouragement, and the blessing of AFT's artistic director, Jeff Herbst, we wrote a new musical about women shipbuilders called *Loose Lips Sink Ships*. It went into AFT's development pipeline and premiered at AFT in 2001 to critical and popular acclaim. Sadly, Fred passed away in May 2001, just after he won the Richard Rogers Production Award with composer James Valcq for *The Spitfire Grill*. I credit Fred for giving me the permission and the courage to start writing. More than ten years later, I have written the book and lyrics for five musicals, including AFT's first-ever commission for my second musical, *See Jane Vote*. My work as an actor with AFT certainly grounded me in the new-work development process, and for me, the transition from actor to writer was a natural one. And because Jacinda, James and I were writing for a specific theatre, with a very specific audience, and even with a specific cast in mind, I learned early on how limitations can help to focus the writing process, as well as the outcome, when it comes to getting new work produced.

Winter Miller
I Asked

I had a fortuitous experience with the *Cherry Lane Mentor Project*. I had a brand new play that I'd written very quickly, in about a week, but because it was unexpected and not in sync with the fellowship calendar, I hadn't submitted it anywhere for development. Some years earlier, I had taken a writing class. 'Pataphysics at the Flea (I highly recommend these weekend intensives!) with Craig Lucas. At the time, he helped me through a hurdle in my play, *The Penetration Play*—just weeks away from opening. I had a lot of respect for Craig and his methods. I took a risk and sent Craig an email and asked if he'd mentor me on this play, as I knew from the website he had mentored Anne Washburn and David Adjmi as part of the Cherry Lane. Next, I emailed Theresa Rebeck, whom I'd met some years earlier when I was a grad student at Columbia and she guest lectured. Theresa was involved with the *Mentor Project* so I asked her advice, how does someone get recommended for candidacy? Theresa was encouraging; she suggested I have Craig call Angelina Fiordellisi and see what the protocol is and I think she generously put in a good word for me. As it happened, that morning, there had been a scheduling conflict with a mentor/mentee team and there was quite suddenly, a hole. Angelina was pacing her office thinking, who's going to fill this slot? The phone rang and it was Craig, phoning to learn how he and I might apply. Some years earlier, unbeknownst to me, a professor of mine had submitted one of my plays to the *Cherry Lane Mentor Project*, and Angelina had very much liked that play. So when this new play came along, she didn't need to vet it, she trusted Craig and believed in me. Immediately, we were slotted. The *Mentor Project* is a real boon to playwrights, I'm not sure it or Angelina get the credit they deserve.

Dan Berkowitz
My Turnpike, My Muse

My writing career, such as it is, owes its existence to serendipity and—literally—a road.

As with most of life, I fell into writing by accident. In my 20s, I was the producer/director/emcee of a weekly musical and comedy cabaret revue in Princeton, NJ. We did a new show each week, with rotating casts (the musical director, choreographer, and I were the only constants), and by mid-week, I'd know that we needed, say, a minute-long "thing" to cover a costume change here, or a three-minute comedy sketch to liven up the show there. I'd jump in my car with a pad and pen, get on the New Jersey Turnpike—where looking at the scenery would drive you mad—and write what we needed.

Flash forward to some years later, when the musical director, who by that time had appeared in the wildly successful revue *A... My Name Is Alice*, agreed to be in the sequel, to be called *A... My Name Is Still Alice*. The creators were looking for sketch material, she recommended me, and they wound up using more stuff of mine than of any other writer's—and the others included heavyweights such as Craig Carnelia, Carol Hall, Michael John LaChiusa, Lynn Nottage, Jimmy Roberts, Mark St. Germain, David Zippel, and the Guild's illustrious prez Stephen Schwartz.

The show premiered at the Old Globe in San Diego before transferring to New York, I got glowing reviews from the California papers for my stuff, and suddenly I was in demand: I was asked to write some things for television, to doctor an off-Broadway musical, eventually to be the LA Regional Rep for The Dramatists Guild.

The bit which probably got the most notice was the show's running gag, in which a miraculous makeup called CoverUp makes it possible for Madonna, Queen Elizabeth, and even the Pope to circulate in the world undetected, as a housewife from La Jolla. I'd originally written it—in my car on the Turnpike—as a bit for the cabaret, and now it's been performed all around the country!

Can anyone really call the Jersey Turnpike "The Road Less Traveled"? I dunno, but in my case it led me to where I am today.

Doug Wright
More Than Just One Benefit

Like many of my peers, I'm often asked to write short sketches for charity functions and benefits. While ostensibly the modest "ten minute play" may not seem like a vehicle mighty enough to cure cancer or clothe the homeless or fund the arts, the money such pithy little pieces can raise is potent indeed. Softie that I am, I habitually say "yes," and not necessarily because I have a big heart; it's fun to procrastinate on a tiny play when a big one is egregiously overdue. About three years ago, I was asked to pen a script on behalf of gay marriage for (I thought) one performance only for a suitably exorbitant ticket price. I was joined on the bill by a roster of similarly passionate and/or gullible playwrights, and the evening was a nice success...so much so, in fact, that an enterprising group of producers mounted the mini-plays under the title "Standing on Ceremony" at the Minetta Lane Theater. So a work I penned for "one night only" got an admittedly brief but very happy commercial run. I urge all my fellow playwrights to do good deeds; sometimes, they do indeed come back to you.

Lee Chamberlin
A Director/Dramatist Exchange

So I was living in a town where I calculated my chances of ever being produced at about 5%, when somehow I'm introduced to a producing artistic director who not only agrees to a reading of my one woman play, but once the reading is over, he's so nuts over it, he promises a production six months hence. Weeks, then months pass with no word from the head over heels producer about the promised production. I inquire only to receive a terse reply awash with transparent platitudes about funding cuts to his theatre. Then I recall the hostile board member the night of the reading who peppered me with not so friendly questions during the otherwise encouraging Q & A. I later learn this one man, who was clearly not in love with my play, threatens to insure a substantial withdrawal of funding from the theatre if it mounts my work. Strong words, funding cuts explained, true story, no production there.

Then one day I scroll The Dramatists Guild e-Newsletter all the way to the end and discover The Guild's Membership Director, Roland Tec, has initiated an exchange between playwrights of solo performance pieces and directors he feels possess imagination and vision. I submit the requested sample single page on a Monday, on Tuesday I'm a lucky participant lottery winner and on Wednesday I book my flight from the heart of darkness to that other city of light, New York.

At the exchange, held at The Guild, I'm next to last of the thirteen playwrights and nine authors to read the previously submitted sample page. An unexpected hush fills the room, which, as we know, can be a good sign or a very, very bad sign.

Of the three directors who later approach me, one introduced my play to The Kitchen Theatre Company in Ithaca, New York. *Objects in the mirror...(are closer than they seem)* was produced a scant year after the exchange and led to an ongoing relationship with The Kitchen Theatre Company. Thanks to the Guild's exchange series, I torched the stack of rejection letters and understood my mother's saying: "there's more than one way to skin a cat." And there's more than one road toward a production of your work.

Larry Dean Harris
Accidental Playwright

Call me an accidental playwright. In 1987 at the age of 25, I was offered a job in New York City in a fancy Madison Avenue advertising agency. But my real "big break" was discovering the art of "second acting" a Broadway show—sneaking in alongside the smokers after intermission. I saw *Burn This* once at full price, but I saw ACT TWO of *Burn This* a dozen times: studying every nuance, every detail from the lighting to the action in the wings. This was my theatre education.

After New York spit me out, I returned to Toledo, Ohio. Over lunch with my first boss who had become a mentor and a dear friend, we discussed the revue Forbidden Broadway. I said "Wouldn't it be cool if someone wrote a show like that about Toledo?" Everyone makes fun of Toledo. But how refreshing if Toledo made fun of itself!

Months later, he called and said "That Toledo show of yours? Well, I sold it to a big sales convention. You've got three months. Get cracking." And he hung up. So not knowing any better, I started writing. The show was mostly bad. But there were kernels of good and even a few gems. Thank God, I found four amazing performers and a brilliant musical director. We pulled it off and got paid. That was the end of that.

Until I was having lunch at a dear friend's restaurant: a deli in a hardware store (only in Toledo). I told her about *Oh, No! Not Toledo!* And she said "That sounds fun.

Why don't you perform it here?" And not knowing any better, I said okay. Every Friday night on a makeshift stage—among the hardware and the antique toys—we played to packed houses. The material got better, and I would update it to reflect current events. The cast—already talented—grew to be amazing and fearless. They would learn a new song an hour before the show and sell it like pros. We ran for years, eventually performing with the Symphony in front of thousands, and even opening for the big guns, The Capital Steps (wiping the smug, patronizing smiles off their faces when the crowd gave us a standing ovation).

Then one day at a party, I said "I think I want to write a play." And a friend, who is a fabulous director, said "If you write it, I'll direct it." And not knowing any better, I wrote a play called *Bible Stories*. We performed it in theatres, a church and even a rock club. When I moved to Los Angeles, not knowing any better, I produced it myself at Celebration Theatre, yielding three LA Weekly Theatre Award nominations and my first review in the LA Times.

I've been with Celebration Theatre ever since and—8 opening nights later—it is still my theatrical home. All because I had people who believed in me, eventually giving me the strength and confidence to believe in myself. And now, as the Guild's representative for Southern California, I get to pay it forward.

Louis Crowder
Swimming Upstream

I ardently believed there was one way to get theatre done, the way it had always been done: research, submit, wait, follow-up, wait, begin again. I'm hard-headed, it took a long time to give up, but I did. I systematically quit the theatre. I stopped sending to competitions first, they seem to be more agenda driven than anything else; stopped sending to festivals, they can be cost-prohibitive to independents; then stopped sending to regional theatres, they rarely respond to 'new' writers and too often when they do it's not kind; then, finally, stopped sending to community theatres, they're a mish-mash of all the above with a dose of nepotism thrown in for good measure. Then came Hurricane Katrina. I'm an artist, I had to do something. I wrote a play that I believed in absolutely. While writing two things happened that made me re-think American theatre and my place in it: I received a mini-grant from the Tennessee Williams festival, and a community theatre producer I approached to produce the new piece smiled at me and said, "Louie, write a play called Naked Boys Reading Poetry and I'll consider producing it for you." (He had just made a lot of money producing the obvious. And my work is very lyrical, heightened poetry. Actually I'm convinced that's why people come see my theatre: lyricism is my hook.) The grant's intrinsic value was in sending me the message that I wasn't a fool and that being a playwright wasn't a foolish thing to do. The producer's comment told me I had no commercial value. So pissed off and re-ignited I went underground, threw away everything I ever knew or thought about the theatre, and reconstructed my game plan: say yes to everything and do something, anything, every day to progress the battle (I'm building a battleship, get on-board or get out of the channel). What I discovered some time later now, after the one Post-Katrina New Orleans play became six, and they're finding their places in the world, is that theatres, mainstream and otherwise, pay attention when the work they didn't want finds its place in the world without them. There are no rules except be adaptable, and nice while doing it.

Andrew Lippa
Marvelous Party

In 2004 I went to a showbiz friend's birthday party. The party was—to borrow a phrase from the NY Times' description of Elizabeth Taylor—equal parts glamour and gemütlichkeit.

I must confess I'm never very comfortable at parties. Call it social anxiety, call it boredom, call it terror—they usually bring out my inner 8th-grader. And not in a good way. Early on at this particular soiree I was introduced to the new-ish beau of a friend. The friend: Successful, near fifty, the life of any party. The beau: Twenty five. I found him CAPTIVATING. Seriously. The kind of captivating that, through the ages, has brought down people like Oscar Wilde. And Cleopatra. And Bill Clinton. Up walks my partner (now husband) David who whispered in my ear "Stop flirting and come meet Bruce Cohen." I obeyed. Bruce Cohen had, by that point in the century, co-produced (with Dan Jinks) the Academy Award-winning film *American Beauty* and had just had a lovely success with the film *Big Fish*. We chatted, were both very charming, and I learned that Bruce was in town that weekend from LA and had little social plans. (Note: It seemed impossible to me that a very successful film producer would have so few social plans. What was WRONG with him?). I told him David and I were hosting a brunch the next day at our apartment—YOU try getting into a restaurant for brunch on the Upper West Side on a Sunday—and that he should join us. Happily, he accepted.

Brunch was forgettable but Bruce wasn't. He went back to LA the next day and I said to David "I loved *Big Fish*. I think it'd make a great musical. Should I call Bruce and discuss this?" I figured: What have I got to lose? People love it when you call them and tell them how much you love something they did. (Showbiz secret: Don't be afraid to tell people—meaningfully tell people—how much you love things they've been a part of. You don't have to be famous. You just have to be sincere.) David said "Call." And so I did. Bruce said he, Dan Jinks and screenwriter (about to be book writer) John August were indeed interested in making *Big Fish* into a musical. I fawned, Bruce fawned, and a month later I was on a plane to LA to meet John. John and I got together for 4 days to discuss and write. It was a "getting to know you/let's see if we're compatible/OMG we both love *Lost In Space*!" kind of get-together. John wrote two scenes, I wrote two songs, we outlined Act One, and ate a lot of sushi. We then went to John's house, played the songs and scenes for Bruce and Dan, and they looked at us and said "Let's do this." Just like that.

The moral: Nothing ventured nothing gained. Thanks to my husband, my friend's soon-to-be ex-boyfriend, and my what-the-hell attitude *Big Fish* opens on Broadway in mid-2013 with Susan Stroman at the helm.

Glamour and gemütlichkeit indeed.

Micheline Auger
Small Pond Is Vast

Right before I moved to New York, I read that it was better to develop oneself as a theater artist in a smaller community, where you'd more opportunities to work and grow, then immediately heading to New York. I thought that was really annoying. I mean, the same temperament that dictates one to become an actor or writer is not the same temperament that says "I'm going to settle! I'm going to be reasonable! I'm gonna take a great big leap into the safe!" But after living in New York for ten years and feeling like I was hitting my head against the wall, I decided to move to Jackson Hole, Wyoming for the summer. I wanted to see how other people lived and I needed a break. I knew only one other person there (an ex-New Yorker) who seemed really, really happy. Glowy even. It was weird. I had also read an article in *The Dramatist* that quoted Paula Vogel as saying that New York was no longer hospitable to artists because you spend all your time working in order to pay your rent and it was too expensive and difficult to make theater here. So I quit my job, subletted my apartment and moved to Jackson Hole, population 9,577, home to the Grand Tetons, three theater companies, an amazing performing arts center and a rodeo. Once I got there, I hooked up with Macey Mott who runs Riot Act Theatre Company. She was teaching a swing dancing class that I was taking and she mentioned that Riot Act was producing a short play festival. I gave her a couple of my plays to read. She liked them and produced them (and produced them at a higher level than I had seen done in other places, L.A. being one of them.)

At the same time, I thought it would be cool to write for *Planet Jackson Hole*, the weekly newspaper there (their version of the *Village Voice*) so I emailed the new editor Matt Irwin, pitched a couple ideas and started a column called "Verbatim," where I would go around town on my bike and tape record locals talking about town politics and then transcribe the conversations or interviews. I also wrote a few other articles and landed a cover story about a group of male exotic dancers from L.A. dancing at the Mangy Moose (good times). A few months later, I was commissioned to develop an experimental theater piece with Riot Act and a group of actors, dancers and musicians that were part of the community.

The summer turned into a year and a half. I had finished two full lengths, a couple shorts, was on a new draft for the commission, and had learned how to white water kayak, mountain bike, road bike, ski better, skateboard (poorly) and say hi to strangers on the street. But finally the itch to return home needed a scratch so I packed my bags and came back to New York. Two and a half years later, I am more a part of the theater community than I ever was and it's because of what I learned in Jackson Hole, population 9,577. I learned that I am an important contributor to my community (as we all are, if we want to be). That I could knock on a door and it would be opened (and if not opened immediately, then eventually, and if not eventually, then where to find a new door, or the tools to build one). And I learned that writing is only one part of being a writer. So in the end, maybe they were right about the small pond (small but vast) so if you're living in one, be thankful, and if moving to one isn't part of your trajectory just yet (or ever), they can be found right here at home, too. And from there, you can go anywhere.

Jeffrey Sweet
The Lives of Others

A fine actress I knew slightly died young. The obituary in The New York Times was tiny. I thought she deserved better and sent a letter saying so to the paper. The Times printed it. Within a few weeks I got a job offer for a TV show. The executive who offered had been a friend of the actress. I never got confirmation that my letter was why, but I cannot figure how else the executive could have known of me at the time except from the letter. Of course, I choose to believe that, though the letter might have drawn this attention, the quality of my work is what landed the job.

I went to a lot of off-off-Broadway in the Seventies. One particular play in previews floored me and I wanted an excuse to talk to its author, so I asked him if I could interview him. Now, I had no paper lined up to interview him for, but I figured if he said yes I could talk to him a good long time. The play was *The Hot L Baltimore* and the writer was Lanford Wilson. The play got great reviews and moved to a commercial run. And I did get an interview out of our conversation. I sold it to Newsday, and the editor liked it well enough to have me interview Richard Rodgers, Sheldon Harnick, Peter Cook and Dudley Moore. With that record I was able to land a contract to write a book about Second City called *Something Wonderful Right Away*. One of the producers at Second City, Joyce Sloane, was on the board of a new theatre in Chicago and, though she had not read any of my work, she recommended me to that company. I ended up doing 14 plays there.

I recognize that neither of these stories offers concrete specific advice, but I think a general principle can be gleaned. In neither case did my luck come from trying to promote or sell anything. Each time, I benefitted from being interested in someone else. If you care about the work of others, others are more likely to care about yours.

Gwydion Suilebhan
Twitter Fed

So many of my fellow playwrights accuse me of frittering away my time on Twitter when I "should" be writing… and sometimes, yes, that's what Twitter is for me: the sort of distraction we all indulge in from time to time when you just can't figure out how to put a button on a scene or work up the courage to cut a character.

More often than not, though, Twitter is a source of inspiring conversation with directors and actors and playwrights around the globe, as well as a kind of virtual networking space in which I often make surprisingly profound connections with artistic directors, dramaturgs, and literary managers at theaters large and small. It's great. You should join me there sometime.

Not convinced? Perhaps you'll be motivated to start choosing an avatar when I tell you that within a few months of spending time on Twitter, I landed a full production of my play *Let X* with a company I never even knew existed… all in 140-character snippets of conversation.

I was introduced to the company—a new outfit called Nothing Special Productions—while tweeting one evening on the #2amt hashtag. (That's the first place to start, for what it's worth, when you DO join Twitter; it's the only 24/7/365 place to meet and tweet with fellow theater makers.) I remember exchanging a few random thoughts about matters theatrical with two of the theater's co-founders, as well as a few other folks who were tweeting. It was a pleasant, if not all that vital, encounter.

Or so I thought. As it happens, that first innocuous exchange was the start of a deeper conversation about the work we were interested in writing, producing, and directing. I didn't know it at the time—I was just enjoying getting to know them—but the company was planning its next project, and my thoughts about matters theatrical inspired them to ask to read some of my work: a request they made, as I recall, through a private direct message on Twitter.

I sent them a few plays, which they read post-haste; they really liked them both, but we agreed that one of them was a slightly better fit. And boom: a match was made. By that point, our conversations moved to email, given the limitations of 140 characters... but Twitter had done its job: breaking down the walls between at least one playwright and one theater, without any of the formal rules and bureaucratic processes and requirements that keep us alienated from each other.

Ready to start tweeting yet?

Teresa Coleman Wash
If We Build It They Will Come

As a young adult I was very active in my church in Atlanta. Very few Sundays went by where you didn't see the choir stand making a joyful noise. One holiday season the choir director asked me to chair the Christmas gathering. With much trepidation and a hint of sarcasm I responded, "Yeah right, so what do you expect me to do, write a play?" He replied, "That's a great idea!"

Somehow I mustered up the courage to take on the challenge and came up with what I thought was a really bad skit. But to my surprise the audience seemed to really enjoy and I was encouraged to write the full length version. There is an old axiom that states, no matter how much you know, the best opportunities in life can be attributed to who you know and so it was with the beginning of my newfound talent. A friend who knew a friend who was an aspiring promoter and was looking for new investments. I took a chance on him and he took a chance on me and eighteen months later the skit I wrote for the church house was on tour. That was the beginning of the rest of my life.

The tour was a huge failure but I had been bitten by the proverbial bug. With my tail tucked between my legs, I decided to start a nonprofit and swore off working with promoters ever again with the goal of writing and producing my own shows. Incidentally, by that time, my church began chartering mission (or satellite) churches in poor neighborhoods to offer more programs to people who lived in at-risk communities. I left the big church and volunteered to work with the small mission church and soon began writing plays for the congregation mostly made up of men who were recovering from drugs and alcohol. Here again, some friends saw my commitment, bought an old union building next door to the mission church (how convenient right?) and gave me keys to the building and complete autonomy to do whatever I wanted to do. We started staging dinner theater productions featuring the men from the church. Today those men are productive citizens with supportive families and good jobs. Although I'm in Dallas and they are in Atlanta, Facebook keeps us connected.

What I've learned from all of this is to bless the person who has found their way without trying to make it your way. There are many paths to working as a playwright but we must be open to the journey that is uniquely designed for us. The most valuable lesson I've learned however is to be very careful who you dismiss. My husband of 12 years who is a National Touring Promoter taught me that.

Karmo Sanders
Go West Young Girl

Being from Maine, I'm already a little off the beaten path. And it seems whenever I pick up a pen I'm headed down the road less traveled, in that my creative process tends to be an unmarked trail. Especially when it comes to marketing.

Jerry Sanders, my collaborator and I had been working on our Broadway Style musical *Gold Rush Girls* for ten years. That's not easy to say out loud, but, it's a musical and they are tricky. We'd been lucky with our re-writing process in that Kate Snodgrass, of Boston Playwrights' hosted a number of readings and helped produce a two week workshop at the New Rep in Watertown, MA. And we'd cultivated a garden of trusted friends with honest feedback. So finally ready to see the musical on its feet, I began the endless pilgrimages to the post office, rounds of competitions, letters to theaters. A bit bumped and bruised along the trail, getting plastered with rejection letters.

But I'm at a point where there's no turning back, no matter what. Even though everyone keeps saying: "What? You're still working on that?!" I couldn't help it. I can't help it. I'm totally in love, dedicated and brewing magic in this passionate excitement. I find myself singing songs from the musical to anybody who'll listen. Uncovering contacts from out of the blue, in the grocery store, spilling over totally enchanted with my characters. These freedom seeking "ladies of the night" women just like me, entrepreneurs, out here in the wilds, gambling on themselves!

And so I kept polishing, working, talking it up and magically one day I found myself at a fabulous party being introduced to Lael Morgan author of, *Good Time Girls,* the book which inspired our musical. I lifted my glass, threw her a toast and burst into the opening number from the show. Then I sang her another one. So began our mutual admiration society.

Now I knew Alaska might be a good initial fit for *Gold Rush Girls*. I'd contacted—and been rejected by—theaters in Anchorage. But when Lael won 2011 Alaska Woman of the Year her book *Good Time Girls* hit the best seller list again. Suddenly we had a buzz, here's *Gold Rush Girls* a musical inspired by the book- ready for an opening.

I was contacted by a little theater who had no budget, but on good faith hired a wonderful dramaturg. And fairy dust got sprinkled. This tiny theater got a Rasmuson and Atwood Foundation Grant for *Gold Rush Girls* and suddenly we're opening. Off Broadway to be sure. Ok yes, off off offff Broadway. But geographically perfect! And it was magic for Anchorage's talent showed up to shine, and shine they did. We opened to a sold out weekend July 27 2012. And *Gold Rush Girls* played to sell out houses the entire six-week run through September 2 as Cyrano's Theatre turned them away at the door.

Magic is alive and well on the road less traveled. Here's toasting all who believe, invite, encourage and celebrate—the joy of it.

Jakob Holder
Unheard Of

There's no expert chainsmith watching over our careers. As playwrights, we see ourselves crafting every link we hope will eventually connect our desks to someone else's stage. And yet, sometimes the chain strengthens without our participation.

My play *Housebreaking* was onstage at the Cherry Lane in 2009 through their Mentor Project. All was going quite well. Audience response was overwhelmingly positive, and a full production in the main season felt all but certain. Then irony usurped inevitability. The play, which deals partially with the effects of economic ruin, was enjoying its two week run nearly in synch with the beginnings of our current recession.

Most of us know this simple story: the production's ready; there just isn't the money to do it.

Part of the Mentor Project's allure is that it offers the quality of a full production without seizing the attractive premiere production credit. As we all know, the world-premiere rights are, beyond the unassailable brilliance of our words, what we relatively unknown playwrights use to entice theatres to take on our relatively unknown work.

Caution encouraged me to be savvy about a subsequent production—to not release the premiere rights to just any company. Obviously, sound advice for someone with leverage. The trouble was that I didn't have any. The one downside to the upside of the Mentor Project's barring of reviewers is that no one seemed to know that I was awaiting a bidding war. I was defending my play from no threat whatsoever.

My chain was rusting over.

Then one day, a year and a half later, I received this email:

"My name is Bastion and I work with Poison Apple Initiative, a theatre company out of Austin. By sheer accident I happened to see *Housebreaking* and fell absolutely in love with your play. We're in the middle of planning our next season and my fellow company members are eager to read the script I've been going on about for months."

Who? What? Never heard of you. Somewhere along the line I may have followed the well-intentioned, wrong-headed advice that giving away premiere rights to an amateur company would be a terrible mistake. Luckily, 18 months had commanded humility. I was thrilled to hear from any director so taken with my play.

Somewhere between first contact and the company's celebration of excellent reviews, nominations and an award, I asked Bastion Carboni what the "sheer accident" was that drew him to see my play. Apparently he was on his way to see Deirdre O'Connor's *Jailbait* at Cherry Lane's then alternate stage—The Cherry Pit—a ten-minute walk from the main space on Commerce Street. By the time he arrived at the wrong theatre he realized he'd never make it in time to the other. And so he took a chance on our humble showcase production.

With apologies to Ms. O'Connor: I'm glad he made such a good mistake and added a strong link to the chain.

David Henry Hwang
Protest And Production

I wrote my first play, *FOB*, to be performed in my college dormitory. Fourteen months later, it opened at the Public Theater in New York. How did this happen?

Through some diligence on my part, but largely as a result of fortuitous circumstances (aka luck), resulting from political protest and community pressure.

FOB revolves around the often-strained tensions between "FOB's," or Fresh Off the Boat Chinese immigrants, and "ABC's," or American-born Chinese. Several months before my dorm premiere, the Public produced a play in which a Caucasian actor was hired to play an Asian character. This "yellow face" casting led to a protest by Asian American actors in 1978, predating by more than a decade the much more public ruckus in 1991 over the casting of Jonathan Pryce as the Eurasian pimp in the Broadway musical *Miss Saigon* (not to mention, 2012's controversy over the musical *The Nightingale* at La Jolla Playhouse).

Joe Papp, the founder of the Public Theater and the New York Shakespeare Festival, who was sympathetic to minorities and the working class, invited the protesters into his office and hired one of them onto his staff with a directive to find plays for Asian actors. Fortunately for me, the Public was one of the theatres to which I sent my script after its dorm production.

I get credit for doing my research about theatres that might actually be interested in my play, including the O'Neill National Playwrights Conference, which chose *FOB* for its summer workshop several weeks after its dorm premiere. The show's director at the O'Neill, Robert Alan Ackerman, also happened to be a Resident Director at the Public, so he too recommended my play to Joe.

The lion's credit for my first production, though, goes to a group of brave actors who exerted community pressure. I am a beneficiary of affirmative action: a slot was created, and I am the writer who got to fill it. As such, I support affirmative action, because it is extremely hard for me to consider my own existence as anything other than a net plus to the American Theatre.

Tammy Ryan
Lost Writer Finds Unexpected Artistic Home

After graduating from Carnegie Mellon University's M.F.A. Playwriting program in 1990, I was not feeling like a writer. My plays had not been well received, and I was struggling to find my voice. Purging my files, I found the first act of a play I'd started there, which I'd entitled *Pig*. After sharing it in class, there'd been silence…and then some halfhearted questions. ("Why is it called…*Pig*?") I put the play away and worked on something that my professor liked better, but my heart wasn't in it. I decided, before quitting writing forever, to finish *Pig* that summer. I needed to write a play I felt passionate about. I finished *Pig* in a mad heat of a few weeks. I remember laughing (sometimes maniacally) alone at my kitchen table. It felt good to finish it, but now what? I sent it to contests and didn't hear back until a year later the Y.E.S. Festival at Northern Kentucky University offered to produce it. The production directed by Mike King was a wonderful experience. But it was like a glass of water in a desert.

In response to the lack of opportunities in Pittsburgh, some playwrights and I started a company called Pyramid Productions. We created a ten minute play festival called *The No Doze Dozen*. It was in one of the *No Doze's* that I met Sheila McKenna—a gifted comic actress who was hilarious in my ten minute play, *Crazy Bone*. During this time, Sheila's mentor, Raymond Laine, a theater professor at Point

Park College, was encouraging her to direct for Playhouse Jr. I saw a few of these shows and was impressed, but still thought of her primarily as a funny actress.

Fast forward to 1998. I get a phone call from John Amplas another professor at Point Park. The Pittsburgh Playhouse, with support from the college, was reviving its professional repertory company and wanted to open their season with one of my plays. They agreed to produce *Pig,* even though it had been previously produced. Amplas said: "How would you feel about Sheila McKenna directing?" They were taking a risk on me, I thought why not take a risk on her.

In the audience on opening night was Ronald Allan-Lindblom the newly hired Artistic Director of The REP. A few months later he called. He wanted to commission my next play. He shared his vision for the Playhouse creating what he called "Pittsburgh product." He wanted people "to think of Tammy Ryan when they hear the name of the Playhouse and to think of the Playhouse when they hear the name Tammy Ryan." What I heard was the sound of a door opening and I ran inside before anyone could change their minds.

Since then the Playhouse has produced seven of my plays, Sheila has become my artistic collaborator and best friend. I can't imagine my life artistically or otherwise without her. A few years after Raymond Laine passed away I found out it was he who had made the decision to call me. I didn't know Raymond at the time. I guess he'd heard something in my early work at the *No Doze Dozen.* He later told Ron Lindblom I was a playwright to champion.

You never know who you have in your corner.

Career Development Professionals

WE'RE LOOKING FOR SOMETHING A LITTLE LESS YOU.

Accountants

Kimerling and Wisdom
150 Broadway, Room 1105
New York, NY 10038
Ross Wisdom, Managing Partner
Phone: (212) 986-0892
www.kwllc.us
rwisdom@kwllc.us
Notes: Est. 1970.
Submission Fee: No

Marks Paneth & Shron LLP
622 3rd Ave.
New York, NY 10017
David R. Marcus, Partner
Phone: (212) 503-8800
Fax: (212) 370-3759
www.markspaneth.com
dmarcus@markspaneth.com
Notes: Est. 1907. Nationally ranked, full-service public accounting firm for individuals and companies in the entertainment industry.
Submission Fee: No

Agents

Abrams Artists Agency
275 Seventh Avenue, 26th fl.
New York, NY 10001
Phone: (646) 486-4600
Fax: (646) 486-0100
www.abramsartists.com/literary.html
literary@abramsartny.com
Notes: Agents: Sarah L. Douglas, Charles Kopelman, Beth Blickers, Morgan Jenness, Maura Teitelbaum, Kate Navin, Ron Gwiazda. Professional recommendation.
Submission Materials: query letter, S.A.S.E., synopsis
Submission Fee: No

Barbara Hogenson Agency, Inc.
165 West End Avenue #19C
New York, NY 10023
Phone: (212) 874-8084
Fax: (212) 595-6748
Bhogenson@aol.com
Notes: Est. 1994. Response time: 2 months.
Submission Materials: professional referral only
Preferred Genre: All genres
Preferred Length: Full-length
Submission Fee: No

Bret Adams Agency
448 W. 44th Street
New York, NY 10036
Phone: (212) 765-5630
www.bretadamsltd.net
morsini@bretadamsltd.net
Notes: Est. 1953. Staff: Bruce Ostler, Mark Orsini; Alexis Williams; Colin Hunt (Literary); Margi Rountree, Ken Melamed,

Michael Golden (Acting). Query must include professional recommendation.
Submission Materials: query letter
Preferred Genre: All genres
Submission Fee: No

Farber Literary Agency Inc.
14 East 75th Street
New York, NY 10021
Ann Farber, President
Phone: (212) 861-7075
Fax: (212) 861-7076
farberlit@aol.com
Notes: Est.1990. Response: 1 month.
Submission Materials: full script, query letter, S.A.S.E., synopsis
Preferred Genre: All genres
Preferred Length: Any length
Submission Fee: No

Fifi Oscard Agency, Inc.
110 West 40 Street
Suite 2100
New York, NY 10018
Phone: (212) 764-1100
Fax: (212) 840-5019
www.fifioscard.com
agency@fifioscard.com
Notes: Est. 1956.
Submission Materials: see website
Preferred Genre: All genres
Preferred Length: Any length
Submission Fee: No

Gage Group Inc.
14724 Ventura Blvd
Sherman Oaks, CA 91403
Phone: (818) 905-3800

Fax: (310) 859-8166
gagegroupla@gmail.com
Notes: Est. 1975. Submissions not returned.
Response: 3 months.
Submission Materials: professional referral
only
Submission Fee: No

Gersh Agency (NY)
41 Madison Ave
33rd Floor
New York, NY 10010
Phone: (212) 634-8105
Fax: (212) 391-8459
qcorbin@gershny.com
Notes: Must be submitted through professional
recommendation.
Submission Fee: No

Harden Curtis Associates
214 W. 29th Street, Suite 1203
New York, NY 10001
Phone: (212) 977-8502
Fax: (212) 975-8420
www.hardencurtis.com
maryharden@hardencurtis.com
Notes: Est. 1995. Response: 2 mos.
Submission Materials: professional referral
only
Preferred Genre: All genres
Preferred Length: Any length
Submission Fee: No

International Creative Management (ICM)
[CA]
10250 Constellation Blvd.
Los Angeles, CA 90067
Phone: (310) 550-4000
www.icmtalent.com/
books@icmtalent.com
Notes: Talent & literary agency.
Submission Materials: see website
Preferred Genre: All genres
Preferred Length: Any length
Submission Fee: No

International Creative Management (ICM)
[NY]
825 8th Ave.
New York, NY 10019
Phone: (212) 556-5600
Fax: (212) 556-5665
books@icmtalent.com
Notes: Talent & literary agency.
Submission Materials: see website

Preferred Genre: All genres
Preferred Length: Any length
Submission Fee: No

International Creative Management (ICM)
[UK]
4-6 Soho Sq.
London W1D 3PZ, United Kingdom
Phone: (442) 074-3208 Ext 00
www.icmtalent.com/
books@icmtalent.com
Notes: Talent & literary agency.
Submission Materials: see website
Preferred Genre: All genres
Preferred Length: Any length
Submission Fee: No

Judy Boals Inc.
307 W. 38th St., #812
New York, NY 10018
Phone: (212) 500-1424
Fax: (212) 500-1426
www.judyboals.com
info@judyboals.com
Notes: Submit via personal recommendation.
Response : 1 month.
Submission Materials: query letter, S.A.S.E.
Submission Fee: No

Kerin-Goldberg Associates
155 E. 55th St., #5-D
New York, NY 10022
Phone: (212) 838-7373
Fax: (212) 838-0774
kgatalent@nyc.rr.com
Notes: Est. 1989. Staff: Ron Ross, Ellison
Goldberg, Chris Nichols.

Paradigm (NY)
360 Park Ave. South
16th Floor
New York, NY 10010
Phone: (212) 897-6400
Fax: (212) 575-6397
www.paradigmagency.com
Notes: Agents: William Craver, Lucy Stille,
Jack Tantleff, Jonathan Mills. Response: 6
months.
Submission Materials: query letter, S.A.S.E.
Submission Fee: No

Peregrine Whittlesey Agency
279 Central Park West
New York, NY 10024
Peregrine Whittlesey, Agent

Phone: (212) 787-1802
Fax: (212) 787-4985
pwwagy@aol.com
Submission Materials: query letter, S.A.S.E.
Submission Fee: No

Robert A. Freedman Dramatic Agency, Inc.
1501 Broadway, suite #2310
New York, NY 10036
Phone: (212) 840-5760
Fax: (212) 840-5776
RFreedmanAgent@aol.com
Notes: Est. 1928. Response: 4 months. Agents: Robert Freedman, Selma Luttinger, Marta Praeger.
Submission Materials: query letter, S.A.S.E.
Preferred Length: Full-length
Submission Fee: No

Soiree Fair Inc.
133 Midland Ave., #10
Montclair, NJ 07042
Karen Gunn, President
Phone: (973) 783-9051
Fax: (973) 746-0426
www.soireefair.com
Soireefair@yahoo.com
Notes: Est. 1995. Material must be unoptioned, unpublished, unproduced and be submitted with professional recommendation.
Submission Materials: query letter, synopsis
Preferred Genre: Plays or Musicals
Preferred Length: Full-length
Special interest: LGBT
Submission Fee: No

Susan Schulman, A Literary Agency
454 W. 44th St.
New York, NY 10036
Susan F. Schulman, Agent
Phone: (212) 713-1633
Fax: (212) 581-8830
schulman@aol.com
Submission Materials: see website
Preferred Genre: All genres
Preferred Length: Full-length

Special interest: Theatre for Young Audiences
Submission Fee: No

The Marton Agency, Inc.
1 Union Square West
#815
New York, NY 10003
Phone: (212) 255-1908
Fax: (212) 691-9061
info@martonagency.com
Notes: Specializes in brokering foreign-language rights to US theater works. Promotes plays to associates abroad, generally after a production has been mounted in the US.
Submission Fee: No

The Shukat Company Ltd.
340 W. 55th St., #1A
New York, NY 10019
Phone: (212) 582-7614
Fax: (212) 315-3752
staff@shukat.com
Submission Materials: 10-pg sample, query letter, S.A.S.E.
Preferred Genre: All genres
Preferred Length: Full-length
Submission Fee: No

William Morris Endeavor (NY)
1325 Avenue of the Americas
New York, NY 10019
Phone: (212) 586-5100
jbz@wmeentertainment.com
Notes: Staff: John Buzzetti, David Kalodner, Derek Zasky, Susan Weaving, Jonathan Lomma, Scott Chaloff.
Submission Materials: professional referral only
Submission Fee: No

Writers & Artists Agency [CA]
8383 Wilshire Blvd., #550
Beverly Hills, CA 90211
Phone: (323) 866-0900
Fax: (323) 866-1899
info@wriart.com
Submission Fee: No

Attorneys

Brooks & Distler
110 E. 59th Street, 23rd fl.
New York, NY 10022
Marsha Brooks, Partner in Law Firm

Phone: (212) 486-1400
Fax: (212) 486-2266
brookslaw@aol.com

Cowan, DeBaets, Abrahams & Sheppard LLP
41 Madison Ave., Fl. 34
New York, NY 10010
Phone: (212) 974-7474
Fax: (212) 974-8474
www.cdas.com
fbimbler@cdas.com

Daniel Aharoni & Partners LLP
575 Madison Ave
New York, NY 10022
Lauren DeBellis Aviv
Phone: (212) 605-0415
Fax: (646) 349-2274
lauren@danielaharoni.com
Notes: Arts Immigration Attorney

David H. Friedlander, Esq.
81 Park Dr.
Mount Kisco, NY 10549
David H. Friedlander
Phone: (914) 241-1277
Fax: (914) 470-2244
www.dfriedlander.com
david@dfriedlander.com

Dinker Biddle & Reath LLP
1500 K Street, MW
Suite 1100
Washington, DC 20005
Janet Fries, Of Counsel
Phone: (202) 842-8800

Fitelson, Lasky, Aslan, Couture and Garmise
551 5th Ave., #605
New York, NY 10176
Phone: (212) 586-4700
Fax: (212) 949-6746
dramalex@aol.com

Frankfurt, Kurnit, Klein and Selz
488 Madison Ave.
New York, NY 10022
S. Jean Ward, Attorney
Phone: (212) 980-0120
Fax: (212) 593-9175
www.fkks.com
sjward@fkks.com

Franklin, Weinrib, Rudell & Vassallo PC
488 Madison Ave.
New York, NY 10022
Elliot H. Brown, Esq, Partner
Phone: (212) 935-5500

Fax: (212) 308-0642
www.fwrv.com
ehb@fwrv.com

Law Office of John J. Tormey III, Esq.
1324 Lexington Avenue, PMB 188
New York, NY 10128
John J. Tormey, Attorney-at-Law
Phone: (212) 410-4142
Fax: (212) 410-2380
www.tormey.org
brightline@att.net
Notes: Entertainment Transactional Legal Work and General Law Practice.

Law Office of Susan J. Steiger, Esq.
60 East 42nd Street, 47th floor
New York, NY 10165
Susan J. Steiger, Attorney
Phone: (212) 880-0865
Fax: (212) 697-0877
Notes: Est. 1982.

Law Offices of Gordon P. Firemark
10940 Wilshire Blvd, 16th Floor
Los Angeles, CA 90024
Gordon P. Firemark, Attorney at Law
Phone: (310) 443-4185
Fax: (310) 477-7676
www.firemark.com
gfiremark@firemark.com
Notes: Additional websites: www.theatrelawyer.com and www.theatreproduceracademy.com.

Law Offices of Jeffrey L. Graubart, P.C.
100 Corson Street, Third Floor
Pasadena, CA 91103
Phone: (626) 304-2800
Fax: (626) 304-2807
www.entertainmentlaw.la
info@jlgraubart.com
Notes: Est. 1970.

Miller Korzenik Sommers LLP
488 Madison Ave
New York, NY 10022
Eric Rayman, Attorney
Phone: (212) 254-6531
Fax: (212) 228-5130
www.mkslex.com
erayman@mkslex.com

Paul, Weiss, Rifkind, Wharton & Garrison
Charles H. Googe, Chair of Entertainment Department

Phone: (212) 373-2391
www.paulweiss.com
cgooge@paulweiss.com

Peter S. Cane, Esq.
230 Park Avenue
Suite 1000
New York, NY 10169
Phone: (212) 922-9800
Fax: (212) 922-9822
www.canelaw.com
peter@canelaw.com

Robert S. Perlstein, Esq.
1501 Broadway
Suite 703
New York, NY 10036
Robert S. Perlstein, Attorney
Phone: (212) 832-9951
Fax: (212) 831-9906
rspesq@judgedee.net
Notes: Clients: major performers, conductors,
singers, actors, musicians, arrangers, orches-
trators, screenwriters, television producers,
authors; emphasis in classical music.

Roberta L. Korus, Attorney at Law
Three Emmalon Ave
North White Plains, NY 10603
Roberta L. Korus, Attorney at Law
Phone: (914) 269-8120
Fax: (914) 831-2174
robertakorus@gmail.com

Ronald A. Lachman
468 N. Camden Dr. #200
Beverly Hills, CA 90210
Phone: (323) 655-6020
www.ronaldlachman.com
ron@ronaldlachman.com

Volunteer Lawyers for the Arts (VLA)
1 E. 53rd St., Fl. 6
New York, NY 10022
Phone: (212) 319-2787
Fax: (212) 752-6575
www.vlany.org
vlany@vlany.org
Notes: Est. 1969. Provider of pro bono legal
and mediation services, educational programs and publications & advocacy to the arts
community in NYC. Fees: based on client's
finances.

Commercial Producers

Araca Group
545 W. 45th Street
10th floor
New York, NY 10036
Phone: (212) 869-0070
Fax: (212) 869-0210
www.araca.com
creative@araca.com
Notes: Est. 1997. Broadway/off Broadway
productions.
Agent Only: Yes
Submission Materials: agent-only
Preferred Genre: Plays or Musicals
Preferred Length: Full-length
Submission Fee: No

Boyett Ostar Productions
268 West 44th Street
4th Floor
New York, NY 10036
Phone: (212) 702-9779
Fax: (212) 702-0899
Agent Only: No
Submission Fee: No

Cameron Mackintosh Inc.
1650 Broadway, #800
New York, NY 10019
Shidan Majidi, Production Associate
Phone: (212) 921-9290
Fax: (212) 921-9271
www.cameronmackintosh.com
smajidi@camack.com
Notes: Mary Poppins, Les Miserables, The
Phantom of the Opera, Oliver!, Oklahoma!,
My Fair Lady, The Witches of Eastwick, Miss
Saigon, CATS.
Agent Only: Yes
Submission Materials: agent-only
Preferred Genre: Musical theatre
Preferred Length: Full-length
Submission Fee: No

Dodger Properties
311 W. 43rd St., #602
New York, NY 10036
Phone: (212) 575-9710
www.dodger.com
info@dodger.com
Notes: Est. 1978. Jersey Boys.

Agent Only: Yes
Submission Materials: agent-only
Preferred Genre: All genres
Preferred Length: Full-length
Submission Fee: No

Jane Harmon Associates
One Lincoln Plaza, Suite 28-0
20 West 64th Street
New York, NY 10023
Jane Harmon
Phone: (212) 362-6836
Fax: (212) 362-8572
harmonjane@aol.com
Notes: Est. 1979. Production: drama/comedy. Submit via mail or email. Response: 3–5 weeks.
Agent Only: No
Submission Materials: query letter, resume, synopsis
Preferred Genre: Plays (No Musicals)
Preferred Length: Full-length
Submission Fee: No

Margery Klain
2107 Locust St.
Philadelphia, PA 19103
Margery Klain, Producer
Phone: (215) 567-1512
Fax: (215) 567-2049
mklain1011@aol.com
Notes: Est. 1985. Material must be unoptioned. Response: 2 months.
Agent Only: Yes
Submission Materials: professional referral only
Preferred Genre: Plays (No Musicals)
Preferred Length: Full-length
Submission Fee: No

Margo Lion Ltd.
246 W. 44th St., Fl. 8
New York, NY 10036
Phone: (212) 869-1112
Fax: (212) 730-0381
www.margolionltd.com
office@margolionltd.com
Notes: Email submissions preferred. Response: 1 year.
Agent Only: Yes

Submission Materials: agent-only
Preferred Genre: All genres
Preferred Length: Full-length
Submission Fee: No

Nederlander Organization
1450 Broadway, Fl. 6
New York, NY 10018
Phone: (212) 840-5577
Fax: (212) 840-3326
www.nederlander.com
kraitt@nederlander.com
Notes: Est. 1912.
Agent Only: Yes
Submission Materials: agent-only
Preferred Genre: All genres
Preferred Length: Full-length
Submission Fee: No

Shubert Organization
234 W. 44th St.
New York, NY 10036
D.S. Moynihan, VP, Creaive Projects
Phone: (212) 944-3700
www.shubertorg.com
vincer@shubertticketing.org
Notes: Est. 1900.
Agent Only: Yes
Submission Materials: agent-only
Preferred Genre: All genres
Preferred Length: Full-length
Submission Fee: No

Stephen Pevner, Inc.
382 Lafayette St., Fl. 8
New York, NY 10003
Stephen Pevner, Producer
Phone: (212) 674-8403
spidevelopment@gmail.com
Agent Only: No

Vienna Waits Productions
1285 Avenue of the Americas
32nd Floor
New York, NY 10019
John Breglio, Esq, Producer
Phone: (917) 584-8341
jbreglio@paulweiss.com
Agent Only: No
Submission Fee: No

Publishers

Anchorage Press Plays Inc.
617 Baxter Ave.
Louisville, KY 40204-1105
Phone: (502) 583-2288
Fax: (502) 583-2288
www.applays.com
applays@bellsouth.net
Notes: Est. 1935. Educational, professional
and amateur venues. Response Time: 6–9 mos.
Agent Only: No
Submission Materials: see website
Preferred Genre: All genres
Preferred Length: Any length
Special interest: Theatre for Young
Audiences
Submission Fee: No

Asian Theatre Journal
2840 Kolowalu St.
Honolulu, HI 96822
Phone: (888) 847-7377
Fax: (800) 650-7811
www.uhpress.hawaii.edu/journals
uhpjourn@hawaii.edu
Notes: Dedicated to performing arts of Asia,
traditional and modern, including original and
translated plays.
Agent Only: No
Submission Materials: query letter
Special interest: Asian-American
Submission Fee: No

Big Dog Publishing
P.O. Box 1400
Tallevast, FL 34270
Dawn Remsing, Editor, Publisher
Fax: (941) 358-7606
www.bigdogplays.com
info@bigdogplays.com
Notes: Est. 2005. Plays for family and school
audiences (K–12). Publishes 25–40 plays/year.
Response time: 2–3 months. Prefer produced/
award-winning work. No email submissions
please.
Agent Only: No
Submission Materials: see website
Preferred Genre: Plays or Musicals
Preferred Length: Any length
Submission Fee: No

Broadway Play Publishing Inc. (BPPI)
56 East 81 Street
New York, NY 10028-0202

www.broadwayplaypubl.com
sara@broadwayplaypubl.com
Notes: Est. 1982. Response time: 2 months
query, 4 months script.
Agent Only: No
Submission Materials: query letter
Preferred Genre: All genres
Preferred Length: Any length
Submission Fee: No

Callaloo
4212 TAMU
Texas A&M University
College Station, TX 77843
Phone: (979) 458-3108
Fax: (979) 458-3275
callaloo.tamu.edu
callaloo@tamu.edu
Notes: Quarterly journal devoted to creative
work by and critical studies of the work of
African-Americans and peoples of African
descent throughout the African Diaspora.
Response time: 6 months.
Agent Only: No
Submission Materials: full script (3 copies),
query letter, S.A.S.E.
Preferred Genre: All genres
Preferred Length: Any length
Special interest: African-American
Submission Fee: No

Capilano Review TCR
2055 Purcell Way
N. Vancouver, BC V7J 3H5, Canada
Phone: (604) 984-1712
Fax: (604) 990-7837
www.thecapilanoreview.ca
contact@thecapilanoreview.ca
Notes: Est. 1972. Unpublished poetry, drama,
visual arts. Response time: 4 months. Please
use Canadian postage for SASE.
Agent Only: No
Submission Materials: see website
Preferred Length: Any length
Submission Fee: No

Confrontation
CW Post Campus English Dept.
Brookville, NY 11548
Joana Semeiks, Editor
Phone: (516) 299-2720
Fax: (516) 299-2735
www.cwpost.liu.edu/cwis/cwp/culture

mtucker@liu.edu
Notes: Material submitted must be unpublished.
Agent Only: No
Submission Materials: full script, S.A.S.E.
Preferred Genre: Plays (No Musicals)
Preferred Length: 10-min./10pgs.
Submission Fee: No

Currency Press
Box 2287
Strawberry Hills
02012, Australia
Phone: (029) 319-5877
Fax: (029) 319-3649
www.currency.com.au
proposals@currency.com.au
Notes: Publisher/distributor of performing arts books on Australian drama, film, music (including play and film scripts) in Australia & New Zealand.
Agent Only: No
Submission Materials: full script, S.A.S.E.
Preferred Genre: Plays (No Musicals)
Preferred Length: One-Act
Submission Fee: No

Dramatic Publishing Company
311 Washington St.
Woodstock, IL 60098
Phone: (800) 448-7469
Fax: (800) 334-5302
www.dramaticpublishing.com/
plays@dramaticpublishing.com
Notes: Est. 1885. Response: 8 months.
Agent Only: No
Submission Materials: full script, S.A.S.E.
Preferred Genre: All genres
Preferred Length: Any length
Submission Fee: No

Dramatics Magazine
2343 Auburn Ave.
Cincinnati, OH 45219
Don Corathers, Editor
Phone: (513) 421-3900
Fax: (513) 421-7077
schooltheatre.org
dcorathers@schooltheatre.org
Notes: Est. 1929. National monthly magazine for High School theater students & teachers, printing 7 one-acts and full-lengths/year. Response: 5 months. Buys one-time, non-exclusive publication rights only.
Agent Only: No

Submission Materials: full script
Preferred Genre: Plays (No Musicals)
Preferred Length: Any length
Submission Fee: No

Dramatists Play Service, Inc.
Attn: Michael Fellmeth
440 Park Avenue South
New York, NY 10016
Phone: (212) 683-8960
www.dramatists.com
fellmeth@dramatists.com
Notes: Performances licensed. All venues except commercial. Response: 6 months.
Agent Only: No
Submission Materials: query letter, synopsis
Preferred Genre: Plays or Musicals
Preferred Length: Full-length
Submission Fee: No

Eldridge Publishing Company Inc.
Box 14367
Tallahassee, FL 32317
Nancy S. Vorhis, Senior Editor
Phone: (850) 385-2463
Fax: (850) 385-2463
www.histage.com
info@95church.com
Notes: Est. 1906. Performances licensed, all venues. Material for non-denominational religous market. Email work to newworks@95church.com. Response, 2 months.
Agent Only: No
Submission Materials: audio CD, full script, query letter, S.A.S.E.
Preferred Genre: Plays or Musicals
Preferred Length: Any length
Special interest: Theatre for Young Audiences
Submission Fee: No

Empire Publishing Service
Box 1344
Studio City, CA 91614
Joseph W. Witt
Phone: (818) 784-8918
empirepubsvc@att.net
Notes: Est. 1960. Publishes performing arts books, including sheet music. Plays must have been produced. No email submissions please. Response: from 3 days to 1 year.
Agent Only: No
Submission Materials: query letter, S.A.S.E.
Preferred Genre: All genres

Preferred Length: Any length
Submission Fee: No

Meriwether Publishing Ltd./Contemporary Drama Service
885 Elkton Drive
Colorado Springs, CO 80907
Mark L. Zapel
Phone: (719) 594-4422
Fax: (719) 594-9916
www.contemporarydrama.com
editor@meriwether.com
Notes: Theatre arts books written by drama educators and professionals, plus DVDs, CDs and videos for classroom use. Submit by US mail.
Agent Only: No
Submission Materials: see website
Preferred Genre: Plays or Musicals
Preferred Length: Any length
Submission Fee: No

Moose Hide Books
684 Walls Rd.
Sault Ste. Marie, ON P6A-5K6, Canada
Richard Mousseau, Publisher
Phone: (705) 779-3331
Fax: (707) 779-3331
www.moosehidebooks.com
rmousseau@moosehidebooks.com
Notes: Response: 1 month.
Agent Only: No
Submission Materials: query letter, S.A.S.E.
Submission Fee: No

NewMusicals.com
22 Grenhart Street
West Hartford, CT 06117
R. J. Chiarappa, Submissions Editor
Phone: (860) 236-0592
Fax: (860) 236-5762
www.newmusicals.com
info@newmusicals.com
Notes: Please Note: We are not accepting any submissions at this time. Please check our website for updates.
Agent Only: No
Submission Materials: see website
Preferred Genre: Musical theatre
Preferred Length: Full-length
Submission Fee: No

Norman Maine Publishing
P.O. Box 1400
Tallevast, FL 34270

Dawn Remsing, Editor, Publishing
Fax: (941) 358-7606
www.normanmaineplays.com
info@normanmaineplays.com
Notes: Est. 2005. Plays for community, professsional and university theatre. Response: 2–3 months. Prefer produced/award-winning work.
Agent Only: No
Submission Materials: see website
Preferred Genre: Plays or Musicals
Preferred Length: Any length
Submission Fee: No

Original Works Publishing
1637 N. Las Palmas Ave
Los Angeles, CA 90028
Jason Aaron Goldberg, President
www.originalworksonline.com
info@originalworksonline.com
Notes: Est. 2000. Submitted material must have been produced. Response: 3–6 months.
Agent Only: No
Submission Materials: see website
Preferred Genre: Plays (No Musicals)
Preferred Length: Any length
Submission Fee: No

PAJ: A Journal of Performance and Art
Box 532, Village Station
New York, NY 10014
Bonnie Marranca, Editor
Phone: (212) 243-3885
Fax: (212) 243-2885
www.mitpressjournals.org/paj
pajpub@mac.com
Notes: Est. 1976. Response: 2 months query, 2 months script. Preferred length: Under 40 pages. Prefer experimental or plays in translation.
Agent Only: No
Submission Materials: query letter, synopsis
Preferred Genre: Plays (No Musicals)
Submission Fee: No

Players Press Inc.
Box 1132
Studio City, CA 91614
Phone: (818) 789-4980
playerspress@worldnet.att.net
Notes: Est. 1960. Response: 2 weeks query, 6 months script. Only published plays and/or musicals that have been produced. A reading is not a production. One production is acceptable if under an Equity contract (professional)

or winner of a playwriting contest. Two productions are required if they are community, school or any form of amateur production.
Agent Only: No
Submission Materials: query letter, S.A.S.E.
Preferred Genre: All genres
Preferred Length: Any length
Submission Fee: No

Playscripts, Inc.
450 Seventh Ave.
Suite 809
New York, NY 10123
Phone: (866) 639-7529
Fax: (888) 203-4519
www.playscripts.com/submit
submissions@playscripts.com
Notes: Est. 1998. Acting editions sold and performances licensed to amateur/professional venues worldwide. Musicals by agent submission only.
Agent Only: Yes
Submission Materials: see website
Preferred Genre: Plays (No Musicals)
Preferred Length: Any length
Submission Fee: No
Deadline(s): Rolling

Poems & Plays
MTSU English Dept.
Murfreesboro, TN 37132
Gaylord Brewer, Editor
Phone: (615) 898-2712
Fax: (615) 898-5098
www.mtsu.edu/english/poemsandplays
gbrewer@mtsu.edu
Notes: Est. 1993. Work must be unpublished. Response: 3 months.
Agent Only: No
Submission Materials: full script, S.A.S.E.
Preferred Genre: Plays (No Musicals)
Preferred Length: 10-min./10pgs.
Submission Fee: No
Deadline(s): See website

Rodgers & Hammerstein Organization Theatricals
229 W. 28th St., Fl. 11
New York, NY 10001
Lissi Borshman, Amateur Licensing Representative
Phone: (212) 564-4000
Fax: (212) 268-1245
www.rnh.com
theatre@rnh.com

Notes: Titles must be returned within 2 weeks after closing in perfect condition. Quotes expire 3 months after created.
Agent Only: No
Submission Materials: application
Submission Fee: No

Samuel French Inc.
45 W. 25th St.
New York, NY 10010
Amy Rose Marsh, Literary Manager
Phone: (212) 206-8990
Fax: (212) 206-1429
www.samuelfrench.com
publications@samuelfrench.com
Notes: Est. 1830. We are the largest play publisher and licenser in the world, with a catalogue of over 5,000 active plays. Recently published plays include 4000 Miles by Amy Herzog and Seminar by Theresa Rebeck. Average response time: 6 months.
Agent Only: No
Submission Materials: see website
Preferred Genre: All genres
Preferred Length: Any length
Submission Fee: No

Smith and Kraus
Box 127
Lyme, NH 03768
Marisa Smith, Publisher
Phone: (603) 643-6431
Fax: (603) 643-1831
www.smithkraus.com
editor@smithkraus.com
Notes: Response: 3 weeks query; 4 months script.
Agent Only: No
Submission Materials: query letter, synopsis
Preferred Genre: Plays (No Musicals)
Preferred Length: Any length
Submission Fee: No

Speert Publishing
Phone: (212) 979-7656
www.speertpublishing.com
espeert@speertpublishing.com
Notes: Self-publishing services for acting editions of original plays. Response: 1 week.
Agent Only: No
Submission Materials: query letter
Preferred Genre: Plays (No Musicals)
Preferred Length: Any length
Submission Fee: No

Steele Spring Theatrical Licensing
3845 Cazador Street
Los Angeles, CA 90065
Phone: (323) 739-0413
Fax: (818) 232-9158
www.steelespring.com
submissions@steelespring.com
Agent Only: No
Submission Materials: full script, synopsis
Preferred Genre: All genres
Preferred Length: Full-length
Submission Fee: No

Tams-Witmark Music Library Inc.
560 Lexington Ave.
New York, NY 10022
Sargent L. Aborn, President
Phone: (212) 688-2525
Fax: (212) 688-3232
www.tams-witmark.com
saborn@tamswitmark.com
Notes: Classic broadway musicals for stage
performance around the world.
Agent Only: No
Submission Materials: see website
Preferred Genre: Musical theatre
Preferred Length: Any length
Submission Fee: No

Theatrefolk
P.O. Box 1064
Crystal Beach, ON L0S-1B0, Canada
Craig Mason, Publisher
Phone: (866) 245-9138
Fax: (877) 245-9138
www.theatrefolk.com/submissions
tfolk@theatrefolk.com
Notes: We publish plays specifically for
student performers. Production: simple.
Response: 6–8 weeks. Please review our sub-
mission policy before submitting.
Agent Only: No
Submission Materials: see website
Preferred Genre: All genres
Preferred Length: Any length
Submission Fee: No
Deadline(s): Year round

TheatreForum
9500 Gilman Dr.
MCO344
La Jolla, CA 92093

Fax: (858) 534-1080
www.theatreforum.org
ashank@ucsd.edu
Notes: Plays must have been professionally
produced. Submit via email.
Agent Only: No
Submission Materials: query letter
Preferred Genre: Plays (No Musicals)
Preferred Length: Full-length
Submission Fee: No

Theatrical Rights Worldwide
570 Seventh Avenue, Suite 2100
New York, NY 10018
Steve Spiegel, President & CEO
Phone: (646) 736-3232
Fax: (212) 643-1322
www.theatricalrights.com
licensing@theatricalrights.com
Notes: Est. 2006. Work must be unpublished.
Response: 3–6 months.
Agent Only: No
Submission Materials: audio CD, full script,
query letter, S.A.S.E.
Preferred Genre: Musical theatre
Preferred Length: Any length
Submission Fee: No

YouthPlays
7199 W. Sunset Blvd. #390
Los Angeles, CA 90046
Jonathan Dorf, Partner
Phone: (424) 703-5315
www.youthplays.com
info@youthplays.com
Notes: We publish plays for young actors
and audiences. Flexible to large cast One-Act
(30–35 minutes) comedies for high school and
middle school actors. Deadline is ongoing for
regular submissions or May 1st for New Voices
One-Act Play Competition for young play-
wrights 19 and under. Please visit our website's
"Submit a Play" page for guidelines and info
on our current needs before submitting.
Agent Only: No
Submission Materials: see website
Preferred Genre: Theatre for Young
Audiences
Preferred Length: Any length
Submission Fee: No
Deadline(s): Ongoing

Career Development Opportunities

AND THE HONORABLE MENTION AS A
THIRD RUNNER-UP TO THE SEMI-FINALIST
IN THE PRELIMINARY ROUND GOES TO . . .

Colonies & Residencies

Altos de Chavon
66 5th Ave., #819D
New York, NY 10011
Phone: (212) 229-5370
Fax: (212) 229-8988
www.altosdechavon.com
altos@earthlink.net
Notes: Est. 1981. 3 1/2 month residencies in
La Romana, Dominican Republic, for visual
artists, writers, musicians, and architects.
Summary of work, critiques of previous work
required.
Agent Only: No
Submission Materials: query letter, synopsis
Submission Fee: Yes
Deadline(s): August 15, 2013

Atlantic Center for the Arts
1414 Art Center Ave.
New Smyrna Beach, FL 32168
Phone: (386) 427-6975
Fax: (386) 427-5669
www.atlanticcenterforthearts.org
program@atlanticcenterforthearts.org
Notes: Est. 1982. Residencies of 3 weeks with
master artists. Workspace includes black box
theater, music/recording studio, dance studio, art & sculpture studios, digital lab and
resource library.
Agent Only: No
Submission Materials: see website
Submission Fee: Yes

Bellagio Center Creative Arts Residencies
Villa Serbelloni, Via Roma 1
Bellagio 22021, Italy
Rob Garris, Managing Director, Bellagio
Programs
Phone: (212) 852-8431
Fax: (212) 852-8438
www.rockfound.org/bellagio
bellagio_ny@rockfound.org
Agent Only: No
Submission Materials: see website
Preferred Genre: All genres
Submission Fee: Yes
Deadline(s): May 1 (yearly); December 1
(yearly)

**Byrdcliffe Arts Colony Artist-in-Residence
(AIR) Program**
34 Tinker St.

Woodstock, NY 12498
Phone: (845) 679-2079
Fax: (845) 679-4529
www.byrdcliffe.org
info@woodstockguild.org
Notes: Est. 1980 Catskill Mountains,
Woodstock, NY. Four, 4-week sessions per
season. Application on website. Additional
phone number May–September ONLY
(845)-679-8540.
Agent Only: No
Submission Materials: see website for
application
Preferred Genre: Plays or Musicals
Preferred Length: Any length
Submission Fee: Yes
Deadline(s): March 1, 2013

Camargo Foundation
1 Ave Jermini
Cassis 13260, France
Phone: 0 (113) 344-2011 Ext 157
Fax: 0 (113) 344-2013 Ext 657
www.camargofoundation.org
apply@camargofoundation.org
Notes: Interdisciplinary residency program
includes thirteen furnished apartments, a ref-
erence library and three art/music studios.
Residencies are one semester. See website for
complete online application requirements.
Agent Only: No
Submission Materials: see website
Preferred Genre: All genres
Preferred Length: Any length
Submission Fee: Yes
Deadline(s): See website

Centrum Artistic Residencies Program
Box 1158
Port Townsend, WA 98368
Phone: (360) 385-3102
www.centrum.org/residencies
lisa@centrum.org
Notes: Est. 1980. Awarded in one week blocks,
residencies may be of any duration, time and
space permitting. Submit proposal of work
focused on with resume and work sample.
Agent Only: No
Submission Materials: see website
Preferred Genre: All genres
Submission Fee: Yes
Deadline(s): Rolling

Dorland Mountain Arts Colony
Box 6
Temecula, CA 92593
Jill Roberts, Colony Manager
Phone: (909) 302-3837
Fax: (951) 582-4973
www.dorlandartscolony.org
info@dorlandartscolony.org
Notes: Est. 1979. Secluded retreat on a scenic
Nature Preserve in southern California 300
acres near Wine Country,
Agent Only: No
Submission Materials: application
Submission Fee: Yes
Deadline(s): May 1, 2013; 9/1/2013

Edward Albee Foundation
Edward Albee Foundation
14 Harrison St.
New York, NY 10013
Jakob Holder, Secretary
Phone: (212) 226-2020
Fax: (212) 226-5551
www.albeefoundation.org
info@albeefoundation.org
Notes: Est. 1966. Residencies of 4–6 weeks
(mid May–mid October) in Montauk, NY, for
writers and visual artists.
Agent Only: No
Submission Materials: see website
Submission Fee: No
Deadline(s): See website

Emlenton Mill
201 Main Street
Emlenton, PA 16373
Phone: (724) 867-0277
www.emlentonmill.com

Gell Center of the Finger Lakes
740 University Ave.
Rochester, NY 14607
Kathy Pottetti, Director Operations/
Programming
Phone: (585) 473-2590
Fax: (585) 442-9333
www.wab.org
Kathyp@wab.org
Agent Only: No
Submission Materials: 10-pg sample
Submission Fee: No

Hawthornden Retreat for Writers
Hawthornden Castle
Lasswade EH18 1EG, Scotland

Phone: 0 (131) 440-2180
Fax: 0 (131) 440-1989
office@hawthornden.com
Notes: Est. 1982. Residencies of 4 weeks
(February–July, September–December) in
17th-century castle, 40-minute bus ride to
Edinburgh. Residents housed in study bed-
rooms. Author must be produced or published.
Agent Only: No
Submission Materials: 10-pg sample,
application
Submission Fee: No
Deadline(s): June 30, 2013

Headlands Center for the Arts
944 Fort Barry
Sausalito, CA 94965
Holly Blake, Residency Manager
Phone: (415) 331-2787
Fax: (415) 331-3857
www.headlands.org
hblake@headlongs.org
Notes: Est. 1987. Hosts 40 residencies for
artists of all disciplines per year from 1 to 3
months. Response: 4–5 months.
Agent Only: No
Submission Materials: see website
Submission Fee: Yes

**Helene Wurlitzer Foundation of New
Mexico**
P.O. Box 1891
Taos, NM 87571
Phone: (575) 758-2413
Fax: (575) 758-2559
www.wurlitzerfoundation.org
HWF@taosnet.com
Notes: Est. 1956. Rent and utility fee free rsi-
dences of 3 months (January–November) for
visual artists, writers and composers. See web-
site for submission guidelines.
Agent Only: No
Submission Materials: application
Submission Fee: No
Deadline(s): See website

International Writing Program (IWP)
430 N. Clinton St.
Iowa City, IA 52242
Christopher Merrill, Director
Phone: (319) 335-0128
Fax: (319) 335-3843
iwp.uiowa.edu
iwp@uiowa.edu

Notes: Est. 1967. For published writers of fiction, poetry, drama, or screenplays who are not US residents but are proficient in English. August–November, 3 month residency.
Agent Only: No
Submission Fee: No

La MaMa Playwright Retreat
74-A E. 4th St.
New York, NY 10003
Phone: (212) 475-7710
web@lamama.org
Notes: Est. 2007.
Agent Only: No
Submission Fee: Yes

Lanesboro Residency Program Fellowships
103 Parkway Ave. N., Box 152
Lanesboro, MN 55949
Phone: (507) 467-2446
Fax: (507) 467-4446
www.lanesboroarts.org
Info@lanesboroarts.org
Notes: Retreat space also available for rent.
Agent Only: No
Submission Materials: see website
Submission Fee: No
Deadline(s): June 30 annually

MacDowell Colony
100 High St.
Peterborough, NH 03458
Courtney Bethel, Admissions Director
Phone: (603) 924-3886
Fax: (603) 924-9142
www.macdowellcolony.org
admissions@macdowellcolony.org
Notes: Est. 1907. Residencies/studios for up to 8 weeks (Jun–Sep, Oct–Jan, Feb–May). Multiple deadlines: September 15, January 15, and April 15. Financial assistance available. Response: 10 weeks
Agent Only: No
Submission Materials: application
Preferred Genre: All genres
Preferred Length: Full-length
Submission Fee: Yes
Deadline(s): Multiple; Multiple

McKnight National Playwriting Residency and Commission
2301 Franklin Ave. E
Minneapolis, MN 55406
Laura Leffler-Mcabe, Artistic Programs Administrator

www.pwcenter.org
info@pwcenter.org
Notes: Commissioning and production of new works from nationally recognized playwrights. Recipient in residence at Center while play is in development.
Agent Only: No
Submission Materials: application
Submission Fee: No
Deadline(s): See website

Millay Colony for the Arts
454 East Hill Rd, Box 3
Austerlitz, NY 12017
Phone: (518) 392-3103
Fax: (518) 392-4944
www.millaycolony.org
apply@millaycolony.org
Notes: Est. 1973. Month-long residencies (April–November) on former estate of Edna St. Vincent Millay for writers, visual artists, composers. No cost for residency. See website for submission guidelines.
Agent Only: No
Submission Materials: see website
Submission Fee: Yes
Deadline(s): See website

Shenandoah International Playwrights
Box 1
Verona, VA 24482
Phone: (540) 248-1868
Fax: (540) 248-7728
www.shenanarts.org
theatre@shenarts.org
Notes: Est. 1977. Up to 12 playwrights (from around the US and the world) work with dramaturgs, directors and actors in July–August, culminating in invited readings.
Agent Only: No
Submission Materials: see website
Preferred Genre: All genres
Preferred Length: Full-length
Submission Fee: Yes
Deadline(s): See website

Sundance Institute Playwrights Retreat at Ucross
180 Varick St.
Suite 1330
New York, NY 10014
Phone: (646) 822-9563
Fax: (310) 360-1969
www.sundance.org/programs/ucross
theatre@sundance.org

Notes: Est. 2001. 18-day retreat for 5 playwrights and 1 theater composer at Ucross Foundation, Clearmont, Wyoming.
Agent Only: No
Submission Fee: No

The Field Artward Bound Residency Program
161 6th Ave., Fl. 14
New York, NY 10013
Pele Bauch, Associate Director, Programming
Phone: (212) 691-6969
Fax: (212) 255-2053
www.thefield.org
pele@thefield.org
Notes: This residency program (free to Field Members) provides individual performing artists the opportunity to enjoy a creative retreat with a group of fellow artists. Retreats are set in beautiful, rural settings so that participants can unplug from the daily grind and focus on their creative process or career development while connecting with peers in an encouraging community. Open only to current Field Members who demonstrate a history of art making, participants are selected via lottery.
Agent Only: No
Submission Materials: application
Preferred Genre: All genres
Preferred Length: Any length
Submission Fee: No
Deadline(s): See website

Tyrone Guthrie Centre
Annaghmakerrig
Newbliss, Ireland
Phone: (353) 475-4003
Fax: (353) 475-4380
www.tyroneguthrie.ie
info@tyroneguthrie.ie
Notes: Est. 1981. Year-round residencies of varying duration in private rooms, studios, self-catering farmyard cottages. Response: 1 month.
Agent Only: No
Submission Materials: application
Submission Fee: Yes

U.S./Japan Creative Artists' Program
1201 15th St. NW, #330
Washington, DC 20005
Phone: (202) 653-9800
Fax: (202) 418-9802
www.jusfc.gov
jusfc@jusfc.gov

Notes: Est. 1979. 5-month residency in Japan for produced professional US artists with financial assistance.
Agent Only: No
Submission Materials: application
Submission Fee: Yes
Deadline(s): See website

Ucross Foundation Residency Program
30 Big Red Ln.
Clearmont, WY 82835
Ruth Salvatore, Residency Manager
Phone: (307) 737-2291
Fax: (307) 737-2322
www.ucrossfoundation.org
info@ucross.org
Notes: Est. 1981. Residencies of 2 weeks to 6 weeks (February–June, July–November) near Big Horn Mountains. Residents are provided living & studio space plus meals.
Agent Only: No
Submission Materials: see website
Submission Fee: Yes
Deadline(s): See website

VCCA (Virginia Center for the Creative Arts)
154 San Angelo Dr.
Amherst, VA 24521
Sheila Pleasants, Director of Artists' Services
Phone: (434) 946-7236
Fax: (434) 946-7239
www.vcca.com
vcca@vcca.com
Notes: Est. 1971. Residencies of 2 weeks–2 months on a beautiful and secluded hilltop in the foothills of the Blue Ridge Mountains near Sweet Briar College. Residencies includes private studios, private bathrooms and all meals. Dinner is in the dining room with up to 25 other writers, artists, and composers. Does not accept scholarly projects. Response time: 2 months.
Agent Only: No
Submission Materials: application, full script
Submission Fee: Yes
Deadline(s): January 15, 2013; May 15, 2013; Sept 15, 2013

William Inge Center for the Arts
Box 708
1057 W. College Ave.
Independence, KS 67301
Peter Ellenstein, Artistic Director

Phone: (620) 331-7768
Fax: (620) 331-9022
www.ingecenter.org
info@ingecenter.org
Notes: Est. 2002. Residencies of 8–9 weeks at William Inge's family home in small Midwestern town; private bedroom in historic 1920s-era house; shared bath. Each playwright receives a week-long professional play development workshop, which culminates in rehearsed reading of a playwright's script. Resident playwrights also teach playwriting 10–12 hours a week at a college and/or high school class. Financial arrangement: stipend of approximately $4,000, plus travel; meals not provided, but housing has a full kitchen. Guidelines: playwrights should have work that has had several professional productions; teaching experience also desirable. Application: send writing sample, description of the project you would like workshopped, resume, references (including in regards to teaching experience), one-page bio, availability over next two years and letter of inquiry. Open Deadline. Notification: 4 months.
Agent Only: No
Submission Materials: see website
Preferred Genre: Plays (No Musicals)
Preferred Length: Full-length
Submission Fee: No
Deadline(s): Rolling

Writers Omi at Ledig House
Art Omni Ledig House
55 5th Ave., Fl. 15

New York, NY 10003
Phone: (212) 206-6060
Fax: (212) 206-6114
www.artomi.org
writers@artomi.org
Notes: Est. 1992. Residencies (March–June, September–November) in Catskill Mountains. Residents provided with separate or combined work/bedroom areas. All meals included. See website for submission guidelines: www.artomi.org/writers/application.php
Agent Only: No
Submission Materials: see website for application
Submission Fee: Yes
Deadline(s): October 20, 2013

Yaddo
Box 395
Saratoga Springs, NY 12866
Phone: (518) 584-0746
Fax: (518) 584-1312
www.yaddo.org
chwait@yaddo.org
Notes: Est. 1900. Residencies of 2 weeks–2 months on 400-acre turn-of-century estate in Saratoga Springs, New York. Free room/board/private studio space. See website for submission materials.
Agent Only: No
Submission Materials: see website
Preferred Genre: All genres
Submission Fee: Yes
Deadline(s): See website

Conferences & Festivals

6 Women Playwriting Festival
Pikes Peak PPAC
Box 1073
Colorado Springs, CO 80901
Lynette Reagan, Festival Coordinator
Phone: (719) 201-7554
Fax: (719) 475-0005
www.sixwomenplayfestival.com
Lynwalks@hotmail.com
Notes: Author must be a woman. Six plays will have full production each with $100 honorarium, 1 of these will be chosen for workshop and author brought to Colorado.
Agent Only: No
Submission Materials: see website
Preferred Genre: Plays (No Musicals)

Preferred Length: 10-min./10pgs.
Special interest: Women's Interest
Submission Fee: No
Deadline(s): September 30, 2013

Actors' Playhouse National Children's Theatre Festival
280 Miracle Mile
Coral Gables, FL 33134
Earl Maulding, Director, TYA
Phone: (305) 444-9293 Ext 615
Fax: (305) 444-4181
www.actorsplayhouse.org
maulding@actorsplayhouse.org
Notes: Est. 1994. Annual 4-day festival. Winning show wins $500 plus production. See website. Production: cast limit 8, touring set.

Agent Only: No
Submission Materials: audio CD, full script, vocal score
Preferred Genre: Theatre for Young Audiences
Preferred Length: 50–60 min.
Special interest: Theatre for Young Audiences
Submission Fee: Yes
Deadline(s): April 1st

Actors Theatre of Louisville, Humana Festival [KY]

316 W. Main St.
Louisville, KY 40202
Amy Wegener, Literary Director
Phone: (502) 584-1265
Fax: (502) 561-3300
www.actorstheatre.org/humana-festival-of-new-american-plays
awegener@actorstheatre.org
Notes: Est. 1976. Festival of 10–12 fully produced new plays (world premieres) running February–April. Unagented writers may submit a synopsis and 10-page sample from script for consideration. Festival also includes 3–4 ten-minute plays; see website for National Ten-Minute Play Contest guidelines and full Humana Festival guidelines.
Agent Only: Yes
Submission Materials: agent-only
Preferred Genre: All genres
Preferred Length: Full-length
Submission Fee: No

Alabama Shakespeare Festival

1 Festival Dr.
Montgomery, AL 36117
Phone: (334) 271-5300
Fax: (334) 271-5348
www.asf.net
swp@asf.net
Notes: Est. 1972. The Southern Writers' Project of the Alabama Shakespeare Festival accepts original scripts and adaptations, not professionally produced, that meet one or more of the following criteria: You are a Southern Writer. Your script is set in the South, or deals specifically with Southern issues, characters, or themes. See website for more information.
Agent Only: No
Submission Materials: see website
Preferred Genre: All genres
Preferred Length: Full-length
Submission Fee: No

American College Theater Festival (ACTF)

Kennedy Center
Washington, DC 20566
Phone: (202) 416-8857
Fax: (202) 416-8802
www.KCACTF.org
kcactf@kennedy-center.org
Notes: Est. 1969. National festival of student productions, selected from regional college festivals.
Agent Only: No
Submission Materials: full script, query letter, S.A.S.E., synopsis
Preferred Genre: All genres
Preferred Length: Any length
Submission Fee: No
Deadline(s): December 1, 2013

Ashland New Plays Festival

Box 3314
Ashland, OR 97520-3314
Gray McKee, President
Phone: (541) 488-7995
Fax: (541) 472-0512
www.ashlandnewplays.org
info@ashlandnewplays.org
Notes: Est. 1992. Four playwrights are chosen each year. Annual weeklong October festival with rehearsals, workshops and 8 staged readings (2 of each winning script) with professional directors and actors. Must speak to U.S. audience. Production: 8-character limit. $1,000 stipend and lodging. Application Fee $10 via US Mail; $15 for online submissions.
Agent Only: No
Submission Materials: see website
Preferred Genre: Plays (No Musicals)
Preferred Length: Full-length
Submission Fee: Yes
Deadline(s): January 15, 2013

Attic Theatre's Denise Ragan Wiesenmeyer One-Act Marathon

5429 W. Washington Blvd.
Los Angeles, CA 90016
Jaime Gray, Literary Manager
Phone: (323) 525-0600
Fax: (323) 525-0661
www.attictheatre.org
litmanager@attictheatre.org
Notes: 3–10 entries selected for production/reading in festival. Panel from Los Angeles theater community chooses 2 winners. Production: cast limit 8, no orchestra, unit set. Response time: 4 months.

Agent Only: No
Submission Materials: see website
Preferred Genre: Plays (No Musicals)
Preferred Length: One-Act
Submission Fee: No
Deadline(s): See website

Baltimore Playwrights Festival
Box 38122
Baltimore, MD 21231
Rodney S. Bonds, Chair
www.baltplayfest.org
chair@baltplayfest.org
Notes: Est. 1981. Plays chosen for 3-week
summer production and selected public
readings.
Agent Only: No
Submission Materials: see website
Preferred Genre: All genres
Preferred Length: Full-length
Submission Fee: Yes
Deadline(s): April 1st; September 30th

**Barter Theatre's Appalachian Festival of
Plays & Playwrights**
P.O. Box 867
Abingdon, VA 24212
Nick Piper, Associate Director—New Play
Development
Phone: (276) 619-3316
Fax: (276) 619-3335
www.bartertheatre.com/festival
apfestival@bartertheatre.com
Notes: Est. 2001 . Appalachian playwrights
or work with Appalachian settings & themes.
Readings of seven new plays with cash reward
plus travel and housing for playwright; and
one mini production (full production, minimal
tech, brief run) selected from previous year's
readings, in a two week festival, judged by
panel. Must be unproduced/unpublished.
Agent Only: No
Submission Materials: full script
Preferred Genre: All genres
Preferred Length: Full-length
Submission Fee: No
Deadline(s): March 1, 2013

Bay Area Playwrights Festival (BAPF)
1616 16th Street
Suite 350
San Francisco, CA 94103
Phone: (415) 626-2176
www.playwrightsfoundation.org
literary@playwrightsfoundation.org

Notes: Est. 1976. 2-week July festival of 5–6
full-length plays by US writers. Submissions
not returned. Response time: 4 months.
Agent Only: No
Submission Materials: full script, query
letter
Preferred Genre: Comedy
Preferred Length: Any length
Submission Fee: No
Deadline(s): See website

Boomerang Theatre Company
P.O. Box 237166, Ansonia Station
New York, NY 10023
Phone: (212) 501-4069
www.boomerangtheatre.org
info@boomerangtheatre.org
Notes: Est. 1999. Annual reading series of
new plays.
Agent Only: No
Submission Materials: 10-pg sample, query
letter, resume, S.A.S.E., synopsis
Preferred Genre: Plays (No Musicals)
Preferred Length: Full-length
Submission Fee: No
Deadline(s): See website

Boston Theater Marathon
949 Commonwealth Avenue
Boston, MA 02215
Phone: (617) 353-6196
www.bu.edu/btm
newplays@bu.edu
Notes: Est. 1999. 50 10-min plays by New
England playwrights by 50 New England
theaters over 10 hours in 1 day. Production:
small orchestra, minimal set. Response time:
4 months. Alternate website: www.bostonplay-
wright.org
Agent Only: No
Submission Materials: full script, S.A.S.E.
Preferred Genre: Comedy
Preferred Length: 10-min./10pgs.
Submission Fee: No
Deadline(s): See website

Centre Stage New Play Festival
Box 8451
Greenville, SC 29604
Brian Haimbach, New Play Fesitval Director
Phone: (864) 233-6733
Fax: (864) 233-6733
www.centrestage.org/content/new-play-
festival-0
brian.haimbach@centrestage.org

Notes: Est. 2002. Submission process is on website. Send detailed synopsis and bio to brian.haimbach@centrestage.org by February 1. Playwrights receive travel and lodging to festival. Winner of festival gets full production. Scripts must be unpublished/unproduced. Cast limit: 5 actors, doubling not recommended.
Agent Only: No
Submission Materials: see website
Preferred Genre: Plays (No Musicals)
Preferred Length: Full-length
Submission Fee: No
Deadline(s): February 1, 2013

Cincinnati Fringe Festival
1120 Jackson Street
Cincinnati, OH 45202
Phone: (513) 300-5669
Fax: (513) 421-3435
www.cincyfringe.com
fringesubmissions@knowtheatre.com
Notes: Est. 2004. Annual Fringe Festival late May/early June. Submissions not returned. Response time: 3 months.
Agent Only: No
Submission Materials: application
Preferred Genre: Plays or Musicals
Preferred Length: Any length
Submission Fee: Yes
Deadline(s): December 30, 2013

Cleveland Public Theatre New Plays Festival
6415 Detroit Ave.
Cleveland, OH 44102
Phone: (216) 631-2727
Fax: (216) 631-2575
www.cptonline.org
cpt@en.com
Notes: Biennial four-week festival of staged readings. Assistance: room/board, travel, per diem. Frequency: biennial. Production: cast of up to 10, simple set.
Agent Only: No
Submission Materials: 10-pg sample, S.A.S.E., synopsis
Preferred Genre: All genres
Preferred Length: Full-length
Submission Fee: No

Collaboraction: Sketchbook Festival
437 N. Wolcott, #201
Attn: SKBK06
Chicago, IL 60622

Anthony Moseley, Executive Artistic Director
Phone: (312) 226-9633
Fax: (312) 226-6107
www.collaboraction.org
becky@collaboraction.org
Notes: Annual festival of short plays. Email submissions. Check website for details.
Agent Only: No
Submission Materials: application, full script
Preferred Genre: Interactive
Preferred Length: Any length
Submission Fee: No
Deadline(s): See website

Cultural Conversations
116 Arts Bldg.
Penn State University School of Theatre
University Park, PA 16802
Susan Russell, Artistic Director
Phone: (814) 863-1451
www.culturalconversations.psu.edu
sbr13@psu.edu
Notes: Est. 2007. Readings of new plays by actors 15–35 addressing themes of local and global diversity. We will not be accepting submissions for 2013. Please check website for updates.
Agent Only: No
Submission Materials: full script
Preferred Genre: Plays (No Musicals)
Preferred Length: Full-length
Submission Fee: No
Deadline(s): See website

Dayton Playhouse FutureFest
1301 E. Siebenthaler Ave.
Dayton, OH 45414
Fran Pesch, FutureFest Program Director
Phone: (937) 424-8477
www.daytonplayhouse.org
dp_futurefest@yahoo.com
Notes: Est. 1991. Adjudicated July festival of new work. Work must be longer than 75 minutes. Submission Fee: $20 (waived for members of the Dramatists Guild). Check website for updates to submission guidelines. Submissions not returned.
Agent Only: No
Submission Materials: full script, synopsis
Preferred Genre: Plays (No Musicals)
Preferred Length: Full-length
Submission Fee: Yes
Deadline(s): August 1, 2013; 10/31/2013

Edinburgh Festival Fringe
180 High St.
EdinburghEH1 1QS
Phone: (441) 312-2600 Ext 26
www.edfringe.com
admin@edfringe.com
Notes: Est. 1947. To participate, you need to organize every aspect of bringing your production to Edinburgh.
Agent Only: No
Submission Materials: see website
Preferred Genre: All genres
Preferred Length: Any length
Submission Fee: Yes
Deadline(s): See website

Firehouse Theatre Project's Festival of New American Plays
1609 W. Broad St.
Richmond, VA 23220
Phone: (804) 355-2001
Fax: (804) 355-0999
www.firehousetheatre.org
info@firehousetheatre.org
Notes: Est. 2003. Submit script and recommendation (theatre professional) by US mail with author's info on removable cover page. Submissions not returned. Response: 9 months.
Agent Only: No
Submission Materials: full script
Preferred Genre: All genres
Preferred Length: Any length
Submission Fee: No
Deadline(s): June 30, 2013

Fresh Fruit Festival
145 E. 27th St., #1-A
New York, NY 10016
Phone: (212) 857-8701
www.freshfruitfestival.com
artisticdirector@freshfruitfestival.com
Notes: Est. 2003. Work submitted must be unproduced in NYC and unoptioned. Response: 2 months.
Agent Only: No
Submission Materials: see website for application
Preferred Genre: Plays or Musicals
Preferred Length: Any length
Special interest: LGBT
Submission Fee: No
Deadline(s): See website

FusionFest
8500 Euclid Ave.
Cleveland, OH 44106
Phone: (216) 795-7000
Fax: (216) 795-7007
www.clevelandplayhouse.com
sgordon@clevelandplayhouse.com
Notes: Est. 1995. Reading series of unoptioned/unproduced new plays. Author must be resident of Ohio. Response: 6 months.
Agent Only: Yes
Submission Materials: agent-only
Submission Fee: No

Indo-American Arts Council Inc. (IACC)
517 East 87th Street, Suite 1B
New York, NY 10128
Phone: (212) 529-2347
Fax: (212) 477-4106
www.iaac.us
aroon@iaac.us
Notes: Est. 1998. Annual film and playwrights festivals.
Agent Only: No
Submission Materials: application, full script, S.A.S.E., synopsis, video
Preferred Genre: Plays (No Musicals)
Preferred Length: Any length
Submission Fee: No
Deadline(s): See website

Inspirato Festival
124 Broadway Ave.
Ste. 112
Toronto, ON M4P-1V8, Canada
Dominik Loncar
Phone: (416) 483-2222
www.inspiratofestival.ca
inspirato@ca.inter.net
Notes: Canada's largest ten-minute play festival has a call out for submissions starting in August. Playwrights are asked to submit a ten-minute play based on a creative challenge. Performances are held in the first two weeks in June.
Agent Only: No
Submission Materials: full script
Preferred Genre: Plays (No Musicals)
Preferred Length: 10-min./10pgs.
Submission Fee: No
Deadline(s): December 17, 2013

International Mystery Writers' Festival
101 Daviess St.
Owensboro, KY 42303

Donna Conkwright, Program Director
Phone: (270) 687-2770
Fax: (270) 687-2775
www.newmysteries.org
dconkwright@riverparkcenter.org
Notes: Est. 2007. Accepts unproduced plays, teleplays or short screenplays in mystery/thriller genre. Submissions not returned. Response: 3 months.
Agent Only: No
Submission Materials: full script
Preferred Genre: Mystery
Preferred Length: Any length
Submission Fee: No
Deadline(s): October 31, 2013

Jewish Ensemble Theater Festival of New Plays

Jewish Ensemble Theater
6600 W. Maple Rd.
West Bloomfield, MI 48322
Christopher Bremer, Managing Director
Phone: (248) 788-2900
Fax: (248) 788-5160
www.jettheatre.org
c.bremer@jettheatre.org
Notes: Est. 1989. Submit by US mail only.
Agent Only: No
Submission Materials: full script, S.A.S.E.
Preferred Genre: Plays or Musicals
Preferred Length: Any length
Submission Fee: Yes
Deadline(s): August 1st each year

Juneteenth Legacy Theatre

605 Water St. #21B
New York, NY 10002
Phone: (212) 964-1904
Fax: (212) 964-1904
www.juneteenthlegacytheatre.com
juneteenthlegacy@aol.com
Notes: Est. 1999. Staged readings on African-American experience in 19th–20th centuries, especially Harlem Renaissance Era, new images of women, gay/lesbian theme. Festival produced in even numbered years.
Agent Only: No
Submission Materials: full script (4 copies)
Preferred Genre: Plays or Musicals
Preferred Length: One-Act
Special interest: African-American
Submission Fee: Yes
Deadline(s): March 15, 2014

Kitchen Dog Theater (KDT) New Works Festival

3120 McKinney Ave., #100
Dallas, TX 75204
Tina Parker, Co-Artistic Director, Administrative Director
Phone: (214) 953-1055
Fax: (214) 953-1873
www.kitchendogtheater.org
tina@kitchendogtheater.org
Notes: Est. 1990. Winner receives production, travel stipend, and royalty; 6 finalists receive reading. Submit by US mail only. Submissions recycled, not returned. Response: 8 months.
Agent Only: No
Submission Materials: full script
Preferred Genre: Plays (No Musicals)
Preferred Length: Full-length
Submission Fee: No
Deadline(s): January 1st

Lark Play Development Center: Playwrights' Week

311 West 43rd Street, Suite 406
New York, NY 10036
Phone: (212) 246-2676
Fax: (212) 246-2609
www.larktheatre.org
submissions@larktheatre.org
Notes: Submissions accepted August–November for a fest of development. Public readings the following fall. See website for submission guidelines and deadlines. Response: 9 months.
Agent Only: No
Submission Materials: application, full script
Preferred Genre: Plays or Musicals
Preferred Length: Full-length
Submission Fee: No

Last Frontier Theatre Conference

Box 97
Valdez, AK 99686
Dawson Moore, Coordinator
Phone: (907) 834-1614
Fax: (907) 834-1611
www.theatreconference.org
dmoore@pwscc.edu
Notes: Est. 1993. Application free. See website for conference fees. Work must not have been professionally produced.
Agent Only: No
Submission Materials: full script
Preferred Genre: Plays (No Musicals)

Preferred Length: Any length
Submission Fee: No
Deadline(s): January 4, 2013

Lavender Footlights Festival
P.O. Box 942107
Miami, FL 33194
Phone: (305) 433-8111
Fax: (305) 672-7818
Ryan@Lavenderfootlights.org
Notes: Est. 2000. Festival of readings with gay and lesbian themes.
Agent Only: No
Submission Materials: full script, S.A.S.E., synopsis
Preferred Genre: Plays (No Musicals)
Preferred Length: Full-length
Special interest: LGBT
Submission Fee: No

Little Festival of the Unexpected
Portland Stage
Box 1458
Portland, ME 04104
Phone: (207) 774-1043
Fax: (207) 774-0576
www.portlandstage.com
dburson@portlandstage.com
Notes: Est. 1989. 1-week fest of new plays (unproduced, unpublished, unoptioned) with writers developing work through staged readings. Production: cast limit 8. US mail submission only.
Agent Only: No
Submission Materials: 10-pg sample, query letter, synopsis
Preferred Genre: Plays (No Musicals)
Preferred Length: Full-length
Submission Fee: No
Deadline(s): Rolling

Long Beach Playhouse New Works Festival
5021 East Anaheim Street
Long Beach, CA 90804
Phone: (562) 494-1014 Ext 526
www.lbplayhouse.org
joblack@dslextreme.com
Notes: Est. 1989. Spring fest of 4 new unproduced plays in staged readings. Production: cast limit 10, limited set. Response: 3 months after festival.
Agent Only: No
Submission Materials: see website
Preferred Genre: Plays (No Musicals)
Preferred Length: Full-length

Submission Fee: Yes
Deadline(s): September 30th; Year Round

Los Angeles Women's Theatre Festival
11411 Cumpston Street
#204
Los Angeles, CA 91601
Phone: (818) 760-0408
Fax: (818) 760-0506
www.lawtf.com
lawtfspotlight@yahoo.com
Notes: The Los Angeles Women's Theatre Festival ("LAWTF") was organized to provide a vehicle for the development of women artists utilizing theatre to educate, enlighten and empower solo artists, audiences and volunteers.
Agent Only: No
Submission Materials: see website
Special interest: Women's Interest
Submission Fee: Yes

Mind the Gap BritBits Short Play Festival
535 W 23rd St.
S11G
New York, NY 10011
Paula D'Alessandris
Phone: (212) 252-3137
allaboard@mindthegaptheatre.com
Notes: Writer must be native British, Scottish, Welsh, Irish or the subject matter must be related to the United Kingdom.
Agent Only: Yes
Submission Materials: agent-only
Preferred Length: 10-min./10pgs.
Submission Fee: Yes
Deadline(s): Ongoing

National Alliance for Musical Theatre (NAMT)
520 8th Ave., #301
New York, NY 10018
Betsy King Militello, Executive Director
Phone: (212) 714-6668
Fax: (212) 714-0469
www.namt.org
info@namt.org
Notes: Est. 1985. Equity Showcase of 8 musicals in 45-minute presentations over 2 days. Participants receive stipend from NAMT. Invitation is industry only. Response: 6 months. See website: www.namt.org/festival-submission.aspx
Agent Only: No

Submission Materials: application, audio CD, full script
Preferred Genre: Musical theatre
Preferred Length: Full-length
Submission Fee: Yes
Deadline(s): See website

National Black Theatre Festival
610 Coliseum Dr.
Winston-Salem, NC 27106
Phone: (336) 723-2266
www.nbtf.org
nbtf@bellsouth.net
Notes: Est. 1989. Biennial (odd years) festival in August of productions about the Black experience.
Agent Only: No
Submission Materials: see website
Preferred Genre: All genres
Preferred Length: Full-length
Special interest: African-American
Submission Fee: No
Deadline(s): See website

New Jersey Playwrights Festival of New Plays
Box 1663
Bloomfield, NJ 07003
Phone: (973) 259-9187
Fax: (973) 259-9188
www.12mileswest.org
info@12mileswest.org
Notes: Annual fest of plays by NJ playwrights. Production: cast of 2–7, unit set. Response: 1 yr.
Agent Only: No
Submission Materials: see website
Preferred Genre: All genres
Preferred Length: Any length
Submission Fee: No

New Play Festival
Denver Center
1101 13th Street
Denver, CO 80204
Chad Henry, Literary Associate
Phone: (303) 572-4456
Fax: (303) 893-3206
www.denvercenter.org
chenry@dcpa.org
Notes: Est. 2005. Rehearsed reading of new work for industry and general audience. At least two full productions of previously work-shopped plays each season. Response: up to 6 months.

Agent Only: No
Submission Materials: full script, S.A.S.E.
Preferred Genre: Plays or Musicals
Preferred Length: Full-length
Submission Fee: No
Deadline(s): Rolling

New Professional Theatre Writers Festival
229 W. 42nd St., #501
New York, NY 10036
Phone: (212) 398-2666
Fax: (212) 398-2924
www.newprofessionaltheatre.org
newprof@aol.com
Notes: Est. 1991. Annual festival of work by African-Americans, Asians, and Latinos. Also business seminars, mentoring, and 2-week residencies.
Agent Only: No
Submission Materials: see website
Preferred Genre: All genres
Preferred Length: Full-length
Submission Fee: No
Deadline(s): See website

New York City 15-Minute Play Fest
American Globe Turnip Fest
145 W. 46th St., Fl. 3
New York, NY 10036
Elizabeth Keefe, Executive Director
Phone: (212) 869-9809
Fax: (212) 869-9807
15minuteplayfestival.org/index.html
liz@americanglobe.org
Notes: Est. 1993. 2-week festival in May of 4–5 new plays each night. Production: cast of 2–10, no set. Response: 2 months. See website for submission guidelines. Additional website: www.americanglobe.org
Agent Only: No
Submission Materials: full script, S.A.S.E.
Preferred Genre: Plays (No Musicals)
Preferred Length: 15 min.
Submission Fee: No
Deadline(s): See website

New York Musical Theatre Festival (NYMF)
242 W. 49th Street, Suite 601
New York, NY 10019
Isaac Robert Hurwitz, Executive Director
Phone: (212) 664-0979
Fax: (212) 664-0978
www.nymf.org
literary@nymf.org

Agent Only: No
Submission Materials: see website
Preferred Genre: Musical theatre
Submission Fee: Yes
Deadline(s): See website

Old Opera House Theatre Company New Voice Play Festival
204 N. George St.
Charles Town, WV 25414
Steven Brewer, Managing and Artistic Director
Phone: (304) 752-4420
www.oldoperahouse.org
ooh@oldoperahouse.org
Notes: Est. 2001. Call or email for application and deadlines. One act play festival—plays 10 to 40 minutes in length.
Agent Only: No
Submission Materials: see website
Preferred Genre: Plays (No Musicals)
Preferred Length: One-Act
Submission Fee: Yes
Deadline(s): March 1, 2013

Penobscot Theatre
131 Main Street
4th Floor
Bangor, ME 04401
Phone: (207) 947-6618
www.penobscottheatre.org
info@penobscottheatre.org
Notes: 2 week New Play Festival featuring readings & workshops.
Agent Only: No
Submission Materials: cover letter
Preferred Genre: All genres
Preferred Length: Any length
Submission Fee: Yes
Deadline(s): See website

Playfest—Harriett Lake Festival of New Plays
812 E. Rollins St., #100
Orlando, FL 32803
Phone: (407) 447-1700
Fax: (407) 447-1701
www.orlandoshakes.org
patrickf@orlandoshakes.org
Notes: Est. 1989. 10 new plays receive readings, 2–3 developmental in Festival of new plays.
Agent Only: No
Submission Materials: see website
Preferred Genre: Plays (No Musicals)

Preferred Length: Full-length
Submission Fee: No
Deadline(s): See website

Premiere Stages Play Festival
Hutchinson Hall, 1000 Morris Ave.,
Union, NJ 07083
Clare Drobot, Producing Associate
Phone: (908) 737-4092
Fax: (908) 737-4636
www.kean.edu/premierestages
premiere@kean.edu
Notes: Est. 2004. Annual fest for playwrights born or living in New Jersey, Connecticut, New York, or Pennsylvania. Four public readings in March, full Equity production of winner in July., and 29 Hour Staged Reading for a second play in June. Frequency: annual. Production: cast limit 8. See website for details.
Agent Only: No
Submission Materials: see website
Preferred Genre: Plays (No Musicals)
Preferred Length: Full-length
Deadline(s): January 15, 2013

Raymond J. Flores Short Play Festival (Around the Block)
5 E. 22nd St., #9-K
New York, NY 10010
Phone: (212) 673-9187
www.aroundtheblock.org
info@aroundtheblock.org
Notes: Est. 2004. Theme: Urban life and dreams. No children's plays. Electronic (e-mail or CD) submissions only. Also include a synopsis please.
Agent Only: No
Submission Materials: application, bio, full script
Preferred Genre: Plays (No Musicals)
Preferred Length: 10-min./10pgs.
Submission Fee: Yes
Deadline(s): November 30, 2013

Samuel French, Inc. Off Off Broadway Short-Play Festival
45 W. 25 St.
New York, NY 10010
Billie Davis, Festival Coordinator
Phone: (212) 206-8990
Fax: (202) 206-1429
www.oob.samuelfrench.com
oobfestival@samuelfrench.com

Notes: Est. 1976. 1-week festival hosted by Samuel French in NYC. 40 plays are selected for production. 6 finalists chosen for publication and representation by Samuel French. Shows must run 30 minutes or less.
Agent Only: No
Submission Materials: application, full script
Preferred Genre: Plays or Musicals
Preferred Length: One-Act
Submission Fee: Yes
Deadline(s): See website

San Francisco Fringe Festival (SFFF)
156 Eddy St.
San Francisco, CA 94102
Phone: (415) 931-1094
Fax: (415) 931-2699
www.sffringe.org
mail@sffringe.org
Agent Only: No
Submission Materials: see website
Preferred Genre: All genres
Preferred Length: Any length
Submission Fee: No
Deadline(s): See website

Seven Devils Playwrights Conference
343 E. 30th St., #19-J
New York, NY 10016
Jeni Mahoney, Artistic Director
Phone: (917) 881-9114
www.idtheater.org
jeni@idtheater.org
Notes: Est. 2001. 2-week play development conference in June. 4–6 new plays selected from open submissions for development in McCall, Idaho. Plays are presented to the public as either fully staged or seated readings.
Agent Only: No
Submission Materials: see website
Preferred Genre: Plays (No Musicals)
Preferred Length: Any length
Submission Fee: Yes
Deadline(s): November 15, 2013

Short Attention Span PlayFEST
Atlantis Playmakers
5261 Whitsett Avenue #20
Valley Village, CA 91607
Phone: (978) 667-0550
www.atlantisplaymakers.com
kdb@atlantisplaymakers.com
Notes: Est. 1998.

Agent Only: No
Submission Materials: see website
Preferred Genre: Plays (No Musicals)
Submission Fee: No
Deadline(s): See website

ShowOff! Ten-Minute Playwriting Festival
Camino Real Playhouse
31776 El Camino Real
San Juan Capistrano, CA 92675
Phone: (949) 248-0808
Fax: (949) 248-0808
www.caminorealplayhouse.org
box_office@sbcglobal.net
Notes: Est. 1993. Material must be unpublished. Response: 3 months.
Agent Only: No
Submission Materials: full script
Preferred Genre: Plays (No Musicals)
Preferred Length: 10-min./10pgs.
Submission Fee: Yes
Deadline(s): See website

Southern Appalachian Repertory Theatre (SART)—ScriptFEST
Box 1720
Mars Hill, NC 28754
Sharon Christensen, SART Board Member & ScriptFEST Coordinator
Phone: (828) 689-1384
Fax: (828) 689-1272
www.sartplays.org
scriptfest@mhc.edu
Notes: Est. 1981. Readings & critique of 4–6 plays in 3-day conference in Asheville and Mars Hill, North Carolina. Submissions must abide the specific guidelines. See website. Response: August/September.
Agent Only: No
Submission Materials: see website
Preferred Genre: Plays or Musicals
Preferred Length: Full-length
Submission Fee: No
Deadline(s): September 30, 2013

Teatro del Pueblo
209 West Page St.
Ste 208
St. Paul, MN 55107
Alberto Justiniano, Artistic Director
Phone: (651) 224-8806
Fax: (651) 298-5796
www.teatrodelpueblo.org
al@teatrodelpueblo.org

Notes: Looking for 15 to 50 min one-act plays dealing with poltical issues pertaining to Latino Social Justice.
Agent Only: No
Submission Materials: full script, synopsis
Preferred Genre: Plays or Musicals
Preferred Length: One-Act
Special interest: Latino
Submission Fee: No
Deadline(s): September 15, 2014

Tennessee Williams/New Orleans Literary Festival
938 Lafayette St., #514
New Orleans, LA 70113
Jessica Ramakrishnan, Contest Coordinator
Phone: (504) 581-1144
Fax: (504) 581-3270
www.tennesseewilliams.net
info@tennesseewilliams.net
Notes: Production: small, minimal.
Agent Only: No
Submission Materials: see website
Preferred Genre: Plays (No Musicals)
Preferred Length: One-Act
Submission Fee: Yes
Deadline(s): See website

The Kentucky Women Writers Conference
Phone: (859) 257-2874
www.kentuckywomenwriters.org
wwk.program@gmail.com
Notes: Will award a national playwriting prize to bring more scripts by women to the stage, especially those featuring majority-female casts. The winner will receive a production by Balagula Theatre in Lexington, Kentucky (www.balagula.com), plus a cash prize of $500. The winning play will be workshopped prior to its world premier for a paying audience in winter. One-act or full-length scripts in English, with a running time between 45 and 90 minutes, that have not been published or commercially produced as of the entry deadline and will not be published or produced before the release of the KWWC production. However, scripts that have been staged in a workshop production or script-in-hand staged readings are eligible.
Agent Only: No
Submission Materials: see website
Special interest: Women's Interest
Submission Fee: No
Deadline(s): See website

The Many Voices Project
1105 W. Chicago Ave.
Chicago, IL 60622
Phone: (312) 633-0630
Fax: (312) 633-0630
www.chicagodramatists.org
iduncan@chicagodramatists.org
Notes: Contest and developmental showcase for US playwrights of color in 2-week July festival of staged readings. Work must be previously unproduced. Response: 2 months.
Agent Only: No
Submission Materials: bio, character breakdown, full script, S.A.S.E.
Preferred Genre: Plays or Musicals
Preferred Length: Any length
Special interest: African-American
Submission Fee: No

Theatre Three [NY] One-Act Play Festival
Box 512, 412 Main St.
Port Jefferson, NY 11777
Jeffrey Sanzel, Executive Artistic Director
Phone: (631) 928-9202
Fax: (631) 928-9120
www.theatrethree.com
jeffrey@theatrethree.com
Notes: Est. 1997. Festival of One-Act Plays. Each season, festival presents 5 to 6 world premieres on the second stage. Non-equity productions. All plays performed 10 times. Preferred length: 35 minute maximum. Frequency: annual. Production: any age, casts up to 10 people, minimal set. Response Time: 3–6 months
Agent Only: No
Submission Materials: see website
Preferred Genre: Plays (No Musicals)
Preferred Length: One-Act
Submission Fee: No
Deadline(s): September 30 (annually)

Trustus Playwrights' Festival
Box 11721
Columbia, SC 29211
Sarah Hammond, Literary Manager
Phone: (803) 254-9732
Fax: (803) 771-9153
www.trustus.org/playwrights.php
shammond@trustus.org
Notes: Est. 1984. Trustus does not accept unsolicited submissions for the general season. Trustus gets to know new writers through its annual Playwrights Festival contest, which accepts queries from December 1 to February

1 each year. Please see the website for application guidelines.
Agent Only: No
Submission Materials: see website
Preferred Genre: Plays (No Musicals)
Submission Fee: Yes
Deadline(s): December 1–February 1 annually

Utah Shakespeare Festival: New American Playwrights Project
351 W. Center St.
Cedar City, UT 84720
Charles Metten, Director, NAPP
Phone: (435) 586-7880
Fax: (435) 865-8003
www.bard.org
metten@bard.org
Notes: August festival of 3 play readings, with writers in residence. Production: cast of 8–10, flexible stage. Unproduced, with single author.
Agent Only: No
Submission Materials: full script
Preferred Genre: Plays (No Musicals)
Preferred Length: Full-length
Submission Fee: Yes
Deadline(s): November 1, 2013

Weathervane Playhouse
1301 Weathervane Lane
Akron, OH 44313
Eileen Moushey, Coordinator, 10 Minute Play Contest
Phone: (330) 836-2323

Fax: (330) 873-2150
www.weathervaneplayhouse.com
10minuteplay@weathervaneplayhouse.com
Notes: Material must be unproduced. See website for details under "Special Events".
Agent Only: No
Submission Materials: see website
Preferred Genre: Plays (No Musicals)
Preferred Length: 10-min./10pgs.
Submission Fee: Yes
Deadline(s): May 1, 2013

Year-End Series (YES) New Play Festival
Northern Kentucky University
One Nunn Drive, Fine Arts 228
Highland Heights, KY 41099
Sandra Forman, Project Director
Phone: (859) 572-6303
Fax: (859) 572-6057
www.nku.edu/~theatre
forman@nku.edu
Notes: Est. 1983. Biennial (odd years) festival in April of 3 new works receive full productions. Playwrights flown in for final week of rehearsals and opening night. Submission deadlines are even number years.
Agent Only: No
Submission Materials: character breakdown, full script, S.A.S.E., synopsis
Preferred Genre: Plays or Musicals
Preferred Length: Full-length
Submission Fee: No
Deadline(s): May 1, 2014; 9/20/2014

Contests

Anna Zornio Memorial Children's Theatre Playwriting Award
UNH Theatre/Dance Dept.
PCAC, 30 Academic Way
Durham, NH 03824
Michael Wood, Administrative Manager
Phone: (603) 862-3038
Fax: (603) 862-0298
www.unh.edu/theatre-dance/zornio
mike.wood@unh.edu
Notes: Est. 1979. Quadrennial cash/production award for unproduced, unpublished children's work for residents of U.S. and Canada.
Agent Only: No
Submission Materials: see website
Preferred Genre: All genres
Preferred Length: Full-length

Special interest: Theatre for Young Audiences
Submission Fee: No
Deadline(s): March 4, 2016

Arts & Letters Prize in Drama
Georgia College
GCSU Campus Box 89
Milledgeville, GA 31061
Phone: (478) 445-1289
Fax: (478) 445-5961
al.gcsu.edu
al@gcsu.edu
Notes: Est. 1999. Response Time: 3 months
Agent Only: No
Submission Materials: see website
Preferred Genre: All genres
Preferred Length: One-Act

Submission Fee: Yes
Deadline(s): See website

Aurora Theatre Company: Global Age Project
2081 Addison St.
Berkeley, CA 94704
Matthew Graham Smith, GAP Producer
Phone: (510) 843-4042
Fax: (510) 843-4826
www.auroratheatre.org
literary@auroratheatre.org
Notes: Celebrating fresh forward-looking visions of global significance. Online submissions only. Response time: 5 months.
Agent Only: No
Submission Materials: full script
Preferred Genre: Plays or Musicals
Preferred Length: Any length
Submission Fee: Yes

Babes With Blades—Joining Sword and Pen
Babes With Blades
7016 N. Greenview, #2
Chicago, IL 60626
Morgan Manasa
www.babeswithblades.org
swordandpen@babeswithblades.org
Notes: Est. 1997. New play development program and contest. Work must include fighting roles for women!
Agent Only: No
Submission Materials: see website
Preferred Genre: All genres
Preferred Length: Full-length
Special interest: Women's Interest
Submission Fee: No

Beverly Hills Theatre Guild Julie Harris Playwright Awards
Beverly Hills Theatre Guild
Box 148
Beverly Hills, CA 90213
Candace Coster, Coordinator
Phone: (310) 273-3390
www.beverlyhillstheatreguild.com
Agent Only: No
Submission Materials: application, full script, query letter
Preferred Genre: Comedy
Preferred Length: Full-length
Submission Fee: No
Deadline(s): November 1, 2013

Bloomington Playwrights Project
107 W. 9th St.
Bloomington, IN 47404
Phone: (812) 334-1188
www.newplays.org
literarymanager@newplays.org
Notes: The BPP hosts two major playwriting competitions. The Woodward/Newman Drama Award, named after Paul Newman and Joanne Woodward in honor of their many great dramas together, offers a $3,000 cash prize and a full production to the best new drama in the world. The Reva Shiner Comedy Award offers a $1,000 cash prize and a full production to the best new comedy. In addition, the BPP has a partnership with Dramatic Publishing and in most instances is able to offer the option of publication.
Agent Only: No
Submission Materials: see website
Preferred Length: Full-length
Submission Fee: Yes
Deadline(s): October 31, 2013; 3/1/2013

Charles M. Getchell Award, SETC
1175 Revolution Mill Drive, Studio 14
Greensboro, NC 27405
Phone: (864) 656-5415
Fax: (864) 656-1013
www.setc.org
info@setc.org
Notes: Submit full script via online application only. See website for eligibility guidelines.
Agent Only: No
Submission Materials: application, full script
Preferred Genre: All genres
Preferred Length: Any length
Submission Fee: Yes
Deadline(s): June 1, 2013

Christopher Brian Wolk Award
Abingdon Theatre
312 W. 36th St., 6th floor
New York, NY 10018
Kim T. Sharp, Literary Manager
Phone: (212) 868-2055
Fax: (212) 868-2056
www.abingdontheatre.org
ksharp@abingdontheatre.org
Notes: Est. 2001. Mail printed copy of unoptioned script, unproduced in NYC, with character breakdown, production history, bio. No Musicals. See website for updated guidelines.

Production: cast limit 8. Response time: 3–6 months.
Agent Only: No
Submission Materials: see website
Preferred Genre: Plays (No Musicals)
Preferred Length: Full-length
Submission Fee: No
Deadline(s): June 1, 2013

Clauder Competition for New England Playwrights
Portland Stage
Box 1458
Portland, ME 04104
Phone: (207) 774-1043
Fax: (207) 774-0576
www.portlandstage.org
dburson@portlandstage.org
Notes: Est. 1981. Competition for unpublished/unproduced work from New England writers (current or former resident; student). Frequency: every 3 years. Production: cast limit 8. We will not be accepting submissions for the 2013 season. Please see website for updates.
Agent Only: No
Submission Materials: full script
Preferred Genre: All genres
Preferred Length: Full-length
Submission Fee: No

Community Theatre Association of Michigan
4026 Lester
Oscoda, MI 48750
Vincent Weiler, Playwriting Contest Chair
Phone: (231) 354-7291
www.communitytheatre.org
vweiler@ioscoresa.net
Notes: Author must be a resident of Michigan. Submit script by US Mail only.
Agent Only: No
Submission Materials: full script, S.A.S.E.
Preferred Genre: Plays (No Musicals)
Preferred Length: Full-length
Submission Fee: Yes
Deadline(s): May 15, 2013

David C. Horn Prize
Yale Univ. Press
Box 209040
New Haven, CT 06520
Alison MacKeen, Editor
Phone: (203) 432-0975
Fax: (203) 436-1064

www.dchornfoundation.org
info@dchornfoundation.org
Notes: Est. 2006. Submissions not returned.
Agent Only: No
Submission Materials: see website
Preferred Genre: Plays (No Musicals)
Preferred Length: Full-length
Submission Fee: No
Deadline(s): See website

David Mark Cohen Playwriting Award
Kennedy Center, Education Div.
Washington, DC 20566
Phone: (202) 416-8857
Fax: (202) 416-8802
www.kcactf.org
skshaffer@kennedy-center.org
Notes: Plays accepted only from college/university participating in KC/ACTF program.
Agent Only: No
Submission Materials: application, full script, synopsis
Preferred Genre: Plays (No Musicals)
Preferred Length: Full-length & 10-min.
Submission Fee: Yes
Deadline(s): See website

Dorothy Silver Playwriting Competition
Mandel Jewish Community Center
26001 S. Woodland Ave.
Beachwood, OH 44122
Deborah Bobrow, Coordinator
Phone: (216) 593-6278
Fax: (216) 831-7796
www.mandeljcc.org
dbobrow@mandeljcc.org
Notes: Award for original works of significant, fresh perspective on Jewish experience. US mail only. Response: 4 months.
Agent Only: No
Submission Materials: audio CD, full script, S.A.S.E.
Preferred Genre: Plays or Musicals
Preferred Length: Full-length
Special interest: Jewish
Submission Fee: No
Deadline(s): See website

Dubuque Fine Arts Players One Act Play Contest
Dubuque Fine Arts Players
P.O. Box 1160
Dubuque, IA 52004
Thomas Boxleiter, Contest Coordinator
Phone: (583) 588-3438

www.dbqoneacts.org
contact@dbqoneacts.com
Notes: Est. 1977. Unproduced/unpublished
material must be sent via US Mail. Production:
cast of 2–5,unit set. Response: 6 months. Cash
prizes. Winning plays are usually produced.
Agent Only: No
Submission Materials: application, full
script (2 copies), SASE
Preferred Genre: Plays (No Musicals)
Preferred Length: One-Act
Submission Fee: Yes
Deadline(s): January 31, 2013

Essential Theatre Playwriting Award
1414 Foxhall Lane #10
Atlanta, GA 30316
Phone: (404) 212-0815
www.essentialtheatre.com
pmhardy@aol.com
Notes: Material must be unproduced of at least
an hour's length. Writer must be resident of
Georgia.
Agent Only: No
Submission Materials: full script
Preferred Genre: Plays or Musicals
Preferred Length: Any length
Submission Fee: No
Deadline(s): See website

FirstStage One-Act Play Contest
Box 38280
Los Angeles, CA 90038
Phone: (323) 350-6271
www.firststagela.org
firststagela@aol.com
Notes: Est. 1983. Staged readings of new/
unproduced work (30 minutes or less).
Submissions not returned. See website for
details. Response : 3 weeks.
Agent Only: No
Submission Materials: full script
Preferred Genre: Plays (No Musicals)
Preferred Length: One-Act
Submission Fee: Yes
Deadline(s): October 15, 2013

**Fort Wayne Civic Theatre—NE Indiana
Playwright Contest**
303 E. Main St.
Fort Wayne, IN 46802
Phillip H. Colglazier, Executive/Artistic
Director
Phone: (260) 422-8641
Fax: (260) 422-6699

www.fwcivic.org
pcolglazier@fwcivic.org
Notes: Current or former resident of Indiana or
within a 90 mile radius of Fort Wayne. Submit
an entry form, play synopsis (1 page), 10 pages
of script, and playwright's bio. Additional
Guidelines: Consult website submission guide-
lines. Entry form available on-line.
Agent Only: No
Submission Materials: see website
Preferred Genre: Plays (No Musicals)
Submission Fee: No
Deadline(s): September 1, 2013

Fred Ebb Award
Roundabout Theatre
231 W. 39th St., #1200
New York, NY 10018
www.fredebbfoundation.org
info@fredebbfoundation.org
Notes: Est. 2005. Named for lyricist Fred Ebb
(1928–2004), award recognizes excellence by
a songwriter or songwriting team that hasn't
yet achieved significant commercial success.
Frequency: annual. Award: $50,000
Agent Only: No
Preferred Genre: Musical theatre
Deadline(s): See website for deadline

FUSION Theatre Company
700 1st Street NW
Albuquerque, NM 87102
Phone: (505) 766-9412
www.fusionabq.org
info@fusionabq.org
Notes: Eighth annual short works fest entitled
"The Seven". Works must be unproduced/
unpublished. Winner flown to New Mexico for
production. See website for details.
Agent Only: No
Submission Materials: see website
Preferred Genre: Plays or Musicals
Preferred Length: 10-min./10pgs.
Submission Fee: Yes
Deadline(s): April 15, 2013

Garrard Best Play Competition
1101 Honor Heights Dr.
Muskogee, OK 74401
Phone: (918) 683-1701
Fax: (918) 683-3070
www.fivetribes.org
5civilizedtribes@sbcglobal.net
Notes: Biennial (even years) competition for
playwrights of Cherokee, Chickasaw, Choctaw,

Creek or Seminole lineage that reflect the history, culture, or traditions of the Five Civilized Tribes.
Agent Only: No
Submission Materials: bio, full script (4 copies), proof of heritage
Preferred Genre: All genres
Special interest: Native American
Submission Fee: No
Deadline(s): See website

Georgia College and State University
Porter Hall CBX 066
Milledgeville, GA 31061
Phone: (478) 445-1980
Fax: (478) 445-1633
www.gcsu.edu/theatre
kbermanth@aol.com
Notes: Work must be unoptioned, unproduced, unpublished and author must be available for a short residency.
Agent Only: No
Submission Materials: see website
Preferred Genre: Plays (No Musicals)
Preferred Length: Full-length
Submission Fee: Yes
Deadline(s): See website

Goshen College Peace Playwriting Contest
1700 S. Main St.
Goshen, IN 46526
Douglas Caskey, Director of Theatre
Phone: (574) 535-7393
Fax: (574) 535-7660
www.goshen.edu/theatre/peace-play
douglc@goshen.edu
Notes: $500 cash prize
Agent Only: No
Submission Materials: full script, resume, synopsis
Preferred Genre: Plays (No Musicals)
Preferred Length: One-Act
Submission Fee: No
Deadline(s): December 31, 2013

Grawemeyer Award for Music Composition
Univ. of Louisville School of Music
Louisville, KY 40292
Marc Satterwhite, Director
Phone: (502) 852-1787
Fax: (502) 852-0520
www.grawemeyer.org/music
GrawemeyerMusic@louisville.edu
Notes: Est. 1984.
Agent Only: No

Submission Materials: see website
Preferred Length: Any length
Submission Fee: Yes

Jackie White Memorial Nat'l. Children's Play Writing Contest
309 Parkade Blvd.
Columbia, MO 65202
Betsy Phillips, Director
Phone: (573) 874-5628
www.cectheatre.org
bybetsy@yahoo.com
Notes: Est. 1988. In memory of Jackie Pettit White (1947–91). All scripts read and recieve evaluation. Please also include author's resume with your submission. Production: at least 7 speaking roles, sets appropriate for community theaters.
Agent Only: No
Submission Materials: application, full script, S.A.S.E.
Preferred Genre: Plays or Musicals
Preferred Length: Full-length
Submission Fee: Yes
Deadline(s): June 1, 2013

Jane Chambers Playwriting Award
Dept. of Perf. Arts, Georgetown U.
108 Davis Center, Box 571063
Washington, DC 20057
Phone: (202) 687-1327
www.athe.org/displaycommon.cfm?an=1&subarticlenbr=138
mer46@georgetown.edu
Notes: Award for plays and performance texts by females that reflect a feminist perspective and contain a majority of opportunities for women performers. Submissions not returned.
Agent Only: No
Submission Materials: application, full script (3 copies), resume, synopsis
Preferred Genre: All genres
Preferred Length: Any length
Special interest: Women's Interest
Submission Fee: No

Jane Chambers Student Playwriting Award
230 W. 56th St., #65-A
New York, NY 10019
jen-scottm@nyc.rr.com
Notes: Award for plays and texts by female students that reflect a feminist perspective and contain a majority of opportunities for women performers. Submissions not returned.
Agent Only: No

Submission Materials: application, full script (2 copies), resume, synopsis
Preferred Genre: All genres
Preferred Length: Full-length
Special interest: Women's Interest
Submission Fee: No

Jean Kennedy Smith Playwriting Award
Kennedy Center, Education Div.
Washington, DC 20566
Gregg Henry, Artistic Director, KCACTF
Phone: (202) 416-8864
Fax: (202) 416-4892
www.kcactf.org
ghenry@kennedy-center.org
Notes: Award for a student-written play addressing issues of disability (as defined by the ADA). Plays accepted only from college/university participating in KC/ACTF program.
Agent Only: No
Submission Materials: see website
Preferred Genre: Plays (No Musicals)
Preferred Length: Any length
Special interest: Disabled
Submission Fee: Yes
Deadline(s): Regional–November 1; National–December 1

John Cauble Short Play Awards Program
Kennedy Center, Education Div.
Washington, DC 20566
Gregg Henry, Artistic Director, KCACTF
Phone: (202) 416-8864
Fax: (202) 416-4892
www.kcactf.org
skshaffer@kennedy-center.org
Notes: Plays accepted only from college/university participating in KC/ACTF program.
Agent Only: No
Submission Materials: application, full script, synopsis
Preferred Genre: Plays (No Musicals)
Preferred Length: One-Act
Submission Fee: Yes
Deadline(s): Regional–November 1

John Gassner Memorial Playwriting Award
NETC
215 Knob Hill Dr.
Hamden, CT 06518
Joseph Juliano, Manager, Operations
Phone: (617) 851-8535
Fax: (203) 288-5938
www.NETConline.org
mail@NETConline.org

Notes: Est. 1967. Honors theater historian John Gassner for his lifetime dedication to all aspects of professional and academic theater. Seeking unproduced/unpublished plays. Response by November 2013.
Agent Only: No
Submission Materials: full script, query letter
Preferred Genre: Plays (No Musicals)
Preferred Length: Full-length
Submission Fee: Yes
Deadline(s): April 15, 2013

KCACTF Ten-Minute Play Award
John F. Kennedy Ctr for the Performing Arts
Washington, DC 20566
Gregg Henry, Artistic Director, KCACTF
Phone: (202) 416-8864
Fax: (202) 416-4892
www.kcactf.org
ghenry@kennedy-center.org
Notes: Plays accepted only from college/university participating in KC/ACTF program.
Agent Only: No
Submission Materials: application, full script, synopsis
Preferred Genre: Plays (No Musicals)
Preferred Length: 10-min./10pgs.
Submission Fee: Yes
Deadline(s): Regional–November 1

Kernodle New Play Award
619 Kimpel Hall
University of Arkansas
Fayetteville, AR 72701
Robert Ford, Director
Phone: (479) 575-2953
Fax: (479) 575-7602
www.theater2.org
kernodle@uark.edu
Notes: Co-administered by Theatre Squared and the Fulbright College of Arts and Sciences, University of Arkansas. Playwrights who live or have lived in Arkansas are strongly encouraged, and we give preference to plays and musicals that reflect the rich diversity of mid-America. Additional website: www.drama.uark.edu
Agent Only: No
Submission Materials: full script, query letter
Preferred Genre: All genres
Preferred Length: Full-length
Submission Fee: No
Deadline(s): November 1, 2013

Laity Theatre Company

3053 Rancho Vista Blvd. Ste. H336
Palmdale, CA 93551
Phone: (888) 732-6092
Fax: (661) 430-5423
www.laityarts.org
contact@laityarts.org
Notes: Seeking unproduced/unpublished
material for readings/workshops thematically
linked to women, theatre for young audiences,
writers of color and people with disabilities.
Agent Only: No
Submission Materials: 15-pg sample, query
letter, synopsis
Preferred Genre: Plays (No Musicals)
Preferred Length: Any length
Submission Fee: No

Latino Playwriting Award

Kennedy Center, Education Div.
Washington, DC 20566
Phone: (202) 416-8857
Fax: (202) 416-8802
www.kcactf.org
skshaffer@kennedy-center.org
Notes: The award will be presented to the
author of the best student-written play by a
Latino student playwright attending a college/
university participating in KCACTF.
Agent Only: No
Submission Materials: application
Preferred Genre: Plays (No Musicals)
Preferred Length: Full-length
Special interest: Latino
Submission Fee: Yes

LiveWire Chicago Theatre

P.O. Box 11226
Chicago, IL 60611
Krista D'Agostino, Literary Manager
Phone: (312) 533-4666
www.livewirechicago.com
livewirechicago@gmail.com
Notes: Annual short play festival surround-
ing a central theme. Work must be previously
unproduced. See website for theme guidelines,
submission criteria, deadlines and more info.
Agent Only: No
Submission Materials: full script
Preferred Genre: Plays (No Musicals)
Preferred Length: 10-min./10pgs.
Submission Fee: No
Deadline(s): See website

Lorraine Hansberry Playwriting Award

Kennedy Center, Education Div.
Washington, DC 20566
Gregg Henry, Artistic Director, KCACTF
Phone: (202) 416-8864
Fax: (202) 416-4892
www.kcactf.org
ghenry@kennedy-center.org
Notes: For the outstanding play written by a
student of African or Diasporan heritage. Plays
accepted only from college/university partici-
pating in KC/ACTF program.
Agent Only: No
Submission Materials: see website
Preferred Genre: Plays (No Musicals)
Preferred Length: Any length
Special interest: African-American
Submission Fee: Yes
Deadline(s): Regional–November 1;
National–December 1

Mark Twain Prize for Comic Playwriting

American Coll. Theater Festival
Education Office., Kennedy Center
Arlington, VA 22210
Gregg Henry, Artistic Director, KCACTF
Phone: (202) 416-8864
Fax: (202) 416-4892
www.kcactf.org
ghenry@kennedy-center.org
Notes: For the outstanding student-written
comedy or play with a significant comic ele-
ment from college/university participating in
KC/ACTF program.
Agent Only: No
Submission Materials: application
Preferred Genre: Comedy
Preferred Length: Any length
Submission Fee: Yes
Deadline(s): Regional–November 1;
National–December 1

McLaren Memorial Comedy Playwriting Competition

Midland MCT
2000 W. Wadley Ave.
Midland, TX 79705
MaryLou Cassidy, McLaren Chair
Phone: (432) 682-2544
Fax: (432) 682-6136
www.mctmidland.org
tracy@mctmidland.org
Notes: Est. 1989. Finalists provided with a
reader's theatre presentation of script to a live
audience and the winner may be produced

as part of an upcoming MCT Season. Prize money awarded. Electronic submissions to our website preferred. Fee and Form must be sent by regular post.
Agent Only: No
Submission Materials: see website
Preferred Genre: Comedy
Preferred Length: Full-length
Submission Fee: Yes
Deadline(s): End of February

MetLife Foundation's Nuestras Voces National Playwriting Com
Repertorio Espanol
138 E. 27th St.
New York, NY 10016
Phone: (212) 225-9950
Fax: (212) 225-9085
www.repertorio.org/opportunities
aav@repertorio.org
Notes: Author must be related to Hispanics in the US. Latino Playwrights and/or plays that deal with subjects relating to Hispanics/Latinos living in the US.
Agent Only: No
Submission Materials: anonymous, application, full script (2 copies)
Preferred Genre: Plays or Musicals
Preferred Length: Full-length
Special interest: Latino
Submission Fee: No
Deadline(s): June 1, 2013

Mississippi Theatre Association
707 Bardwell Road
Starkville, MS 39759
Phone: (812) 320-3534
www.mta-online.org
tklee1976@gmail.com
Notes: This competition is open to all Mississippi writers either in state or abroad. Submit via online form available on website.
Agent Only: No
Submission Materials: application, full script, synopsis
Preferred Genre: All genres
Preferred Length: One-Act
Submission Fee: No
Deadline(s): December 17, 2013

Musical Theater Award
Kennedy Center, Education Div.
Washington, DC 20566
Gregg Henry, Artistic Director, KCACTF
Phone: (202) 416-8864

Fax: (202) 416-4892
www.kcactf.org
ghenry@kennedy-center.org
Notes: For the outstanding musical theater or music theater piece written and/or developed at a college or university. At least one member of the Composer/Lyricist/Librettist team must be a student or faculty member at a college/university participating in KC/ACTF program.
Agent Only: No
Submission Materials: application
Preferred Genre: Musical theatre
Preferred Length: Any length
Submission Fee: Yes
Deadline(s): Regional–November 1; National–December 2

Naples Players ETC
701 5th Ave. S.
Naples, FL 34102-6662
Phone: (239) 434-7340
www.naplesplayers.com
venus46@naples.net
Notes: Writer must reside in Collier, Lee, Charlotte, Glades or Hendry counties in Florida and may not be a member of the anonymous judging panel.
Agent Only: No
Submission Materials: see website
Preferred Genre: Comedy
Preferred Length: One-Act
Submission Fee: No

National Latino Playwriting Award
Arizona Theatre Company
343 S. Scott Avenue
Tucson, AZ 85701
Phone: (520) 884-8210
www.arizonatheatre.org
kmonberg@arizonatheatre.org
Notes: Must be resident of US, or Mexico; Latino.
Agent Only: No
Submission Materials: see website
Preferred Genre: All genres
Preferred Length: Full-length
Special interest: Latino
Submission Fee: No
Deadline(s): See website

National Science Playwriting Award
Kennedy Center, Education Division
Washington, DC 20566
Gregg Henry, Artistic Director, KC/ACTF
Phone: (202) 416-8864

Fax: (202) 416-4892
www.kcactf.org
ghenry@kennedy-center.org
Notes: Award for the outstanding student-written play on themes of science, technology and the impact of both on our lives from college/university participating in KCACTF program.
Agent Only: No
Submission Materials: see website
Preferred Genre: Plays (No Musicals)
Preferred Length: Any length
Submission Fee: Yes
Deadline(s): Regional–November 1; National–December 1

National Student Playwriting Award
John F. Kennedy Center for the Perf
Washington, DC 20566
Gregg Henry, Artistic Director, KCACTF
Phone: (202) 416-8864
Fax: (202) 416-4892
www.kcactf.org
ghenry@kennedy-center.org
Notes: For the outstanding student-written, full-length play premiering at a college or university participating in KC/ACTF program.
Agent Only: No
Submission Materials: application
Preferred Genre: Plays (No Musicals)
Preferred Length: Full-length
Submission Fee: Yes
Deadline(s): Regional–November 1; National–December 1

National Ten-Minute Play Contest
Actors Theatre of Louisville
316 W. Main St.
Louisville, KY 40202
Sarah Lunnie, Literary Associate
Phone: (502) 584-1265
Fax: (502) 561-3300
actorstheatre.org/participate/submit-a-play/national-ten-minute-play-contest
slunnie@actorstheatre.org
Notes: Est. 1989. Characters in submitted plays should be in age range 18–28. See website for full submission guidelines.
Agent Only: No
Submission Materials: full script
Preferred Genre: Plays (No Musicals)
Preferred Length: 10-min./10pgs.
Submission Fee: No
Deadline(s): See website

North Carolina New Play Project (NCNPP)
Greensboro Playwrights Forum
Greensboro Cultural Center
200 N. Davie St., Box 2
Greensboro, NC 27401
Stephen Hyers, Director
Phone: (336) 335-6426
Fax: (336) 373-2659
www.playwrightsforum.org
stephen@playwrightsforum.org
Notes: Work must be unpublished/unproduced. Email submission. Author must be a resident of North Carolina. Production: small cast, simple set. Response: 6 months.
Agent Only: No
Submission Materials: full script
Preferred Genre: Plays (No Musicals)
Preferred Length: Full-length
Submission Fee: No
Deadline(s): See website

Ohioana Career Award
274 E. 1st Ave., #300
Columbus, OH 43201
Linda R. Hengst, Executive Director
Phone: (614) 466-3831
Fax: (614) 728-6974
www.ohioana.org
ohioana@ohioana.org
Notes: Est. 1943. Award to native Ohioan for outstanding professional accomplishments in arts and humanities.
Agent Only: No
Submission Materials: see website
Submission Fee: No
Deadline(s): December 31st of each year

Ohioana Citations
274 E. 1st Ave., #300
Columbus, OH 43201
Linda Hengst, Executive Director
Phone: (614) 466-3831
Fax: (614) 728-6974
www.ohioana.org
ohioana@ohioana.org
Notes: Est. 1945. Award for outstanding contributions and accomplishments in specific area of arts and humanities. Must be native or at least five year resident of Ohio.
Agent Only: No
Submission Materials: see website
Submission Fee: No
Deadline(s): December 31st of each year

Ohioana Pegasus Award
274 E. 1st Ave., #300
Columbus, OH 43201
Linda Hengst, Executive Director
Phone: (614) 466-3831
Fax: (614) 728-6974
www.ohioana.org
ohioana@ohioana.org
Notes: Est. 1964. Award for unique or out-standing contributions or achievements in arts and humanities, given at discretion of trustees. Must be Ohio native or at least five year resident.
Agent Only: No
Submission Materials: see website
Submission Fee: No
Deadline(s): December 31st of each year

One-Act Playwriting Competition
900 N. Benton Ave.
Springfield, MO 65802
Dr. Mick Sokol, Associate Professor, Theatre
Phone: (417) 873-6821
Fax: (417) 873-7572
www.drury.edu
msokol@drury.edu
Notes: Est. 1984.
Agent Only: No
Submission Materials: full script, S.A.S.E.
Preferred Genre: Plays (No Musicals)
Preferred Length: One-Act
Submission Fee: No
Deadline(s): December 1, 2014

Paul Stephen Lim Playwriting Award
Kennedy Center, Education Division
Washington, DC 20566
Gregg Henry, Artistic Director, KC/ACTF
Phone: (202) 416-8864
Fax: (202) 416-4892
www.kcactf.org
ghenry@kennedy-center.org
Notes: Award for the outstanding student-written play by a student of Asian or Pacific Rim heritage from college/university participating in KCACTF program.
Agent Only: No
Submission Materials: see website
Preferred Genre: Plays (No Musicals)
Preferred Length: Any length
Special interest: Asian-American
Submission Fee: Yes
Deadline(s): Regional–November 1;
National–December 1

Paula Vogel Award for Playwriting
John F. Kennedy Center for the Performing Arts
Washington, DC 20566
Gregg Henry, Artistic Director, KCACTF
Phone: (202) 416-8864
Fax: (202) 416-4892
wwww.kennedy-center.org/educatioctf
ghenry@kennedy-center.org
Notes: Est. 2003. Award for the outstanding student-written play that explores issues of gender, diversity, sexuality and tolerance. Plays accepted only from college/university participating in KC/ACTF program.
Agent Only: No
Submission Materials: application
Preferred Genre: All genres
Preferred Length: Any length
Submission Fee: Yes
Deadline(s): Regional–November 1;
National–November 2

PEN/Laura Pels International Foundation Awards for Drama
588 Broadway, #303
New York, NY 10012
Paul Morris, Director
Phone: (212) 334-1660
Fax: (212) 334-2181
www.pen.org
awards@pen.org
Notes: Est. 1998. Award to US playwright in mid-career writing in English. See website for details.
Agent Only: No
Submission Materials: see website
Submission Fee: No
Deadline(s): February 1, 2013

Playwrights First
The National Arts Club
15 Gramercy Park S
New York, NY 10003
Emily Andren, Director of Public Relations
Phone: (212) 410-9234
emilyandren@earthlink.net
Notes: July 1 2013 winner announced. No submissions before August 1 please. No electronic submissions. $1000 grant for winners and professional reading where appropriate, introductions to actors, literary managers, directors, etc.. No adaptations or translations. One author per play—original, full-length, unproduced prior to submission, in English.
Agent Only: No

Submission Materials: full script, resume, synopsis
Preferred Genre: Plays (No Musicals)
Preferred Length: Full-length
Submission Fee: No
Deadline(s): October 15, 2013

Public Access Television Corp. (PATC)
1111 Marcus Ave., #LL27
Lake Success, NY 11042
Shirley Bruno, Executive Director
Phone: (516) 629-3710
Fax: (516) 629-3704
www.patv.org
info@patv.org
Notes: Est. 1998. TV opportunity only. One-act play competition. Fees: $5 Frequency: annual Production: cast of 2–3 adults,unit set. Response Time: 2 months. Submissions will be accepted as of Fall 2013.
Agent Only: No
Submission Materials: see website
Preferred Genre: Comedy
Preferred Length: One-Act
Submission Fee: Yes

Quest for Peace Playwriting Award
Kennedy Center, Education Division
Washington, DC 20566
Gregg Henry, Artistic Director
Phone: (202) 416-8864
Fax: (202) 416-4892
www.kcactf.org
ghenry@kennedy-center.org
Notes: Award for the oustanding student-written play grappling with issues of war and peace, the Middle East, and the impact here at home from college/university participating in KCACTF program.
Agent Only: No
Submission Materials: see website
Preferred Genre: Plays (No Musicals)
Preferred Length: Any length
Submission Fee: Yes
Deadline(s): Regional–November 1; National–December 1

Reverie Productions
c/o Brooklyn Creative League
540 President Street, 3rd Floor
Brooklyn, NY 11215
Phone: (212) 244-7803
Fax: (212) 244-7813
www.reverieproductions.org
kimberly@reverieproductions.org

Notes: Est. 2002. Response: April.
Agent Only: No
Submission Materials: application, full script, S.A.S.E.
Preferred Genre: Plays (No Musicals)
Preferred Length: Any length
Submission Fee: Yes
Deadline(s): See website

Richard Rodgers Awards for Musical Theater
633 W. 155th St.
New York, NY 10032
Phone: (212) 368-5900
Fax: (212) 491-4615
www.artsandletters.org
academy@artsandletters.org
Notes: Est. 1978. Awards for musicals by writers and composers not already established in field.
Agent Only: No
Submission Materials: application, audio CD, full script, S.A.S.E., synopsis
Preferred Genre: Musical theatre
Submission Fee: No
Deadline(s): See website

Robert Chesley Award
828 N. Laurel Ave.
Los Angeles, CA 90046
Victor Bumbalo, President
Phone: (323) 658-5981
www.chesleyfoundation.org
VictorTom@aol.com
Notes: Est. 1991. In honor of Robert Chesley (1943–90) to recognize gay and lesbian themed work. Nominations open in early fall.
Agent Only: No
Submission Materials: full script, S.A.S.E.
Preferred Genre: Plays (No Musicals)
Preferred Length: Full-length
Special interest: LGBT
Submission Fee: No
Deadline(s): Early fall

Robert J. Pickering Award for Playwriting Excellence
89 Division St.
Coldwater, MI 49036
Phone: (517) 279-7963
Fax: (517) 279-8095
Notes: Est. 1984. Award for unproduced plays and musicals.
Agent Only: No
Submission Materials: full script, S.A.S.E.

Preferred Genre: Plays or Musicals
Preferred Length: Full-length
Submission Fee: No
Deadline(s): December 31, 2013

Rosa Parks Playwriting Award
Kennedy Center, Education Division
Washington, DC 20566
Gregg Henry, Artistic Director, KCACTF
Phone: (202) 416-8864
Fax: (202) 416-4892
www.kcactf.org
ghenry@kennedy-center.org
Notes: Awarded for the outstanding student or faculty written play on the theme of civil rights and social justice from college/university participating in KC/ACTF program.
Agent Only: No
Submission Materials: see website
Preferred Genre: Plays (No Musicals)
Submission Fee: Yes
Deadline(s): Regional–November 1; National–December 1

Ruby Lloyd Apsey Award
Theatre UAB
ASC 255
1720 2nd Ave South
Birmingham, AL 35294
Lee E. Shackleford, Chair, Apsey Play Search
Phone: (205) 975-8755
Fax: (205) 934-8076
www.uab.edu/theatre/apsey
leeshack@uab.edu
Notes: Biennially (even years) UAB seeks new/full-length work on racial or ethnic issues, with ethnically diverse casting. Prefer recyclable hard copy sent by US mail, but we do accept electronic submissions provided each submission is a single file containing a brief synopsis of the play and a cover letter giving highlights of the author's theatre experience.
Agent Only: No
Submission Materials: full script
Preferred Genre: Plays (No Musicals)
Preferred Length: Full-length
Submission Fee: No
Deadline(s): September 12, 2014

Santa Cruz Actors' Theatre Play Contests
1001 Center St., #12
Santa Cruz, CA 95060
Phone: (831) 425-1003
Fax: (831) 425-7560
www.sccat.org/

admin@santacruzactorstheatre.org
Notes: Est. 1985. Contests for full and ten minute long play as well as for young playwrights.
Agent Only: No
Submission Materials: see website
Preferred Genre: Plays (No Musicals)
Preferred Length: Any length
Submission Fee: Yes
Deadline(s): See website

Scholastic Art & Writing Awards
557 Broadway
New York, NY 10012
Phone: (212) 343-7729
Fax: (212) 389-3939
www.artandwriting.org
info@artandwriting.org
Notes: Est. 1923. National awards in 2 categories (grades 7–8; grades 9–12), selected from regional contests. Regional deadlines vary. Regional Gold Key works are considered for national awards.
Agent Only: No
Submission Materials: application, full script
Preferred Genre: Plays (No Musicals)
Preferred Length: 10-min./10pgs.
Submission Fee: No
Deadline(s): See website

SETC High School New Play Award
1175 Revolution Mill Dr., Suite 14
Greensboro, NC 27405
Nancy Gall-Clayton, Chair, High School Playwriting Contest
Phone: (336) 272-3645
Fax: (336) 272-8810
www.setc.org/theatre/high-school-new-play-project
nancygallclayton@earthlink.net
Notes: Author must be a student & resident of Alabama, Florida, Georgia, Kentucky, Mississippi, North Carolina, South Carolina, Tennessee, Virginia or West Virginia and work must be unpublished/unproduced.
Agent Only: No
Submission Materials: see website
Preferred Genre: Plays (No Musicals)
Preferred Length: One-Act
Submission Fee: No
Deadline(s): See website

Southern Rep's The Ruby Prize
333 Canal St Box 34

New Orleans, LA 70130
Amiee Hayes, Artistic Director
Phone: (504) 523-9857
Fax: (504) 523-9859
www.southernrep.com
theruby@southernrep.com
Notes: The Ruby Prize has been suspended for 2013 and will return in 2014. Submission details for the next Ruby Prize will be announced in 2013. Must be a US citizen and self-identified woman of color. Open to established or emerging playwrights. No collaborations, translations, one-acts, or works previously submitted to Southern Rep. For musicals, only playwright is eligible. No plays written as a result of commission or that have had a previously professional production (workshop/non-professional OK.) If selected as prize-winner or finalist, playwright agrees that their work may be included in annual Ruby Prize publication (non-exclusive).
Agent Only: No
Submission Materials: see website
Preferred Genre: Plays or Musicals
Preferred Length: Full-length
Special interest: Women's Interest
Submission Fee: No
Deadline(s): See website

STAGE International Script Competition
Professional Artists Lab
CNSI-MC 6105
3241 Elings Hall Building 266

University of California
Santa Barbara, CA 93106-6105
www.stage.cnsi.ucsb.edu
stage@cnsi.ucsb.edu
Notes: The professional Artists Lab and the California NanoSystems Institute at UCSB collaborate on STAGE- Scientists, Technologists and Artists Generating Exploration for the best new play about science and/or technology. See website for full info: www.stage.cnsi.ucsb.edu. The STAGE International script Competition is biennial; guidelines/deadlines may alter with each cycle.
Agent Only: No
Submission Materials: see website
Preferred Length: Full-length
Submission Fee: No

Stanley Drama Award
Wagner College
One Campus Road

Staten Island, NY 10301
Phone: (718) 420-4338
Fax: (718) 390-3323
www.wagner.edu/stanley_drama
todd.price@wagner.edu
Notes: Est. 1957. Work must be unoptioned, unproduced, unpublished. Response: 6 months. See website for details.
Agent Only: No
Submission Materials: audio CD, full script, S.A.S.E.
Preferred Genre: Plays or Musicals
Preferred Length: Full-length
Submission Fee: Yes
Deadline(s): October 1, 2013

Summerfield G. Roberts Award
1717 8th St.
Bay City, TX 77414
Janet Knox, Administrative Assistant
Phone: (979) 245-6644
Fax: (979) 244-3819
www.srttexas.org/
srttexas@srttexas.org
Notes: Award for creative writing about the Republic of Texas, to encourage literature & research about the events and personalities of 1836–46.
Agent Only: No
Submission Materials: full script, S.A.S.E.
Submission Fee: No
Deadline(s): January 15, 2013

Susan Smith Blackburn Prize
3239 Avalon Pl.
Houston, TX 77019
Phone: (713) 308-2842
Fax: (713) 654-8184
www.blackburnprize.org
play@blackburnprize.com
Notes: Est. 1978. Plays accepted only from specified source theaters in US, UK and Ireland. Writers should bring their work to the attention of the theatre companies listed on website.
Agent Only: No
Submission Materials: full script, S.A.S.E.
Preferred Genre: Comedy
Preferred Length: Any length
Submission Fee: No
Deadline(s): See website

TeCo Theatrical Productions New Play Competition
215 South Tyler Street

Dallas, TX 75208
Teresa Coleman Walsh, Executive Artistic
Director
Phone: (214) 948-0716
Fax: (214) 948-3706
www.tecotheater.org
teresa@tecotheater.org
Notes: Est. 1993. Author must be resident of
Dallas. Submit unoptioned/unpublished/unpro-
duced by US mail. Production: cast limit 4,
minimal set and costume changes. Response:
2 months.
Agent Only: No
Preferred Genre: Plays (No Musicals)
Preferred Length: One-Act
Submission Fee: No
Deadline(s): December 1, 2013

Ten Minute Musicals Project
Box 461194
West Hollywood, CA 90046
Michael Koppy, Producer
www.TenMinuteMusicals.org
info@TenMinuteMusicals.org
Notes: Est. 1989. Production: cast limit 10.
Agent Only: No
Submission Materials: audio CD, full script,
S.A.S.E., vocal score
Preferred Genre: Musical theatre
Preferred Length: 10-min./10pgs.
Submission Fee: No
Deadline(s): August 31, 2013

Theater for Youth Playwriting Award
John F. Kennedy Center for the Performing
Arts
Washington, DC 20566
Phone: (202) 416-8857
Fax: (202) 416-8802
www.kcactf.org
skshaffer@kennedy-center.org
Notes: Award for student-written play appeal-
ing to young people in grades K–12. Plays
accepted only from college/univ. participating
in KC/ACTF program.
Agent Only: No
Submission Materials: application
Preferred Genre: Plays (No Musicals)
Preferred Length: Any length
Special interest: Theatre for Young
Audiences
Submission Fee: Yes

Theatre Oxford 10-Minute Play Contest
PO Box 1321
Oxford, MS 38655
Phone: (662) 236-5052
Fax: (662) 234-9266
www.10minuteplays.com
10minuteplays@gmail.com
Notes: Est. 1998. Production: casts 2–4,
minimal set, props. Only winners & finalists
will be contacted. Work must be unoptioned,
unproduced, unpublished. Submissions not
returned.
Agent Only: No
Submission Materials: full script
Preferred Genre: Plays (No Musicals)
Preferred Length: 10-min./10pgs.
Submission Fee: Yes
Deadline(s): See website

University of Central Missouri Competition
Theater Dept., Martin 113
Warrensburg, MO 64093
Phone: (660) 543-4020
Fax: (660) 543-8006
www.ucmo.edu/theatre/about/write.cfm
wilson@ucmo.edu
Notes: Est. 2001. Has produced children's
plays for over 25 years. Now focused on
world-premiere originals, through national
competition.
Agent Only: No
Submission Materials: see website
Special interest: Theatre for Young
Audiences
Submission Fee: Yes
Deadline(s): See website

**University of Wyoming Amy & Eric Burger
Essays on Theatre**
Univ. of Wyoming c/o Dr. Jim Volz
Theatre & Dance, PO Box 6850
Fullerton, CA 92834
Jim Volz, President, Consultant for the Arts
jvolz@fullerton.edu
Notes: Seek unpublished essays (between
1800 & 7500 words) on Theatre/Drama for
award. Email Dr. Volz (jvolz@fullerton.edu)
for submission requirements. Winner notified
by June 2013. $2,500 prize. Dramatists Guild
Members have been past winners.
Agent Only: No
Submission Materials: 2 copies of essay
Preferred Genre: All genres
Submission Fee: No
Deadline(s): March 12, 2013

Urban Stages Emerging Playwright Award
555 8th Ave.
Suite #1800
New York, NY 10018
Phone: (212) 421-1380
Fax: (212) 421-1387
www.urbanstages.org
urbanstage@aol.com
Notes: Est. 1986. Material must be unoptioned/unproduced/unpublished. Production: cast limit 6. Response: 6 months.
Agent Only: No
Submission Materials: full script
Preferred Genre: Plays (No Musicals)
Preferred Length: Full-length
Submission Fee: No

Vermont Playwrights Award
Valley Players
P.O. Box 441
Waitsfield, VT 05673
Sharon Kellermann, Coordinator
Phone: (802) 583-6767
www.valleyplayers.com
valleyplayers@madriver.com
Notes: Est. 1982. Must be resident of Maine, New Hampshire, Vermont. Work must be unoptioned, unpublished, unproduced.
Agent Only: No
Submission Materials: application, full script, S.A.S.E.
Preferred Genre: Plays (No Musicals)
Preferred Length: Full-length
Submission Fee: No
Deadline(s): February 1, 2013

Walter H. Baker High School Playwriting Contest
45 W. 25th Street, 2nd Floor
New York, NY 10010
Amy R. Marsh, Literary Manager
Phone: (212) 206-8990
Fax: (212) 627-7753
www.samuelfrench.com/contests-and-festivals
publications@bakersplays.com
Notes: Est. 1989. For student playwrights currently enrolled in High School. The application must be accompanied by a teacher/mentor signature. Plays can be about any subject, but playwrights may submit 1–3 plays, up to 60 pages each. Plays must be submitted electronically. Please visit our website for more information.

Agent Only: No
Submission Materials: application, full script
Preferred Genre: All genres
Preferred Length: One-Act
Submission Fee: No
Deadline(s): January 18, 2013

Write a Play! NYC Contest
Young Playwrights Inc
Post Office Box 5134
New York, NY 10185
Amanda Junco, Associate Director
Phone: (212) 594-5440
Fax: (212) 684-4902
www.youngplaywrights.org
admin@youngplaywrights.org
Notes: Contest open to all NYC students in 3 categories: elementary, middle and high school. All receive certificate of merit, written evaluation, and invitation to awards ceremony.
Agent Only: No
Submission Materials: full script
Preferred Genre: Plays (No Musicals)
Preferred Length: Full-length
Submission Fee: No
Deadline(s): See website

Young Playwrights Inc. National Playwriting Competition
Young Playwrights, Inc.
Post Office Box 5134
New York, NY 10185
Amanda Junco, Associate Director
Phone: (212) 594-5440
Fax: (212) 684-4892
www.youngplaywrights.org
admin@youngplaywrights.org
Notes: Est. 1981. Young Playwrights Inc. identifies and develops young (18 and younger) US playwrights by involving them as active participants in the highest quality professional productions of their plays. See website for competition guideline.
Agent Only: No
Submission Materials: full script, S.A.S.E.
Preferred Genre: No musicals or adaptations
Preferred Length: Any length
Submission Fee: No
Deadline(s): See website

Grants & Fellowships

Alabama State Council on the Arts
201 Monroe St.
Montgomery, AL 36130
Phone: (334) 242-4076
Fax: (334) 240-3269
www.arts.alabama.gov
randy.shoults@arts.alabama.gov
Notes: Artist Fellowships and Artist in
Education Residency in performing artists,
literature, and visual artists. Must be a 2-year
resident of Alabama.
Agent Only: No
Submission Fee: No
Deadline(s): March 1, 2013

Alaska State Council on the Arts (ASCA)
411 W. 4th Ave., #1-E
Anchorage, AK 99501
Phone: (888) 278-7424
Fax: (907) 269-6601
www.eed.state.ak.us/aksca
aksca_info@eed.state.ak.us
Notes: Est. 1966. Opportunities include quar-
terly career opportunity grants and biennial
Connie Boochever Artist Fellowships (Aug 31
deadline, odd yrs).
Agent Only: No
Submission Materials: 10-pg sample, audio
CD
Preferred Genre: All genres
Preferred Length: Full-length
Submission Fee: No
Deadline(s): See website for various
deadlines

Alavi Foundation
500 Fifth Ave, Suite 2320
New York, NY 10110
Phone: (212) 944-8333
Fax: (212) 921-0325
www.alavifoundation.org
Notes: The Foundation's mission is to promote
charitable and philanthropic causes through
educational, religious, and cultural programs.
It supports organizations that sustain interfaith
harmony and promote Islamic culture and
Persian language, literature, and civilization.
Grants are awarded in the areas of colleges
and universities, Persian schools, Islamic organizations, disaster relief, support for the arts,
and scholarly research. It also has established a
book distribution program for those unable to
purchase books related to Islamic/Persian culture on their own.
Agent Only: No
Submission Fee: No

American-Scandinavian Foundation (ASF)
58 Park Ave.
New York, NY 10016
Phone: (212) 879-9779
Fax: (212) 249-3444
www.amscan.org
grants@amscan.org
Notes: Grants for short visits and fellowships
for full year of study or research in Denmark,
Finland, Iceland, Norway or Sweden by U.S.
citizens/residents. Proficient in host language
preferred.
Agent Only: No
Submission Materials: see website
Submission Fee: Yes
Deadline(s): November 1, 2013

Arch & Bruce Brown Foundation
502 West Pico Road
Palm Springs, CA 92262
Arch Brown, President
Phone: (760) 202-1125
www.aabbfoundation.org
ArnoKrue@aol.com
Notes: The Foundation holds annual writ-
ing competitions for full-length works for the
stage [comedies, dramas, musicals, operas,
song cycles] that are based on, or inspired by,
History. $1,000 first prize (not limited to a sin-
gle winner) will be announced late May, 2013.
The Foundation also offers $1,000 Production
Grants to Producing Organization to aid in
producing historic works. For more informa-
tion see www.aabbfoundation.org.
Agent Only: No
Submission Materials: see website
Special interest: LGBT
Submission Fee: No
Deadline(s): See website

Arthur Foundation
19 Riverside Drive
Suite 6
Riverside, IL 60546
Thomas A. Hett, Director of Programs
Phone: (708) 443-5710
Fax: (708) 443-5717
www.arthurfdn.org/index.php

Notes: The Foundation's grantmaking is focused on improving the health of the population. Funding is awarded to organizations that provide accessible, affordable, and appropriate health services to vulnerable populations. Funding is awarded to projects that provide academic resources for schools, curricular enhancements in the visual and performing arts, educational opportunities to the disabled, programs that encourage college attendance, and those that train and educate doctors, nurses, teachers, and charitable organization managers. Education grants fall under the Foundation's Initiative for Educational Excellence program targeted at schools located in the City of Berwyn, the town of Cicero, and the western suburbs of Chicago. The Foundation asks potential applicants to send a two- or three-page letter outlining briefly the project, the amount of funding sought, and time frame in which the funds are needed.
Agent Only: No
Submission Fee: No

Artist Trust
1835 12th Ave.
Seattle, WA 98122
Miguel Guillien, Program Manager
Phone: (206) 467-8734
Fax: (206) 467-9633
www.artisttrust.org
miguel@artisttrust.org
Notes: Grants for Artist Projects (GAP) program. Assistance: $1,500 unrestricted award. Response time: 4 months. Must be resident of Washington.
Agent Only: No
Submission Materials: 12-pg sample, application, audio CD
Preferred Genre: All genres
Submission Fee: No
Deadline(s): May

Aurand Harris Fellowship
c/o 8950 Koch Field Road at Silver Saddle
Flagstaff, AZ 86004
Mina H. Casmir, CTFA VP—Grants
www.childrenstheatrefoundation.org
info@childrenstheatrefoundation.org
Notes: Est. 1958. For individuals with specific projects or with specific plans for developing excellence in children's theater.
Agent Only: No
Submission Materials: see website
Preferred Genre: All genres

Special interest: Theatre for Young Audiences
Submission Fee: No

Baird Foundation
P.O Box 0672
Milwaukee, WI 53201
Phone: 1 (800) 792-2473
www.rwbaird.com/about-baird/culture/baird-foundation.aspx
Notes: The Foundation is the philanthropic arm of Robert W. Baird & Co., a financial services firm. The Foundation provides direct support to health, education, the arts, and other quality of life causes, often with a focus on diversity and helping individuals achieve their full potential. The Foundation has offices in 100 locations across the United States, and in Europe and Asia. Grants are awarded in to organizations in Hamburg, Germany, Hong Kong, London, and China as well as the United States.
Agent Only: No
Submission Fee: No

Chaim Schwartz Foundation
www.chaimschwartz.org
Notes: The Foundation is dedicated to preserving and enriching Yiddishkeit, the Yiddish language, culture, theater, and art. Named after Chaim Schwartz, a poet, Yiddishist, and social activist, the Foundation was created by his daughter, to carry on his life's work. Proposals may be project specific or for general support. The Foundation is particularly interested in projects that continue on the social justice heritage of Yiddishkeit.
Agent Only: No
Submission Materials: query letter
Special interest: Jewish
Submission Fee: No

Charles Lafitte Foundation
818 Linden Lane
Brielle, NJ 08730
Jennifer Vertetis, President and Executive Director
charleslafitte.org
Jennifer@charleslafitte.org
Notes: Founded in 1999 to help people help themselves and the others around them lead healthy, satisfying, and enriched lives. The Foundation believes that exposure to the arts is vital to fostering and sustaining healthy communities. Goals for arts funding include:

cultivating new talent; supporting established artists; providing educational programs that encourage children's creativity; furthering equal access to the arts; and establishing therapeutic arts programs. The Foundation accepts letters of inquiry throughout the year. It prefers to underwrite specific projects with distinct goals, and targets grants that will have notable impact and make a material difference. The Foundation looks for creativity, innovation, and initiative when awarding funds. Grantmaking should promote inclusiveness and diversity. The Foundation likes projects that remove barriers to full economic and/or social participation in society.
Agent Only: No
Submission Materials: see website
Submission Fee: No

Children's Theater Foundation Grants
www.childrenstheatrefoundation.org
Notes: The Children's Theater Foundation offers grants to small and mid-sized theater companies that produce children's plays. The grants offset cost of children's theater productions, enable theater's to purchase scripts and royalties, and provide better rehearsal facilities for their young performers. If you belong to a community theater and would like more information about obtaining a grant from the Foundation, please visit our website.
Agent Only: No
Preferred Genre: Theatre for Young Audiences
Special interest: Theatre for Young Audiences
Submission Fee: No

Connecticut Office of the Arts (DECD)
One Constitution Plaza
2nd Fl.
Hartford, CT 06103
Tamara Dimitri, Program Specialist
Phone: (860) 256-2800
Fax: (860) 256-2811
www.cultureandtourism.org
tamara.dimitri@ct.gov
Notes: Artistic fellowship for resident of Connecticut.
Agent Only: No
Submission Materials: see website
Submission Fee: No
Deadline(s): See website

Delaware Division of the Arts
820 N. French St.
Wilmington, DE 19801
Phone: (302) 577-8278
Fax: (302) 577-6561
www.artsdel.org
kristin.pleasanton@state.de.us
Notes: Invidual artists fellowships. Must be 18+ and resident of Delaware.
Agent Only: No
Submission Materials: 10-pg sample, application, S.A.S.E.
Submission Fee: No
Deadline(s): See website

Don and Gee Nicholl Fellowships
1313 Vine St.
Hollywood, CA 90028
Joan Wai, Program Manager
Phone: (310) 247-3010
Fax: (310) 247-3794
www.oscars.org/nicholl
nicholl@oscars.org
Notes: Est. 1986. Film competition for screenwriters who haven't earned more than $5K in film or TV. Up to five $30K fellowships each year.
Agent Only: No
Submission Materials: application, full script
Preferred Genre: Screenplays
Preferred Length: Full-length
Submission Fee: Yes

Foundation Center
www.foundationcenter.org
Notes: Grant Source for Individuals provides online access to accurate, up-to-date information on foundations that fund: Educational support—scholarships, fellowships, loans, and internships, Students and graduates of specific schools, Arts and cultural support, Awards, prizes, and grants by nomination
Agent Only: No
Submission Fee: No

Fulbright Program for US Scholars
3007 Tilden St. NW, #5-L
Washington, DC 20008
Phone: (202) 686-7859
Fax: (202) 362-3442
www.cies.org
info@cies.iie.org

Notes: Est. 1947. Grants for US faculty or professionals to research or lecture abroad for 2–12 months in 140 countries.
Agent Only: No
Submission Materials: see website
Submission Fee: No
Deadline(s): See website

Helen McCloy / MWA Scholarship for Mystery Writing

www.mysterywriters.
com/?q=AwardsPrograms-McCloy
mccloy.MWA@gmail.com
Notes: The Helen McCloy/MWA Scholarship for Mystery Writing seeks to nurture talent in mystery writing-in fiction, nonfiction, play-writing, and screenwriting. The scholarship is open to U.S. citizens or permanent residents only. Membership in Mystery Writers of America is not required to apply. Because the McCloy Scholarship is intended for serious aspiring mystery writers who wish to improve their writing skills, we expect that most applicants will be college students or adult learners.
Agent Only: No
Submission Materials: see website
Preferred Genre: Mystery
Preferred Length: Full-length
Submission Fee: No
Deadline(s): February 28, 2013; 2/28/2014

Hodder Fellowship

185 Nassau Street
Princeton, NJ 08542
Mary O'Connor, Assistant to the Chair
Phone: (609) 258-4840
Fax: (609) 258-2230
www.princeton.edu/arts/fellows/
oconnorm@princeton.edu
Notes: 1-year fellowship for Academic Year 2013-14. Fellows may be writers, composers, choreographers, visual artists, performance artists, or other kinds of artists or humanists who have "much more than ordinarily intellectual and literary gifts". They are selected more for promise than for performance. Apply by November 1, 2013 through the Princeton Human Resources website: www.princeton. edu/jobs; search for Open Positions and enter key word "Hodder Fellows".
Agent Only: No
Submission Materials: see website
Submission Fee: No
Deadline(s): November 1, 2013

Iowa Arts Council

600 E. Locust
Des Moines, IA 50319
Phone: (515) 242-6194
Fax: (515) 242-6498
www.iowaartscouncil.org
Linda.lee@iowa.gov
Notes: Application must be downloaded from website. Applicant must be a resident of Iowa. Response: Approximately 4-6 weeks.
Agent Only: No
Submission Fee: No
Deadline(s): See website

Jerome Playwright-in-Residence Fellowships

2301 Franklin Ave E
Minneapolis, MN 55406
Laura Leffler-McCabe, Artistic Programs Administrator
www.pwcenter.org
info@pwcenter.org
Notes: Fellowships to emerging playwrights for one year residency (Jul-Jun) in Minnesota using Center services. Apply online.
Agent Only: No
Submission Materials: see website
Submission Fee: No
Deadline(s): See website

John Simon Guggenheim Memorial Foundation

90 Park Ave.
New York, NY 10016
Keith B. Lewis, Program Manager
Phone: (212) 687-4470
Fax: (212) 697-3248
www.gf.org
fellowships@gf.org
Notes: Est. 1925. Fellowship to scholars and artists for research or creation.
Agent Only: No
Submission Materials: see website
Submission Fee: No
Deadline(s): See website

Jonathan Larson Performing Arts Foundation

Box 672, Prince St. Sta.
New York, NY 10012
Phone: (212) 529-0814
Fax: (212) 253-7604
www.americantheatrewing.org/larsongrants/
jlpaf@aol.com

Notes: Est. 1996. Annual grants to theater composers, lyricists, book writers and to theaters developing new musicals by former Larson award recipients. Response: 4 months.
Agent Only: No
Submission Materials: application, S.A.S.E.
Preferred Genre: Musical theatre
Preferred Length: Full-length
Submission Fee: No
Deadline(s): See website

Kleban Award
424 W. 44th St.
New York, NY 10036
Phone: (212) 757-6960
Fax: (212) 265-4738
www.newdramatists.org/kleban_award.htm
newdramatists@newdramatists.org
Notes: Award to lyricists and librettists working in the American musical theater.
Agent Only: No
Submission Materials: application
Preferred Genre: Musical theatre
Preferred Length: Full-length
Submission Fee: No
Deadline(s): Sepember 15 each year

Laidlaw Foundation
300 Bloor Street East
Suite 2000
Toronto, ON M4W 3L4, Canada
Anna Skinner, Program Manager, Youth Organizing
Phone: (416) 964-3614 Ext 307
Fax: (416) 975-1428
www.laidlawfdn.org
Notes: The Canadian Foundation promotes positive youth development through inclusive youth engagement in the arts, environment, and in the community. It recognizes that all young people need the unconditional support of significant adults in their lives and need multiple opportunities to locate an individual talent and the resources necessary to develop that talent. The Foundation invests in innovative ideas, convenes interested parties, shares its learning and advocates for change in support of young people becoming healthy, creative, and fully engaged citizens. The Foundation's core values include youth engagement, diversity, social inclusion, and civic engagement.
Agent Only: No
Submission Fee: No

Laura Jane Musser Fund: Intercultural Harmony Program
www.musserfund.org/index.asp?page_seq=25
Notes: The Intercultural Harmony Program, an initiative of the Laura Jane Musser Fund, promotes mutual understanding and cooperation between groups and citizens of different cultural backgrounds within defined geographical areas through collaborative, cross-cultural projects. Support is provided to nonprofit organizations in Colorado, Hawaii, Michigan, Minnesota, Ohio, and Wyoming that include members of various cultural communities working together on projects with common goals. These projects must be intercultural, rather than focused on just one culture, and must demonstrate tangible benefits in the larger community. Funded projects can be carried out in a number of areas, including the arts, community service, and youth activities. Planning or implementation grants of up to $20,000 are provided for new projects within their first three years of operation.
Agent Only: No
Submission Fee: No

Lincoln & Therese Filene Foundation
World Trade Center West
155 Seaport Blvd.
Boston, MA 02210
Alane Harrington Wallis, Charitable Foundations Manager
Phone: (617) 439-2498
www.filenefoundation.org
Notes: The Foundation makes grants primarily to Massachusetts organizations with some consideration given to other New England-based programs. Funding is targeted toward programs and projects that enable those who are disadvantaged in various ways to help themselves and others; that reduce social conflicts and create harmonious communities; that encourage informed civic participation on local, state, and regional levels; and that promote participation in the performing arts. Grants are awarded in the following areas: civic education; human development and self-sufficiency; music education and performing arts; and public education and broadcasting.
Agent Only: No
Submission Fee: No
Deadline(s): March 1 & September 1

Louisiana Cultural Economy Foundation
1540 Canal Street, Suite 201

New Orleans, LA 70112
Lisa Picone, Economic Opportunity Fund
Director
Phone: (504) 895-2800
Fax: (504) 910-3001
www.culturaleconomy.org
lisa@culturaleconomy.org
Notes: Grants are made to individuals, businesses and organizations based in Louisiana.
Agent Only: No
Submission Materials: see website
Submission Fee: No
Deadline(s): See website for deadlines

Louisiana Division of the Arts
Box 44247
Baton Rouge, LA 70804
Phone: (225) 342-8180
Fax: (225) 342-8173
www.crt.state.la.us/arts
dbelanger@crt.state.la.us
Agent Only: No
Submission Materials: see website
Preferred Genre: Plays or Musicals
Preferred Length: Any length
Submission Fee: No
Deadline(s): First Monday in March

Marin Arts Council Fund for Artists
555 Northgate Dr., #270
San Rafael, CA 94903
Phone: (415) 499-8350
Fax: (415) 499-8537
www.marinarts.org
marinarts@marinarts.org
Notes: Est. 1985. Career Development Grants to individual artists for professional development.
Agent Only: No
Submission Materials: application
Preferred Genre: All genres
Preferred Length: Any length
Submission Fee: No
Deadline(s): See website

Massachusetts Cultural Council (MCC)
10 St. James Ave., Fl. 3
Boston, MA 02116
Phone: (617) 727-3668
Fax: (617) 727-0044
www.massculturalcouncil.org
dan.blask@art.state.ma.us
Notes: Grants alternating between dance, drawing, prose, painting, poetry, traditional arts (even years) and crafts, film/video, music,

photography, playwriting, sculpture (odd years).
Agent Only: No
Submission Materials: application
Submission Fee: No
Deadline(s): See website

McKnight Advancement Grants
www.pwcenter.org/fellows_advancement.php
Notes: The McKnight Advancement Grants recognize playwrights whose work demonstrates exceptional artistic merit and excellence in the field, and whose primary residence is in the state of Minnesota. Two grants of $25,000 each will be awarded in 2012-13, funded by the Minneapolis-based McKnight Foundation as part of its Arts Program. The grants are intended to significantly advance recipients' playwriting development and their careers. Additional funds of $2,000 can be used to support a play development workshop and other professional expenses.
Agent Only: No
Submission Fee: No

McKnight Theater Artist Fellowship
2301 Franklin Ave. E.
Minneapolis, MN 55406
Phone: (612) 332-7481
Fax: (612) 332-6037
www.pwcenter.org
info@pwcenter.org
Notes: Fellowships to theater artists other than writers whose work demonstrates exceptional artistic merit and potential.
Agent Only: No
Submission Materials: application
Submission Fee: No
Deadline(s): See website

Meyer Memorial Trust
425 NW 10th Aveneu
Suite 400
Portland, OR 97209
Phone: (503) 228-5512
www.mmt.org/program/responsive-grants
mmt@mmt.org
Notes: The Trust's Responsive Grant program supports nonprofits that deliver significant social benefit throughout the state of Oregon and in Clark County, Wash. Grants are awarded for a wide array of activities in the areas of human services, health, affordable housing, community development, conservation and environment, public affairs, arts and

culture, and education. Responsive grants are awarded for project support, expansions, organizational capacity building, and capital construction projects. Letters of inquiry may be submitted throughout the year.
Agent Only: No
Submission Materials: see website
Submission Fee: No

Michener Center for Writers
702 E. Dean Keeton St.
Austin, TX 78705
Phone: (512) 471-1601
Fax: (512) 471-9997
www.utexas.edu/academic/mcw
mcw@www.utexas.edu
Notes: Est. 1993. Financial assistance for full-time students in MFA program. Author must have BA. Playwrights submit 1 full length or 2 one act plays.
Agent Only: No
Submission Materials: application
Preferred Genre: All genres
Preferred Length: Any length
Submission Fee: Yes
Deadline(s): December 15, 2013

Mid Atlantic Arts Foundation
201 N. Charles St., #401
Baltimore, MD 21201
Phone: (410) 539-6656
Fax: (410) 837-5517
www.midatlanticarts.org
info@midatlanticarts.org
Notes: Est. 1999. Artists & Communities program offers matching support for partnerships between artists in New Jersey, New York, Pennsylvania with nonprofit orgs in Washington D.C., Delaware, Maryland, New Jersey, New York, Pennsylvania, Virginia, US Virgin Islands, and West Virginia.
Agent Only: No
Submission Materials: see website
Submission Fee: No

Missouri Arts Council
815 Olive Street
Suite 16
St. Louis, MO 63101
Phone: (314) 340-6845
Fax: (314) 340-7215
www.missouriartscouncil.org
moarts@ded.mo.gov
Agent Only: No
Submission Materials: application

Submission Fee: No
Deadline(s): Last Monday in February

NEH Division for Research Program/ Collaborative Research
1100 Pennsylvania Ave NW
Washington, DC 20506
Phone: (202) 606-8461
Fax: (202) 606-8204
www.neh.gov/grants/guidelines/collaborative.html
mhall@neh.gov
Agent Only: No
Submission Materials: see website
Submission Fee: No

New York Coalition of Professional Women in the Arts & Media
Box 2537, Times Sq. Sta.
New York, NY 10108
Phone: (212) 592-4511
www.wamcoalition.org/
collaboration@nycwam.org
Notes: Est. 1990. NYCWAM Collaboration Award is to encourage professional women in the arts and media to work collaboratively with other women on the creation of new works.
Agent Only: No
Submission Materials: 15–20-pg sample
Preferred Genre: Plays or Musicals
Preferred Length: Any length
Special interest: Women's Interest
Submission Fee: No
Deadline(s): See website for biannual deadline

New York State Council on the Arts (NYSCA)
175 Varick St., Fl. 3
New York, NY 10014
Phone: (212) 627-4455
Fax: (212) 620-5911
www.nysca.org
mwhite@nysca.org
Agent Only: No
Submission Materials: see website
Submission Fee: No

New York Theatre Workshop (NYTW) Playwriting Fellowship
83 E. 4th St.
New York, NY 10003
Phone: (212) 780-9037
Fax: (212) 460-8996
www.nytw.org

rachels@nytw.org

Notes: We are currently not accepting applications for Fellowships. Please visit Website for updates.

Agent Only: No

Submission Materials: see website

Submission Fee: No

Norfolk Southern Foundation

www.nscorp.com/nscportal/nscorp/
Community/NS%20Foundation/

Notes: The Norfolk Southern Foundation supports nonprofit organizations that focus on educational, cultural, environmental, social safety net, and economic development opportunities within the region served by Norfolk Southern, primarily in the Eastern, Midwestern, and Southern United States. The Foundation offers grants in the following principal areas: educational programs, primarily at the post-secondary level; community enrichment focusing on cultural and artistic organizations; human services that support basic needs; and environmental programs.

Agent Only: No

Submission Fee: No

Deadline(s): Between July 15 and September 30, annually

North Carolina Arts Council

Department of Cultural Resources
Raleigh, NC 27699

Phone: (919) 807-6500

Fax: (919) 807-6532

www.ncarts.org
ncarts@ncmail.net

Agent Only: No

Submission Materials: see website

Submission Fee: No

Deadline(s): March 1 (orgs); Nov 1 (artists)

North Dakota Council on the Arts

1600 E. Century Ave., Suite 6
Bismarck, ND 58503
Jan Webb, Executive Director

Phone: (701) 328-7590

Fax: (701) 328-7595

www.nd.gov/arts
comserv@nd.gov

Notes: Est. 1984. Fellowships for visual/media arts (2013); literary/musical artists (2014). See website for more information.

Agent Only: No

Submission Materials: see website

Submission Fee: No

Deadline(s): See website

Page 73 Productions

138 S. Oxford St. #4E
Brooklyn, NY 11217
Liz Jones, Executive Director

Phone: (718) 398-2099

Fax: (718) 398-2794

www.page73.org
info@page73.org

Notes: Est. 1997. Committed to developing and producing the work of emerging playwrights, specifically those who have yet to receive a professional production in New York City. Page 73 produces one or two professional premieres or workshop presentations each season, and runs three primary development programs: a weeklong summer residency on the campus of Yale University for four or five playwrights, a yearlong writers group called "Interstate 73," and the P73 Playwriting Fellowship which provides development support to one early-career playwright annually. See website for requirements on what to submit and who is eligible.

Agent Only: No

Submission Materials: see website

Preferred Genre: All genres

Preferred Length: Any length

Submission Fee: No

Deadline(s): May 1 annually

Pew Fellowships in the Arts (PFA)

Pew Center for Arts & Heritage
1608 Walnut St., 18th Floor
Philadelphia, PA 19103

Phone: (267) 350-4920

Fax: (267) 350-4997

www.pcah.us/fellowships
pfa@pcah.us

Notes: Est. 1991. As of 2010, a nomination process determines who is invited to apply. All disciplines are considered each year. For more info, see website.

Agent Only: No

Submission Materials: application

Submission Fee: No

Playwrights' Center Many Voices
Playwriting Residency

The Playwrights' Center
2301 Franklin Ave. E.
Minneapolis, MN 55406

Phone: (612) 332-7481 Ext 15

Fax: (612) 332-6037

www.pwcenter.org
info@pwcenter.org
Notes: Mentorships available to beginning playwrights of color from Minnesota. Fellowships available to emerging playwrights of color from Minnestoa and nationally. See website for details/award amounts and submission guidelines.
Agent Only: No
Submission Materials: see website
Preferred Genre: Plays or Musicals
Preferred Length: Full-length
Submission Fee: No
Deadline(s): Refer to website

Playwrights' Center McKnight Advancement Grants
2301 Franklin Ave E
Minneapolis, MN 55406
Laura Leffler-McCabe, Artistic Programs Administrator
Phone: (612) 332-7481
www.pwcenter.org
info@pwcenter.org
Notes: Grants to advance a writer's art and career.
Agent Only: No
Submission Materials: application
Submission Fee: No
Deadline(s): See website

Princess Grace Foundation USA Playwriting Fellowship
150 E. 58th St., Fl.25
New York, NY 10155
Phone: (212) 317-1470
Fax: (212) 317-1473
www.pgfusa.org
grants@pgfusa.org
Notes: Est. 1982. 10-week residency with New Dramatists; stipend; and publication/representation by Samuel French for 1 winning playwright.
Agent Only: No
Submission Materials: application
Preferred Genre: Comedy
Preferred Length: Full-length
Submission Fee: No
Deadline(s): See website

Public Theater/Emerging Writers Group
425 Lafayette Street
New York, NY 10003
www.publictheater.org
EWGquestions@publictheater.org

Notes: Targets playwrights at the earliest stages in their careers.
Agent Only: No
Submission Materials: see website
Preferred Genre: All genres
Preferred Length: Full-length
Submission Fee: No

Radcliffe Institute Fellowships
8 Garden Street
Cambridge, MA 02138
Phone: (617) 496-1324
Fax: (617) 495-8136
www.radcliffe.edu/fellowships
fellowships@radcliffe.edu
Notes: To support scholars, scientists, artists, and writers of exceptional promise and demonstrated accomplishments to pursue work in academic and professional fields and in the creative arts.
Agent Only: No
Submission Materials: see website
Submission Fee: Yes
Deadline(s): See website

Rhode Island State Council on the Arts
1 Capitol Hill, Fl. 3
Providence, RI 02908
Cristina DiChiera, Director, Individual Artists Program
Phone: (401) 222-3880
Fax: (401) 422-3018
www.arts.ri.gov
cristina.dichiera@arts.ri.gov
Notes: Applicants MUST be Rhode Island residents. Annual fellowship in play/screenwriting.
Agent Only: No
Submission Materials: application
Submission Fee: No
Deadline(s): April 1, 2013; 10/1/2013

Richard H. Driehaus Foundation
Contact: Peter Handler
333 N. Michigan Ave.
Suite 510
Chicago, IL 60601
Phone: (312) 641-5772
Fax: (312) 641-5736
www.driehausfoundation.org
Notes: The Foundation's program for small Chicago theater and dance companies is designed specifically to address the needs of small professional companies. Proposals will only be accepted from companies that

emphasize professional presentation instead of education or community outreach. To qualify, companies must have annual operating budgets of less than $150,000, must be based in the Chicago area, and must have produced at least one show in the Chicago area.
Agent Only: No
Submission Fee: No

Seventh Generation Fund for Indian Development
www.7genfund.org
Notes: The Seventh Generation Fund for Indian Development is dedicated to promoting and maintaining the uniqueness of Native peoples and the sovereignty of tribal Nations throughout the Americas. The Fund's primary grantmaking program areas include the following: Arts and Cultural Expression, Environmental Health and Justice, Human Rights, Sustainable Communities, Intergenerational Leadership, and Women's Leadership.
Agent Only: No
Submission Materials: see website for application
Submission Fee: No
Deadline(s): February 1, June 1, and October 1, annually.

South Dakota Arts Council
711 E. Wells Ave.
Pierre, SD 57501
Phone: (605) 773-3301
Fax: (605) 773-5657
artscouncil.sd.gov
sdac@state.sd.us
Notes: Est. 1966. Must be a resident of South Dakota. Submit application and sample online only. Response: 3 months.
Agent Only: No
Submission Materials: 10-pg sample, application
Submission Fee: No
Deadline(s): See website

Surdna Foundation
330 Madison Ave
30th Floor
New York, NY 10017
Phone: (212) 557-0010
www.surdna.org/what-we-fund/thriving-cultures/80.html
Notes: Under the Foundation's Thriving Cultures priority area, the Teens Artistic Advancement Initiative seeks to address the isolation and lack of opportunities for artistic advancement for young people from disadvantaged communities. Of particular interest are programs that offer unwavering institutional commitment to teens as evidenced by the consistent availability of resources and staff. Programs that offer increasingly complex and long-term opportunities to create art with accomplished artists, those with high quality, experienced faculty and guest artists and professional artistic development opportunities for staff are a priority.
Agent Only: No
Submission Fee: No

Ted Arison Family Foundation USA
10800 Biscayne Blvd.
Room 950
Miami, FL 33161
Madelon Rosenberg
Phone: (305) 891-0017
www.arison.co.il/group/en/Content.aspx?PageName=The+Ted+Arison+Family+Foundation+
Notes: The Foundation's worldview is rooted in three Jewish values: charity, acts of loving kindness, and Tikkun olam (transformation of the world). The Foundation believes in acting as a role model, creating a better human environment based on fundamental human values, investing in improving the quality of life, and developing public infrastructures and programs based on the commitment to excellence. The Foundation contributes to various projects and to hundreds of nonprofits that operate in seven key spheres: health; education; children and youth; culture, art and sports; populations in distress; disabilities; and scholarships and research.
Agent Only: No
Submission Fee: No

The Moody's Foundation
Manager Philanthropy Programs
7 World Trade Center
250 Greenwich Street
New York, NY 10007
Phone: (212) 553-3667
www.moodys.com/cust/default.asp
Notes: The Foundation is the philanthropic arm of Moody's Corporation, the parent company of Moody's Investors Services. The Corporation provides credit ratings and research covering debt instruments and

securities. The Corporation believes it's important to contribute to the communities in which it operates. It focuses its grantmaking on four areas: education, health and human services, arts and culture, and civic programs. Arts, culture, and civic grants are aimed at enriching the quality of life in communities where employees live and work. Grants are made to organizations in New York City, San Francisco, and London.
Agent Only: No
Submission Fee: No

U.S. Bancorp Foundation
www.usbank.com/cgi_w/cfm/about/
community_relations/grant_guidelines.cfm
Notes: The U.S. Bancorp Foundation supports nonprofit organizations that improve the quality of life for the residents of the communities served by the bank in Arizona, Arkansas, California, Colorado, Idaho, Illinois, Indiana, Iowa, Kansas, Kentucky, Minnesota, Missouri, Montana, Nebraska, Nevada, North Dakota, Ohio, Oregon, South Dakota, Tennessee, Utah, Washington, Wisconsin, and Wyoming. The Foundation's areas of interest include affordable housing, self-sufficiency, economic development, education, and artistic and cultural enrichment.
Agent Only: No
Submission Fee: No
Deadline(s): Vary by area of interest and location

U.S. Dept. of State Fulbright Program for US Students
809 United Nations Plaza
New York, NY 10017
Phone: (212) 984-5330
www.us.fulbrightonline.org
wjackson@iie.org
Notes: Est. 1946. Funds for graduate study, research, or teaching. Students in US colleges must apply thru campus Fulbright Advisers. Those not enrolled in US may apply directly to IIE.
Agent Only: No
Submission Materials: see website
Submission Fee: No
Deadline(s): October annually

Undiscovered Voices Scholarship
The Writer's Center
4508 Walsh Street
Bethesda, MD 20815

Laura Spencer
Notes: The Writer's Center seeks promising writers earning less than $25,000 annually to apply. This scholarship program will provide complimentary writing workshops to the selected applicant for a period of one year, but not to exceed 8 workshops in that year (and not to include independent studies). The Writer's Center believes writers of all backgrounds and experiences should have an opportunity to devote time and energy toward the perfection of their craft. The recipient will be able to attend writing workshops offered by The Writer's Center free of charge. In addition, he or she will give a reading from his or her work at the close of the scholarship period (June 2013) and will be invited to speak with local high school students on the craft of writing. Please submit: a cover letter signed by the candidate that contains the statement: "I understand and confirm I meet all eligibility requirements of the Undiscovered Voices Scholarship." The cover letter should include information on the impact this scholarship would have on the candidate, contact information for two references who can speak to the candidate's creative work and promise, a work sample in a single genre (Eight pages of poetry, no more than one poem per page, 10 pages of fiction, double-spaced, no more than one work or excerpt, 10 pages of nonfiction (essay, memoir, etc), double-spaced, no more than one work or excerpt, 15 pages of a script or screenplay).
Agent Only: No
Submission Fee: No

Vermont Arts Council
136 State St., Drawer 33
Montpelier, VT 05633
Phone: (802) 828-3293
Fax: (802) 828-3363
www.vermontartscouncil.org
srae@vermontartscouncil.org
Notes: Est. 1994. Grants for artists and organizations. Application submission is online only. Must be a Vermont resident. Response: 2 months.
Agent Only: No
Submission Materials: see website
Submission Fee: No
Deadline(s): See website

Verve Grants for Spoken Word Poets—Minnesota
www.intermediaarts.org/verve-grants-program-overview
Notes: Intermedia Arts' VERVE grant program provides funding for emerging Minnesota spoken word poets who are interested in artistic advancement and leadership in their communities. Through financial assistance, professional encouragement, and recognition within a culturally and socioeconomically diverse group of literary artists, this program strengthens and supports Minnesota's literary community.
Agent Only: No
Submission Fee: No

William Penn Foundation
Square, 11th Floor
100 North 18th Street
Philadelphia, PA 19103
Feather Houston, President
Phone: (215) 988-1830
www.williampennfoundation.org
moreinfo@williampennfoundation.org

Notes: The Foundation's grantmaking focuses on improving the quality of life in the greater Philadelphia region through efforts that foster rich cultural expression, strengthen children's futures, and deepen connections to nature and community. Grants are awarded in the following topic areas: children, youth, and families; environment and communities; and arts and culture. Funding priorities for arts and culture grants include growing a robust cultural community and leveraging strategic opportunities. Virtually all of the Foundation's grantmaking takes place in the counties of Bucks, Camden, Chester, Delaware, Montgomery, and Philadelphia. The Foundation will also consider requests for projects that, although administered by an organization located outside of the region, are expressly for the benefit of the region and its constituents. The Foundation occasionally makes grants to national organizations for work performed by local affiliates.
Agent Only: No
Submission Materials: see website
Submission Fee: No

Theaters

12 Miles West Theatre Company
62 Park Avenue
Rutherford, NJ 07070
Robert Cox, Artistic Director
Phone: (201) 636-2127
www.12mileswest.org
info@12mileswest.com
Notes: Est. 1992. Cast of 2–12, unit set.
Response Time: 1 yr
Agent Only: No
Submission Materials: see website
Preferred Genre: All genres
Preferred Length: Any length
Submission Fee: No

16th Street Theater
1619 Wesley Ave
Berwyn, IL 60402
Ann Filmer, Artistic Director
www.16thstreettheater.org/
scriptsubmissionpolicy.html
scripts@16thstreettheater.org
Notes: Preference for Illinois resident writers able to commit to being "playwright-in-residence." We look for diverse voices, and we produce at least one "Latino" play per year. No Musicals. No romantic comedies. No Theatre

for Young Audiences.
Agent Only: No
Submission Materials: see website
Preferred Genre: Plays (No Musicals)
Preferred Length: Full-length
Special interest: American
Submission Fee: No

24th Street Theatre
1117 West 24th St
Los Angeles, CA 90007-1725
Allegra Padilla, Arts Administrator
Phone: (213) 745-6516
www.24thstreet.org
theatre@24thstreet.org
Agent Only: No
Special interest: Theatre for Young Audiences
Submission Fee: No

52nd Street Project
789 10th Ave
New York, NY 10019
Lisa Kerner, General Managment Associate
Phone: (212) 333-5252
Fax: (212) 333-5598
www.52project.org

kerner@52project.org
Agent Only: No
Submission Fee: No

A Noise Within (ANW)
3352 E Foothill Blvd
Pasadena, CA 91107
Geoff Elliot, Co-Artistic Director
Phone: (626) 356-3100
Fax: (626) 356-3120
www.anoisewithin.org
info@anoisewithin.org
Notes: Est. 1991. Response Time: 8 mos.
Agent Only: No
Submission Materials: full script
Preferred Genre: Adaptation
Preferred Length: Full-length
Submission Fee: No

A. D. Players
2710 W. Alabama St.
Houston, TX 77098
Lee Walker, Literary Manager
Phone: (713) 526-2721
Fax: (713) 439-0905
www.adplayers.org
lee@adplayers.org
Notes: Est. 1967. Production cast limit 10
(mainstage)/8 (children's), piano only, limited
sets. Response Time: 3–6 mos. Email profes-
sional recommendation.
Agent Only: No
Submission Materials: 10-pg sample, query
letter, synopsis
Preferred Genre: Plays or Musicals
Preferred Length: Full-length
Submission Fee: No

Abingdon Theatre Company
312 W. 36th St., Fl. 6
New York, NY 10018
Kim T. Sharp, Literary Manager
Phone: (212) 868-2055
Fax: (212) 868-2056
www.abingdontheatre.org
ksharp@abingdontheatre.org
Notes: Est. 1993. Production: cast limit 8.
Response Time: 3–6 months. Deadline is
ongoing. No musicals. Work must be unpro-
duced/unoptioned in NYC.
Agent Only: No
Submission Materials: see website
Preferred Genre: Plays (No Musicals)
Preferred Length: Full-length
Submission Fee: No

About Face Theatre
1222 W. Wilson Ave., Fl. 2
Chicago, IL 60640
Bonnie Metzgar, Artistic Director
Phone: (773) 784-8565
Fax: (773) 784-8557
www.aboutfacetheatre.com
literary@aboutfacetheatre.com
Notes: About Face Theatre creates excep-
tional, innovative, and adventurous plays to
advance the national dialogue on gender and
sexual identity, and to challenge and entertain
audiences in Chicago, across the country, and
around the world.
Agent Only: No
Submission Materials: see website
Preferred Genre: All genres
Preferred Length: Any length
Special interest: Women's Interest
Submission Fee: No

Absinthe-Minded Theatre Company
1484 Stadium Ave.
Bronx, NY 10465
Ralph Scarpato, Producing Artistic Director
Phone: (212) 714-4696
www.myspace.com/absmind
rscarp@aol.com
Notes: Seeking edgy material.
Agent Only: No
Submission Materials: see website
Preferred Genre: All genres
Submission Fee: No

Act II Playhouse
56 E. Butler Pike
Ambler, PA 19002
Tony Braithwaite, Producing Artistic Director
Phone: (215) 654-1011
Fax: (215) 654-9050
www.act2.org
tony@act2.org
Notes: Est. 1998. 130-seat SPT. Act II
Playhouse, a non-profit 501(c)(3) organization in Ambler, is committed to creating and
programming world-class theatre in a venue
whose intimacy draws audiences and actors
into dynamic interaction. Act II produces new,
classic, and contemporary plays and musicals
that reflect the highest artistic standards.
Agent Only: No
Preferred Genre: Comedy

ACT Theater (A Contemporary Theatre)
700 Union St.

Seattle, WA 98101
Phone: (206) 292-7660
Fax: (206) 292-7670
www.acttheatre.org
amontgomery@acttheatre.org
Notes: Est. 1965. Authors from Washington, Oregon, Alaska, Idaho and Montana only. Response Time: 6 mos.
Agent Only: No
Submission Materials: 10-pg sample, synopsis
Preferred Genre: All genres
Preferred Length: Full-length
Submission Fee: No

Acting Company
Box 898, Times Square Station
New York, NY 10108
Phone: (212) 258-3111
Fax: (212) 258-3299
www.theactingcompany.org
mail@theactingcompany.org
Notes: Est. 1972. Prefer solo one-acts on US historical figures for HS tours and full-length adaptations of classic novels. Production: Cast limit 13.
Agent Only: Yes
Submission Materials: agent-only
Preferred Genre: Educational
Preferred Length: Any length
Special interest: Theatre for Young Audiences
Submission Fee: No

Actors Art Theatre (AAT)
6128 Wilshire Blvd., #110
Los Angeles, CA 90048
Jolene Adams, Artistic Director
Phone: (323) 969-4953
www.actorsart.com
actorsart@actorsart.com
Notes: Est. 1994. 32-seat theater developing plays thru workshops and labs. Produces 1 original play each year, plus one-acts and solos under Equity 99-seat. Production: no orchestra. Response Time: 1 yr.
Agent Only: No
Preferred Genre: Plays (No Musicals)

Actors Collective
447 W. 48th St., Ste. 1W
New York, NY 10036
Catherine Russell, Managing Director
Phone: (212) 445-1016
Fax: (212) 445-1015

www.snappletheater.com
postarvis@aol.com
Notes: Est. 1981. Production: cast limit 8. Response time: 1 month.
Agent Only: No
Submission Materials: query letter, S.A.S.E., synopsis
Preferred Genre: All genres
Preferred Length: Full-length
Submission Fee: No
Deadline(s): September

Actor's Express
887 W. Marietta St. NW, #J-107
Atlanta, GA 30318
Freddie Ashley, Artistic Director
Phone: (404) 875-1606
Fax: (404) 875-2791
www.actors-express.com
freddie@actorsexpress.com
Notes: Est. 1988. Readings, workshops, production. Assistance: room/board,travel. Response Time: 6 months.
Agent Only: Yes
Submission Materials: full script
Preferred Genre: All genres
Preferred Length: Any length
Submission Fee: No

Actors Theatre of Louisville [KY]
316 W. Main St.
Louisville, KY 40202
Amy Wegener, Literary Director
Phone: (502) 584-1265
Fax: (502) 561-3300
www.actorstheatre.org
awegener@actorstheatre.org
Notes: Est. 1964. Best time to submit: April–July for full-length scripts, Sept. 1–Nov. 1 postmark window for the National Ten-Minute Play Contest (entries capped at the first 500 ten-minute plays received). See website for full guidelines. Response Time: 12 months.
Agent Only: Yes
Preferred Length: Full-length & 10-min.
Submission Fee: No

Adventure Stage Chicago (ASC)
1012 N. Noble St.
Chicago, IL 60642
Tom Arvetis, Producing Artistic Director
Phone: (773) 342-4141
Fax: (773) 278-2621
www.adventurestage.org
tom@adventurestage.org

Notes: Est. 1998. Production: ages 18 and older, cast limit 10. Response Time: 1 month. Hard copies only. No open submission for the 2012–2013 season. See website for updates.
Agent Only: No
Submission Materials: character breakdown, query letter, synopsis
Preferred Genre: Theatre for Young Audiences
Preferred Length: Any length
Special interest: Theatre for Young Audiences
Submission Fee: No

Airmid Theatre Company
844 Bay Shore Ave
West Islip, NY 11795
Tricia McDermott, Artistic Director
Phone: (631) 704-2888
www.airmidtheatre.org
info@airmidtheatre.org
Notes: The Airmid Theatre Company recovers, collects, and produces classic works by women. With these plays at the heart of its mission, the company creates a safe home for women theatre artists, and ignites broad public recognition of the essential contribution women have made to the worlds of theatre, dramatic literature and society.
Agent Only: No
Submission Materials: see website
Special interest: Women's Interest
Submission Fee: No

Allenberry Playhouse
1559 Boiling Springs Road
Boiling Springs, PA 17007
Phone: (717) 960-3211
Fax: (717) 960-5280
www.allenberry.com
Aberry@allenberry.com
Notes: Production: age 20–60, cast of 6–10, orchestra limit 5.
Agent Only: No
Submission Materials: 20-pg sample, query letter
Preferred Genre: Musical theatre
Preferred Length: Any length
Submission Fee: No

Alley Theatre
615 Texas Ave. 18th Floor
Houston, TX 77002
Jacey Little, Literary Associate
Phone: (713) 228-9341

Fax: (713) 222-6542
www.alleytheatre.org
jaceyl@alleytheatre.org
Notes: Est. 1947. The Alley Theatre is unable to accept any unsolicited scripts at this time. See website for updates.
Agent Only: No
Submission Materials: see website
Preferred Genre: All genres
Preferred Length: Full-length
Submission Fee: No

Alliance Theatre
1280 Peachtree St. NE
Atlanta, GA 30309
Celise Kalke, Director of New Projects
Phone: (404) 733-4650
Fax: (404) 733-4625
www.alliancetheatre.org
allianceinfo@woodruffcenter.org
Notes: Est. 1968. Produces world premiere musical and plays, and productions of national significance including theatre for youth and families. No unsolicited scripts except for residents of Georgia.
Agent Only: Yes
Submission Materials: agent-only
Preferred Genre: All genres
Preferred Length: Full-length
Special interest: Theatre for Young Audiences
Submission Fee: No

American Folklore Theatre (AFT)
Box 273
Fish Creek, WI 54212
Phone: (920) 854-6117
Fax: (920) 854-9106
www.folkloretheatre.com
dmaier@folkloretheatre.com
Notes: Est. 1990. Original musical works for families. Production: cast of 3–10. Must have professional recommendation.
Agent Only: No
Submission Materials: 10-pg sample, character breakdown, S.A.S.E., synopsis
Preferred Genre: Musical theatre
Preferred Length: One-Act
Submission Fee: No

American Music Theater Festival/Prince Music Theater
1412 Chestnut Street
Philadelphia, PA 19102
Marjorie Samoff, Producing Director

Phone: (215) 972-1000
Fax: (215) 569-3231
www.princemusictheater.org
info@princemusictheater.org
Agent Only: No
Preferred Genre: Musical theatre
Submission Fee: No

And Toto Too
P.O. Box 12192
Denver, CO 80212
Phone: (720) 280-7058
www.andtototoo.org
submissions@andtototoo.org
Notes: A theatre company that strives to challenge assumptions and generalizations by playwrights in any genre except musicals and children's plays. Plays must never have been produced in Colorado and must have 6 characters or fewer and minimal set requirements.
Agent Only: No
Submission Materials: see website
Special interest: Women's Interest
Submission Fee: No

Animated Theaterworks Inc.
240 Central Park S., #13-B
New York, NY 10019
Elysabeth Kleinhans, President
Phone: (212) 757-5085
Fax: (212) 247-3826
www.animatedtheaterworks.org
info@animatedtheaterworks.org
Notes: Est. 1999. Readings and showcase productions of unpublished/unproduced, new and developing works. Production: cast limit 6, unit set. Response Time: 6 months.
Agent Only: No
Submission Materials: 10-pg sample, query letter, synopsis
Preferred Genre: Plays (No Musicals)
Preferred Length: Any length
Submission Fee: No

Arden Theatre Company
40 N. 2nd St.
Philadelphia, PA 19106
Phone: (215) 922-8900
Fax: (215) 922-7011
www.ardentheatre.org
scripts@ardentheatre.org
Notes: Est. 1988. 7 shows/yr in 2 houses. Response Time: 4–6 months.
Agent Only: Yes
Submission Materials: see website

Preferred Genre: Adaptation
Preferred Length: Full-length
Submission Fee: No

Arena Players Repertory Theatre
269 West 18th Street
Deer Park, NY 11729
Fred De Feis, Producer
Phone: (516) 293-0674
www.arenaplayers.org
arena109@aol.com
Notes: Est. 1950. Award. Production: cast of 2–10. Response time: 6 months. Unproduced/unpublished.
Agent Only: No
Submission Materials: full script, query letter, S.A.S.E., synopsis
Preferred Genre: Plays (No Musicals)
Preferred Length: Full-length
Submission Fee: No

Arena Stage
1101 6th St. SW
Washington, DC 20024
Phone: (202) 554-9066
Fax: (202) 488-4056
www.arenastage.org
info@arenastage.org
Notes: Est. 1950. Arena Stage is currently not accepting script submissions at this time. See website for changes.
Agent Only: Yes
Submission Materials: agent-only
Preferred Genre: All genres
Preferred Length: Full-length
Submission Fee: No

Arizona Theatre Company
Box 1631
Tucson, AZ 85702
Phone: (520) 884-8210
Fax: (520) 628-9129
www.arizonatheatre.org
kmonberg@arizonatheatre.org
Notes: Est. 1966. National Latino Playwriting Award. Details on website.
Agent Only: Yes
Submission Materials: see website
Preferred Genre: Plays or Musicals
Preferred Length: Full-length
Submission Fee: No

Arizona Women's Theatre Company
6501 E, Greebway Parkway
Suite 103, PMB 338
Scottsdale, AZ 85254

Phone: (480) 422-5386
www.azwtc.org
info@azwtc.org
Notes: Produces contemporary, provocative, thought provoking plays written by women, by and with women from the community. Provide an innovative, intimate, progressive forum for women's voices with plays not previous produced in the Phoenix Metro area.
Agent Only: No
Submission Materials: see website
Preferred Genre: Plays (No Musicals)
Special interest: Women's Interest
Submission Fee: No

Arkansas Repertory Theatre
Box 110
Little Rock, AR 72201
Phone: (866) 6TH-EREP
Fax: (501) 378-0012
www.therep.org
bhupp@therep.org
Notes: Production: small cast. Response Time: 3 months query, 6 months script.
Agent Only: No
Submission Materials: query letter, synopsis
Preferred Genre: All genres
Preferred Length: Full-length
Submission Fee: No

Ars Nova
511 W. 54th St.
New York, NY 10019
Phone: (212) 489-9800
Fax: (212) 489-1908
www.arsnovanyc.com
artistic@arsnovanyc.com
Notes: Founded in memory of Gabe Weiner, Ars Nova develops/produces theatre, comedy, music melding disciplines and giving voice to new generation of artists. Response time: 6 months.
Agent Only: No
Submission Materials: see website
Preferred Genre: All genres
Preferred Length: Any length
Submission Fee: No

ART Station
P.O. Box 1998
Stone Mountain, GA 30086
Jon Goldstein, Literary Manager
Phone: (770) 469-1105
Fax: (770) 469-0355
www.artstation.org

jon@artstation.org
Notes: Est. 1986. Work about Southern experience for Southern, suburban, senior audience. Production: cast limit 6. Response time: 1 yr. Regular mail submission only. No email submissions, please.
Agent Only: No
Submission Materials: 10-pg sample, S.A.S.E., synopsis
Preferred Genre: Comedy
Preferred Length: Full-length
Submission Fee: No

Artists Repertory Theatre
1515 SW Morrison Street
Portland, OR 97205
Stephanie Mulligan, Literary Manager
Phone: (503) 241-9807 Ext 110
Fax: (503) 241-8268
www.artistsrep.org
info@artistsrep.org
Notes: Est. 1981. 7 shows per season on 2 stages, plus staged readings. Response time: 3 months query, 6 months script, please see website for submission guidelines.
Agent Only: No
Submission Materials: query letter, S.A.S.E., synopsis
Preferred Genre: Plays (No Musicals)
Preferred Length: Full-length
Submission Fee: No

ArtsPower National Touring Theatre
271 Grove Ave. Bldg. A
Velena, NJ 07044
Phone: (973) 239-0100
Fax: (973) 239-0165
www.artspower.org
gblackman@artspower.org
Notes: Tourable theater presenting unpublished one-act plays and musicals for young and family audiences. Production: cast limit 4.
Agent Only: No
Submission Materials: audio CD, S.A.S.E., synopsis
Preferred Genre: Plays or Musicals
Preferred Length: One-Act
Special interest: Theatre for Young Audiences
Submission Fee: No

Asolo Repertory Theatre
5555 N. Tamiami Tr.
Sarasota, FL 34243
Phone: (941) 351-9010

Fax: (941) 351-5796
www.asolo.org
lit_intern@asolo.org
Notes: Est. 1960. Email preferred.
Agent Only: No
Submission Materials: query letter
Preferred Genre: All genres
Preferred Length: Any length
Submission Fee: No

Atlantic Theater Company
76 9th Ave., #537
New York, NY 10011
Phone: (212) 691-5919
Fax: (212) 645-8755
www.atlantictheater.org
literary@atlantictheater.org
Notes: Est. 1985. 4-show mainstage season,
2-show second stage season. Response time: 6
months. Submit through professional recom-
mendation, agent or inquiry.
Agent Only: Yes
Submission Materials: 20-pg sample, audio
CD, full script, query letter, S.A.S.E.
Preferred Genre: Plays or Musicals
Preferred Length: Full-length
Submission Fee: No

Attic Ensemble
The Barrow Mansion
83 Wayne St.
Jersey City, NJ 07302
Phone: (201) 413-9200
www.atticensemble.org
info@atticensemble.org
Notes: Est. 1970. Production: cast 4–8, char-
acter ages 15–65, unit set or conceptual.
Agent Only: No
Submission Materials: full script, S.A.S.E.
Preferred Genre: All genres
Preferred Length: Full-length
Submission Fee: Yes

Axis Theatre Company
1 Sheridan Sq.
New York, NY 10014
Brian Barnhart, Producing Director
Phone: (212) 807-9300
Fax: (212) 807-9039
www.axiscompany.org
info@axiscompany.org
Notes: Est. 1997.
Agent Only: No
Submission Materials: see website
Submission Fee: No

Bailiwick Chicago
6201 N. Hermitage
Chicago, IL 60660
Phone: (773) 969-6201
Fax: (773) 883-2017
www.bailiwickchicago.com
info@bailiwickchicago.com
Notes: Not interested in 1–3 person cast, looking for larger projects. We do more musicals
than plays. Every year we workshop a few
original works, directed by company members,
and one full production of a new work. Please
check our website to see the kinds of shows
we produce. Do not submit via US Mail, only
electronic submissions will be considered.
Agent Only: No
Submission Materials: see website
Preferred Genre: Plays or Musicals
Preferred Length: Full-length
Special interest: Multi-Ethnic
Submission Fee: No

Barksdale Theatre
114 W. Broad Street
Richmond, VA 23220
Phone: (804) 783-1688
Fax: (804) 288-6470
www.barksdalerichmond.org
TheatreIVandBarksdale@gmail.com
Notes: Est. 1953. Production: small cast, no fly
or wing space. Response time: 6 months query,
1 year script.
Agent Only: No
Submission Materials: full script, query
letter, synopsis
Preferred Genre: Plays (No Musicals)
Preferred Length: Full-length
Submission Fee: No

Barrow Group
312 W. 36th St., #6B
New York, NY 10018
Becca Worthington, Literary Manager
Phone: (212) 760-2615
Fax: (212) 760-2962
www.barrowgroup.org
lit@barrowgroup.org
Notes: Est. 1986. Offers 1–2 mainstage shows/
year, plus readings and workshops. Response:
1 month query, 4 months script.
Agent Only: No
Submission Materials: see website
Submission Fee: No

Bay Street Theatre
Box 810
Sag Harbor, NY 11963
Phone: (631) 725-0818 Ext 108
Fax: (631) 725-0906
www.baystreet.org
mail@baystreet.org
Notes: Est. 1991. Mainstage season and play
reading series. Production: cast limit 9, unit
set, no fly/wing space. Response time: 6
months.
Agent Only: Yes
Submission Materials: agent-only
Preferred Genre: Plays (No Musicals)
Preferred Length: Full-length
Submission Fee: No

Berkeley Repertory Theatre
999 Harrison Street
Berkeley, CA 94710
Julie McCormick, Literary Associate
Phone: (510) 647-2900
Fax: (510) 647-2976
www.berkeleyrep.org
JMcCormick@berkeleyrep.org
Notes: Est. 1968. Response time: 6–9 months.
Only accepts scripts from agents and Bay Area
playwrights.
Agent Only: No
Submission Materials: full script
Preferred Genre: All genres
Preferred Length: Full-length
Submission Fee: No

Berkshire Public Theater
Box 860, 30 Union St.
Pittsfield, MA 01202
Agent Only: No
Submission Fee: No

Berkshire Theatre Festival
P.O. Box 797
Stockbridge, MA 01262
Phone: (413) 298-5536
Fax: (413) 298-3368
www.berkshiretheatregroup.org
info@berkshiretheatregroup.org
Notes: Est. 1928. New works, small musicals.
Production: cast of up to 8. Will respond only
if interested. Submissions not returned.
Agent Only: No
Submission Materials: E-mail only
Preferred Genre: Plays or Musicals
Preferred Length: Any length
Submission Fee: No

Black Dahlia Theatre Los Angeles
5453 W. Pico Blvd.
Los Angeles, CA 90019
Phone: (323) 525-0085
www.thedahlia.com
info@thedahlia.com
Agent Only: No
Submission Materials: see website
Preferred Genre: All genres
Preferred Length: Any length
Submission Fee: No

Black Rep
1717 Olive St., Fl. 4
St. Louis, MO 63103
Phone: (314) 534-3807
Fax: (314) 534-4035
www.theblackrep.org
ameerch@theblackrep.org
Notes: Est. 1976.
Agent Only: No
Submission Materials: 5-pg sample, query
letter, resume, synopsis
Preferred Genre: Plays (No Musicals)
Preferred Length: Full-length
Special interest: African-American
Submission Fee: No

Black Spectrum Theatre
119-07 Merrick Boulevard
Jamaica, NY 11434
Phone: (718) 723-1800
Fax: (718) 723-1806
www.blackspectrum.com
info@blackspectrum.com
Agent Only: No
Submission Materials: full script
Preferred Genre: All genres
Preferred Length: Full-length
Submission Fee: No

Black Swan Theater
109 Roberts Street
Asheville, NC 28801
Phone: (828) 254-6057
Fax: (828) 251-6603
www.blackswan.org
swanthtre@aol.com
Notes: Est. 1988. Develops new scripts &
revisits classics. Production: modest cast,
simple set. Response time: 3 months. Material
must be unpublished.
Agent Only: No
Submission Materials: full script
Preferred Genre: All genres

Preferred Length: Any length
Submission Fee: No
Deadline(s): See website

Bond Street Theatre
2 Bond St.
New York, NY 10012
Joanna Sherman, Artistic Director
Phone: (212) 254-4614
Fax: (212) 460-9378
www.bondst.org
info@bondst.org
Notes: Response time: 1 month. We look for scripts with minimal dialogue that can be expressed through the gestural arts.
Agent Only: No
Submission Materials: query letter, S.A.S.E., synopsis
Preferred Genre: Movement-based
Preferred Length: Any length
Special interest: Women's Interest
Submission Fee: No

Brat Productions
56 S. 2nd St.
Philadelphia, PA 19106
Phone: (215) 627-2577
Fax: (215) 627-4304
www.bratproductions.org
brat@bratproductions.org
Notes: Est. 1996. New work, experimental/immersive theatre ideas considered by query; invite to follow if interested. Production: cast limit 7, unit set. Response time: 1 month query, 6 months script.
Agent Only: No
Submission Materials: query letter
Preferred Genre: Plays or Musicals
Preferred Length: Full-length
Submission Fee: No

Brava! for Women in the Arts
2781 24th St.
San Francisco, CA 94110
Phone: (415) 641-7657
Fax: (415) 641-7684
www.brava.org
info@brava.org
Notes: Committed to the artistic expression of women, people of color, and youth. Specializes in creation of new work, especially by lesbians and women of color. Brava is currently not accepting scripts at this time. Please check website for updates.
Agent Only: No

Submission Materials: see website
Special interest: Women's Interest
Submission Fee: No

Break A Leg Productions
Box 20503, Hammarskjold Ctr.
New York, NY 10017
Phone: (212) 330-0406
Fax: (212) 750-8341
www.breakalegproductions.com
breakalegproductionsnyc@yahoo.com
Agent Only: No
Submission Materials: see website
Submission Fee: No

Bridge Theatre Company
244 W. 54th St.
12th Fl.
New York, NY 10019
Phone: (212) 246-6655
www.thebridgetheatrecompany.com
esther@thebridgetheatrecompany.com
Notes: Development through reading, workshops, moving towards off-off Broadway production. Author must be Canadian or the work about Canada in some way.
Agent Only: No
Submission Materials: 10-pg sample, query letter, synopsis
Preferred Genre: Plays (No Musicals)
Preferred Length: Any length
Submission Fee: No

Burning Coal Theatre Company
224 Polk Street
Raleigh, NC 27604
Jerome Davis, Artistic Director
Phone: (919) 834-4001
Fax: (919) 834-4002
www.burningcoal.org
coalartisticdir@ncrrbiz.com
Notes: Est. 1995. 3–4 staged readings/year, Response time: 6 months. Author must be resident or connected to North Carolina. Submit via mail only.
Agent Only: No
Submission Materials: see website
Preferred Genre: Plays (No Musicals)
Preferred Length: One-Act
Submission Fee: No
Deadline(s): December 16, 2013

Caldwell Theatre Company
7901 N. Federal Hwy.
Boca Raton, FL 33487

Phone: (561) 241-7432
Fax: (561) 997-6917
www.caldwelltheatre.com
patricia@caldwelltheatre.com
Notes: Est. 1975. Playsearch series reads
4 plays annually. Production: cast up to 8.
Response time varies.
Agent Only: No
Submission Materials: see website
Preferred Genre: Plays or Musicals
Preferred Length: Full-length
Submission Fee: No

Capital Repertory Theatre
111 N. Pearl St.
Albany, NY 12207
Phone: (518) 462-4531
Fax: (518) 465-0213
www.capitalrep.org
info@capitalrep.org
Notes: Est. 1981.
Agent Only: No
Submission Materials: see website
Submission Fee: No

Celebration Theatre
7985 Santa Monica Blvd., #109-1
Los Angeles, CA 90046
Charls Hall, Literary Manager
Phone: (323) 957-1884
Fax: (888) 898-9374
www.celebrationtheatre.com
admin@celebrationtheatre.com
Notes: Est. 1982. Deadline rolling. See website for guidelines. Production: cast limit 12.
Response if interested.
Agent Only: No
Submission Materials: bio, full script, synopsis
Preferred Genre: Plays or Musicals
Preferred Length: Any length
Special interest: LGBT
Submission Fee: No
Deadline(s): Rolling

Center Stage [MD]
700 N. Calvert St.
Baltimore, MD 21202
Phone: (410) 986-4042
Fax: (410) 986-4046
www.centerstage.org
gwitt@centerstage.org
Notes: Est. 1963. Seeking unproduced scripts.
Agent Only: No

Submission Materials: 10-pg sample, audio CD, query letter, S.A.S.E., synopsis
Preferred Genre: Plays (No Musicals)
Preferred Length: Full-length
Submission Fee: No
Deadline(s): See website

Center Stage Community Playhouse
Box 138
Westchester Square Station
Bronx, NY 10461
Phone: (212) 823-6434
www.centerstageplayhouse.org
info@centerstageplayhouse.org
Notes: Est. 1969. Nonprofit community theater seeks unoptioned, unpublished, unproduced work. Response time: 2 months.
Agent Only: No
Submission Materials: query letter, S.A.S.E.
Preferred Genre: Adaptation
Preferred Length: Any length
Submission Fee: No

Center Theatre Group (CTG)
601 W. Temple St.
Los Angeles, CA 90012
Mike Sablone, Literary Manager/Resident Dramaturg
Phone: (213) 972-8033
Fax: (213) 972-0746
www.centertheatregroup.org
scripts@ctgla.org
Notes: Est. 1967. Includes Ahmanson Theatre and Mark Taper Forum at Music Center in L.A. and Kirk Douglas Theatre in Culver City.
Response time: 6 weeks.
Agent Only: No
Submission Materials: 10-pg sample, query letter, S.A.S.E., synopsis
Preferred Genre: All genres
Preferred Length: Any length
Submission Fee: No

Charleston Stage
Box 356
Charleston, SC 29402
Phone: (843) 577-5967
Fax: (843) 577-5422
www.charlestonstage.com
jwiles@charlestonstage.com
Notes: Est. 1977. In residence at the Historic Dock Street Theater. Not accepting new work at this time.
Agent Only: No
Submission Materials: see website

Preferred Genre: All genres
Preferred Length: Full-length
Special interest: Latino
Submission Fee: No
Deadline(s): May 21, 2013; 6/15/2013

Charter Theatre
Box 3505
Reston, VA 20195
Phone: (202) 333-7009
www.chartertheatre.org
Agent Only: No
Submission Materials: see website
Special interest: Asian-American
Submission Fee: No

Cherry Lane Theatre
38 Commerce St.
New York, NY 10014
Phone: (212) 989-2020
Fax: (212) 989-2867
www.cherrylanetheatre.org
company@cherrylanetheatre.org
Notes: Currently not accepting unsolicited material.
Agent Only: Yes
Submission Materials: see website
Submission Fee: No

Chicago Theater Company
500 E. 67th St.
Chicago, IL 60637
Phone: (773) 493-5360
Fax: (773) 493-0360
Agent Only: No
Submission Fee: No

Children's Theatre Company (CTC)
2400 3rd Ave. S.
Minneapolis, MN 55404
Phone: (612) 874-0500 Ext 134
Fax: (612) 874-8119
www.childrenstheatre.org
eadams@childrenstheatre.org
Notes: Est. 1965.
Agent Only: Yes
Submission Materials: agent-only
Preferred Genre: Plays or Musicals
Preferred Length: Full-length
Special interest: Theatre for Young Audiences
Submission Fee: No

Children's Theatre of Cincinnati [OH]
5020 Oaklawn Drive

Cincinnati, OH 45227
Angela Powell Walker, Artistic Director
Phone: (513) 569-8080
Fax: (513) 569-8084
www.thechildrenstheatre.com
angela.powellwalker@thechildrenstheatre.com
Agent Only: No
Submission Materials: audio CD, full script
Preferred Genre: Theatre for Young Audiences
Preferred Length: 50–60 min.
Submission Fee: No
Deadline(s): Summer

Childsplay, Inc
900 S. Mitchell Dr.
Tempe, AZ 85281
David Saar, Artistic Director
Phone: (480) 921-5700
Fax: (480) 921-5777
www.childsplayaz.org
info@childsplayaz.org
Notes: Est. 1977. 6 mainstage and 3 touring productions/year. Opportunities include Whiteman New Plays Program. Production: cast of 2–12.
Agent Only: No
Submission Materials: 10-pg sample, S.A.S.E., synopsis
Preferred Genre: Plays or Musicals
Preferred Length: Any length
Special interest: Theatre for Young Audiences
Submission Fee: No

Cider Mill Playhouse
2 S. Nanticoke Ave.
Endicott, NY 13760
Phone: (607) 748-7363
www.cidermillplayhouse.com
cmpartdir@gmail.com
Notes: Est. 1976. Production: small cast, unit set, no fly space. Response time: 6 months.
Agent Only: Yes
Submission Materials: agent-only
Submission Fee: No

Cincinnati Playhouse in the Park
PO Box 6537
Cincinnati, OH 45206
Phone: (513) 345-2242
Fax: (513) 345-2254
www.cincyplay.com

Notes: Est. 1960. Equity LORT B+ and D. Tony Award winner 2004 & 2007. Agent submission of full script. Non-agent submission—please see website for guidelines. Response: 8 months.
Agent Only: No
Submission Materials: see website
Preferred Genre: Plays or Musicals
Preferred Length: Full-length
Submission Fee: No

Cinnabar Theater
3333 Petaluma Blvd. N.
Petaluma, CA 94952
Phone: (707) 763-8920
Fax: (707) 763-8929
www.cinnabartheater.org
elly@cinnabartheater.org
Notes: Est. 1970. Will consider operas.
Agent Only: No
Submission Materials: see website
Submission Fee: No

Circle Theatre [TX]
230 W. Fourth St.
Ft. Worth, TX 76102
Phone: (817) 877-3040
Fax: (817) 877-3536
www.circletheatre.com
plays@circletheatre.com
Notes: Est. 1981. Professional contemporary theater in an intimate setting. Queries accepted, email preferred, for works with production history.
Agent Only: No
Submission Materials: query letter
Preferred Genre: Plays or Musicals
Preferred Length: Full-length
Submission Fee: No

Circle Theatre of Forest Park [IL]
7300 W. Madison St.
Forest Park, IL 60130
Phone: (708) 771-0700
Fax: (708) 771-1826
www.circle-theatre.org
circletheatre@gmail.com
Notes: Est. 1985. Opportunities include new play festival of shorts and full-lengths.
Agent Only: No
Submission Materials: see website
Preferred Genre: All genres
Preferred Length: Any length
Submission Fee: No

Citizen Pell Theater Group
30 The Hamlet
Pelham, NY 10803
Phone: (917) 428-1955
www.citizenpell.com
citizenpell@yahoo.com
Agent Only: No
Submission Materials: see website
Submission Fee: No

City Garage
2525 Michigan Avenue, Building T1
Santa Monica, CA 90404
Charles Duncombe, Producing Director
Phone: (310) 319-9939
Fax: (310) 396-1040
www.citygarage.org
citygarage@citygarage.org
Notes: Est. 1987. Material should be non-realistic, experimental, social and political work. Production: Simple, nonrealistic sets. Response time: 2 weeks letter, 6 weeks script.
Agent Only: No
Submission Materials: query letter, synopsis
Preferred Genre: Experimental
Preferred Length: Full-length
Submission Fee: No

City Theatre [FL]
444 Brickell Ave., #229
Miami, FL 33131
Phone: (305) 755-9401
Fax: (305) 755-9404
www.citytheatre.com
summershorts@citytheatre.com
Notes: Est. 1996. Summer Shorts festival/guest artist residency , Short Cuts educational tours, Festival Reading Series and Kid Shorts Project. Submissions not returned.
Agent Only: No
Submission Materials: full script
Preferred Genre: Plays (No Musicals)
Preferred Length: One-Act
Submission Fee: No

City Theatre Company [PA]
1300 Bingham St.
Pittsburgh, PA 15203
Carlyn Aquiline, Literary Manager/ Dramaturg
Phone: (412) 431-4400
Fax: (412) 431-5535
www.citytheatrecompany.org
caquiline@citytheatrecompany.org

Notes: Est. 1974. Produces new and contemporary full-length solo work, translations, adaptations with emphasis on under-represented voices. Production: cast limit 6, prefer 4 or fewer. See website for list of materials to submit.
Agent Only: No
Submission Materials: No Email, query letter
Preferred Genre: Plays or Musicals
Preferred Length: Full-length
Submission Fee: No

Cleveland Play House
8500 Euclid Ave.
Cleveland, OH 44106
Laura Kepley, Associate Artistic Director
Phone: (216) 795-7000
Fax: (216) 795-7005
www.clevelandplayhouse.com
sgordon@clevelandplayhouse.com
Notes: Est. 1916. Response time: 2 mos query, 6 mos script.
Agent Only: No
Submission Materials: 10-pg sample, query letter, resume, S.A.S.E., synopsis
Preferred Genre: Plays (No Musicals)
Preferred Length: Full-length
Submission Fee: No

Cleveland Public Theatre
6415 Detroit Ave.
Cleveland, OH 44102
Raymond Bobgan, Executive Artistic Director
Phone: (216) 631-2727
Fax: (216) 631-2575
www.cptonline.org
rbobgan@cptonline.org
Notes: Est. 1983. Looking for experimental, poetic, political, intellectually/spiritually challenging work. Response time: 9 months.
Agent Only: No
Submission Materials: see website
Preferred Genre: Experimental
Preferred Length: Any length
Submission Fee: No

Clubbed Thumb
141 E. 3rd Street
#11H
New York, NY 10009
Clubbed Thumb Info
Phone: (212) 802-8007
Fax: (212) 533-9286
www.clubbedthumb.org

info@clubbedthumb.org
Notes: Accepts submissions of plays that are funny, strange, and provocative, with a running time of an hour to an hour and a half with no intermission. Plays must be unproduced in New York City and must have a reasonable representation of women, both in quantity and quality of roles. We prefer medium sized ensemble casts; at least 3 character. The director of the piece will be chosen by mutual consent of playwright and Clubbed Thumb. We are committed to play development, and therefore produce only plays that are actively being worked on with the expectation that the rehearsal process will prove beneficial to the playwright's writing process. Submit unbound scripts. NOTE: No e-mail submissions.
Agent Only: No
Submission Materials: see website
Preferred Length: 90 min./no intermission
Special interest: Women's Interest
Submission Fee: No

Colony Theatre Company
555 N. Third St.
Burbank, CA 91502
Phone: (818) 558-7000
Fax: (818) 558-7110
www.colonytheatre.org
barbarabeckley@colonytheatre.org
Notes: Est. 1975. Production: cast limit 4.
Agent Only: Yes
Submission Materials: agent-only
Preferred Genre: Plays (No Musicals)
Preferred Length: Full-length
Submission Fee: No

Congo Square Theatre Company
2936 N. Southport #210
Chicago, IL 60657
Phone: (773) 296-0968
www.congosquaretheatre.org
tpatton@congosquaretheatre.org
Agent Only: No
Submission Materials: see website
Submission Fee: No

Contemporary American Theatre Company (CATCO)—Phoenix, Inc
55 East State Street
Columbus, OH 43215
Phone: (614) 645-7558
www.catco.org
jputnam@catco.org

Notes: Est. 1984. 5–6 plays/season. Merged with Phoenix Theatre for Children www.phoenix4kids.org. Production: cast limit 10, set limit 2. Response: 6 months.
Agent Only: No
Submission Materials: 10-pg sample, synopsis
Preferred Genre: Plays or Musicals
Preferred Length: Any length
Special interest: Theatre for Young Audiences
Submission Fee: No
Deadline(s): Year round

Cornerstone Theater Company
708 Traction Ave.
Los Angeles, CA 90013
Laurie Woolery, Associate Artistic Director
Phone: (213) 613-1700
Fax: (213) 613-1714
www.cornerstonetheater.org
lwoolery@cornerstonetheater.org
Notes: Est. 1986. Collaborating with playwrights to develop new works with community. Our development process is focused on playwrights engaged in a deep collaboration with community over a 18–24 month process. So PLEASE go to our website first before submitting plays. Read our Mission Statement and see examples of our work. Response 8 months.
Agent Only: No
Submission Materials: 5-pg sample, query letter
Preferred Length: Any length
Submission Fee: No

Crossroads Theatre Company [NJ]
P.O. Box 238
7 Livingston Ave.
New Brunswick, NJ 08901
Marshall Jones, Producing Artistic Director
Phone: (732) 545-8100
Fax: (732) 907-1864
www.crossroadstheatrecompany.org
membership@crossroadstheatrecompany.org
Notes: Est. 1978
Agent Only: No
Submission Materials: see website
Preferred Genre: Plays or Musicals
Submission Fee: No

Dad's Garage Theatre Co.
280 Elizabeth St., #C-101
Atlanta, GA 30307
Kevin Gillese, Artistic Director
Phone: (404) 523-3141
Fax: (404) 688-6644
www.dadsgarage.com
kevin@dadsgarage.com
Notes: Est. 1995.
Agent Only: No
Submission Materials: 10-pg sample, query letter, synopsis
Preferred Genre: Comedy
Preferred Length: Any length
Submission Fee: No

Dallas Children's Theater
5938 Skillman St.
Dallas, TX 75231
Artie Olaisen, Artistic Associate
Phone: (214) 978-0110
Fax: (214) 978-0118
www.dct.org
artie.olaisen@dct.org
Notes: Est. 1984. Professional Theatre performed for a youth and family audience.
Agent Only: No
Submission Materials: character breakdown, query letter, synopsis
Preferred Genre: Plays or Musicals
Preferred Length: Full-length
Special interest: Theatre for Young Audiences
Submission Fee: No
Deadline(s): Rolling

Dallas Theater Center
2400 Flora Street
Dallas, TX 75201
Kevin Moriarty, Artistic Director
Phone: (214) 526-8210
Fax: (214) 521-7666
www.dallastheatercenter.org
mel.lopez@dallastheatercenter.org
Notes: Est. 1959. Response: 1 year
Agent Only: No
Submission Materials: 10-pg sample, synopsis
Preferred Genre: All genres
Preferred Length: Any length
Submission Fee: No

Danisarte
PO Box 286146, 1617 Third Ave.
New York, NY 10128
Alicia Kaplan, Producing Artistic Director
Phone: (212) 561-0191
www.danisarte.org
Danisarte@aol.com

Notes: Est. 1992. Seeking unpublished/unproduced works. Production: cast limit 4
Agent Only: No
Submission Materials: query letter, S.A.S.E.
Preferred Genre: All genres
Preferred Length: 50–60 min.
Special interest: Theatre for Young Audiences
Submission Fee: No

Deaf West Theatre (DWT)
5114 Lankershim Blvd.
North Hollywood, CA 91601
Phone: 818-508-8389 TTY
Fax: (818) 762-2981
www.deafwest.org
info@deafwest.org
Notes: Est. 1991.
Agent Only: No
Submission Fee: No

Delaware Theatre Company
200 Water St.
Wilmington, DE 19801
Phone: (302) 594-1104
Fax: (302) 594-1107
www.delawaretheatre.org
literary@delawaretheatre.org
Notes: Est. 1978. Season usually 5–6 readings/productions. Production: cast limit 10, small orchestra, unit set. Response: 6 months.
Agent Only: Yes
Submission Materials: see website
Preferred Genre: All genres
Preferred Length: Full-length
Submission Fee: No

Detroit Repertory Theatre
13103 Woodrow Wilson St.
Detroit, MI 48238
Barbara Busby, Literary Manager
Phone: (313) 868-1347
Fax: (313) 868-1705
www.detroitreptheatre.com
bbdetrepth@aol.com
Notes: Est. 1957. Production: age 18–65, casts no larger than 5–7 characters. We do not double cast. We prefer "diversity centered" rather than non-traditional. Response: 6 months.
Agent Only: No
Submission Materials: full script, S.A.S.E.
Preferred Genre: Plays (No Musicals)
Preferred Length: Full-length
Submission Fee: No

Dicapo Opera Theatre
184 E. 76th St.
New York, NY 10021
Michael Capasso, General Director
Phone: (212) 288-9438
Fax: (212) 744-1082
www.dicapo.com
michael.capasso@dicapo.com
Notes: Limited run performances.
Agent Only: No
Submission Materials: see website
Preferred Genre: Opera
Submission Fee: No

Directors Company
311 W. 43rd St., #307
New York, NY 10036
Phone: (212) 246-5877
directorscompany.org
directorscompany@aol.com
Agent Only: No
Submission Materials: see website
Submission Fee: No

Diversionary Theatre
4545 Park Blvd., #101
San Diego, CA 92116
John E. Alexander, Executive Director
Phone: (619) 220-6830
Fax: (619) 220-0148
www.diversionary.org
submissions@diversionary.org
Notes: Est. 1986. 3rd oldest LGBT theater in US. 6-show season and new-work readings in 106-seat space. Apply online. Response: 6 months.
Agent Only: No
Submission Materials: synopsis
Preferred Genre: All genres
Preferred Length: Any length
Special interest: LGBT
Submission Fee: No

Dixon Place
161A Christie Street
New York, NY 10002
Ellie Covan, Founding Director
Phone: (212) 219-0736
Fax: (212) 219-0761
www.dixonplace.org
submissions@dixonplace.org
Notes: Est. 1986. Nonprofit laboratory theater for New York-based performing and literary artists to create and develop new works in front of a live audience. Rolling deadline.

Agent Only: No
Submission Materials: see website
Preferred Genre: Experimental
Preferred Length: Any length
Submission Fee: No

Do Gooder Productions
233 East 86th Street, Suite 2A
New York, NY 10023
Phone: (212) 581-8852
www.dogooder.org
dgp@dogooder.org
Notes: Not accepting unsolicited scripts at this time.
Agent Only: No
Submission Fee: No

Dorset Theatre Festival
Box 510
Dorset, VT 05251
Phone: (802) 867-2223
Fax: (802) 867-0144
www.dorsettheatrefestival.org
dina@dorsettheatrefestival.org
Notes: Dorset only accepts scripts of writers in residence or by invitation.
Agent Only: No
Submission Materials: see website
Submission Fee: No

Dramatic Women
111 Skylie Circle
Santa Barbara, CA 93109
Phone: (805) 965-5826
dramaticwomen.org
ellena@silcom.com
Notes: Founded in 1993 to explore and promote the participation of women in all areas of theatre & to produce original scripts by locally-based writers. In the many years that followed we have produced the work of 30 playwrights, 21 of them women, and 31 directors, 22 of them women. Preference given to residents of Santa Barbara County.
Agent Only: No
Submission Materials: see website
Special interest: Women's Interest
Submission Fee: No

Dream Theatre
484 W. 43rd St., #14-Q
New York, NY 10036
Andrea Leigh, Artistic Director
Phone: (212) 564-2628
andrealeigh88@hotmail.com

Notes: Est. 2001. New works, especially by/for women, that have not been optioned or produced in NYC. Mailed submissions not returned. Email preferred. Response: 6 months.
Agent Only: No
Submission Materials: full script, synopsis
Preferred Genre: Plays (No Musicals)
Preferred Length: Any length
Submission Fee: No
Deadline(s): Ongoing

Drilling Company
236 W. 78th Street
3rd floor
New York, NY 10024
Hamilton Clancy, Artistic Director
Phone: (212) 873-9050
Fax: (917) 330-4234
www.drillingcompany.org
DrillingCompany@aol.com
Notes: Est. 1999. Commissions and workshops new work. Response: 3 months.
Agent Only: No
Submission Materials: see website
Preferred Genre: Plays (No Musicals)
Preferred Length: Any length
Submission Fee: No

DUO Multicultural Arts Center
62 East 4th Street
New York, NY 10003
Michelangelo Alasa, Artistic Director
Phone: (212) 598-4320
www.duotheater.org
duotheater@gmail.com
Notes: Develop and produce theater works by Latino playwrights while employing Latino directors, actors and designers.
Agent Only: No
Special interest: Latino
Submission Fee: No

East West Players
120 N. Judge John Aiso St.
Los Angeles, CA 90012
Jeff Liu, Literary Manager
Phone: (213) 625-7000
Fax: (213) 625-7111
www.eastwestplayers.org
jliu@eastwestplayers.org
Notes: Est. 1965. 4 mainstage productions/season in addition to readings. Submissions by US mail only. Response: 12–18 months.
Agent Only: No

Submission Materials: full script, resume, S.A.S.E., synopsis
Preferred Genre: Plays or Musicals
Preferred Length: Full-length
Special interest: Asian-American
Submission Fee: No

Emelin Theatre for the Performing Arts
153 Library Lane
Mamaroneck, NY 10543
Phone: (914) 698-3045
Fax: (914) 698-1404
www.emelin.org
info@emelin.org
Notes: Est. 1972. Production: small cast, no fly. Response: 6 months.
Agent Only: Yes
Submission Materials: professional referral only
Preferred Genre: All genres
Preferred Length: Any length
Submission Fee: No

Emerging Artists Theatre (EAT)
15 West 28th St., 3rd Floor
New York, NY 10001
Paul Adams, Artistic Director
Phone: (212) 247-2429
www.emergingartiststheatre.org
eattheatre@gmail.com
Notes: Develop and produce new work. Submit by email. Production: age 20–70, cast 2–10. Response: 3–6 months.
Agent Only: No
Submission Materials: see website
Preferred Genre: All genres
Preferred Length: One-Act
Special interest: LGBT
Submission Fee: No
Deadline(s): See website

Enrichment Works
5605 Woodman Ave., # 207
Valley Glen, CA 91401
Phone: (818) 780-1400
Fax: (818) 780-0300
www.enrichmentworks.org
dwbabcock@enrichmentworks.org
Notes: Est. 1999. Tours in L.A. schools, libraries, museums and community venues. Production: cast limit 3, touring set. Response: 6 months.
Agent Only: No
Submission Materials: full script, S.A.S.E.
Preferred Genre: Musical theatre

Preferred Length: One-Act
Special interest: Theatre for Young Audiences
Submission Fee: No

Ensemble Studio Theatre (EST)
549 W. 52nd St.
New York, NY 10019
Phone: (212) 247-4982
Fax: (212) 664-0041
www.ensemblestudiotheatre.org
est@ensemblestudiotheatre.org
Notes: Est. 1972.
Agent Only: No
Submission Materials: see website
Preferred Genre: All genres
Preferred Length: Any length
Submission Fee: No

Ensemble Theatre [TX]
3535 Main St.
Houston, TX 77002
Phone: (713) 807-4316
Fax: (713) 520-1269
www.ensemblehouston.com
ejmorris@ensemblehouston.com
Notes: Est. 1976. Produces contemporary and classical works devoted to the portrayal of the African-American experience. Production: cast limit 5, touring set. Response: 3 months.
Agent Only: No
Submission Materials: 10-pg sample, audio CD, query letter, S.A.S.E., synopsis
Preferred Genre: Plays or Musicals
Preferred Length: Any length
Special interest: African-American
Submission Fee: No

First Stage Children's Theater
325 W. Walnut St.
Milwaukee, WI 53212
Phone: (414) 267-2929
Fax: (414) 267-2930
www.firststage.org
jfrank@firststage.org
Notes: Est. 1987. Response : 3 months query, 9 months script.
Agent Only: No
Submission Materials: query letter, resume, synopsis
Preferred Genre: All genres
Preferred Length: Any length
Special interest: Theatre for Young Audiences
Submission Fee: No

Flat Rock Playhouse
Box 310
Flat Rock, NC 28731
Phone: (828) 693-0403
Fax: (828) 693-6795
www.flatrockplayhouse.com
frp@flatrockplayhouse.org
Agent Only: No
Submission Materials: full script
Preferred Genre: Plays or Musicals
Preferred Length: Full-length
Submission Fee: No

Florida Repertory Theatre
2267 1st St.
Fort Myers, FL 33901
Phone: (239) 332-4665
Fax: (239) 332-1808
www.floridarep.org
jasonparrish@floridarep.org
Notes: Est. 1989. 8 mainstage plays
September–June. Production: cast limit 10,
orchestra 4–5, sets limit 2. Response: 1 year.
Agent Only: Yes
Submission Materials: agent-only
Preferred Genre: All genres
Preferred Length: Full-length
Submission Fee: No

Folger Theatre
201 E. Capitol St., SE
Washington, DC 20003
Phone: (202) 675-0344
Fax: (202) 608-1719
www.folger.edu/whatsontype.cfm?wotypeid=2
tswoape@folger.edu
Notes: Est. 1986.
Agent Only: No
Submission Materials: see website
Submission Fee: No

Ford's Theatre Society
511 10th St., NW
Washington, DC 20004
Phone: (202) 638-2941
Fax: (202) 638-6269
www.fordstheatre.org
literary@fords.org
Notes: Est. 1968. 4–5 shows/year, including perhaps 1 original play or musical. Prefer
plays and musicals that explore the American
Experience and celebrate Abraham Lincoln's
ideals and leadership principles. Production:
orchestra limit 8. Response: 1 year.

Agent Only: Yes
Submission Materials: see website
Preferred Genre: All genres
Preferred Length: Full-length
Submission Fee: No

Fountain Theatre
5060 Fountain Ave.
Los Angeles, CA 90029
Simon Levy, Producing Director
Phone: (323) 663-2235
Fax: (323) 663-1629
www.fountaintheatre.com
fountaintheatre1@aol.com
Notes: Submit work with professional recom-
mendation. Production: cast limit 12, unit set,
no fly space. Response: 3 months.
Agent Only: No
Submission Materials: query letter, synopsis
Preferred Genre: Plays (No Musicals)
Preferred Length: Any length
Submission Fee: No

Freed-Hardeman University
Theater Dept., 158 E. Main St.
Henderson, TN 38340
Phone: (731) 989-6780
Fax: (731) 989-6938
www.fhu.edu
cthompson@fhu.edu
Agent Only: No
Submission Materials: 30-pg sample,
S.A.S.E., synopsis
Preferred Genre: Plays (No Musicals)
Preferred Length: Any length
Submission Fee: No

GableStage
1200 Anastasia Ave.
Coral Gables, FL 33134
Phone: (305) 446-1116
Fax: (305) 445-8645
www.gablestage.org
jadler@gablestage.org
Notes: Est. 1979. 6 productions/year.
Agent Only: No
Submission Materials: query letter
Preferred Genre: Plays (No Musicals)
Preferred Length: Full-length
Submission Fee: No

Galli Theatre for Personal Growth
66 West 38th Street
#40E
New York, NY 10018

Daisy Jane, Executive Director at Galli
Theater Wiesbaden
Phone: (212) 731-0668
www.gallitheaterny.com
newyork@galli-group.com
Agent Only: No
Submission Fee: No

Geffen Playhouse
10886 LeConte Ave
Los Angeles, CA 90024
Phone: (310) 208-6500
Fax: (310) 208-0341
www.geffenplayhouse.com
amy@geffenplayhouse.com
Notes: Est. 1995. Response Time: 6 months
Agent Only: Yes
Submission Materials: agent-only
Submission Fee: No

George Street Playhouse
9 Livingston Ave.
New Brunswick, NJ 08901
Phone: (732) 846-2895
Fax: (732) 247-9151
www.georgestplayhouse.org
sgoldman@georgestplayhouse.org
Notes: No longer accepting unsolicited scripts
or material.
Agent Only: Yes
Preferred Genre: No translation or
adaptation
Preferred Length: Any length
Submission Fee: No

Geva Theatre Center
75 Woodbury Blvd.
Rochester, NY 14607
Phone: (585) 232-1366
Fax: (585) 232-4031
www.gevatheatre.org
Notes: Est. 1972. Productions, readings,
workshops of classics, musicals, new works.
Response: 3 months query; 6 months script.
Agent Only: No
Submission Materials: 10-pg sample, query
letter, S.A.S.E., synopsis
Preferred Genre: Plays or Musicals
Preferred Length: Any length
Submission Fee: No

Goodman Theatre
170 N. Dearborn St.
Chicago, IL 60601
Phone: (312) 443-3811

Fax: (312) 443-3821
www.goodmantheatre.org
PlaySubmissions@GoodmanTheatre.org
Notes: Est. 1925. Response: 6–8 weeks.
Agent Only: Yes
Submission Materials: agent-only
Preferred Genre: All genres
Preferred Length: Full-length
Submission Fee: No

Goodspeed Musicals
6 Main St
P.O. Box A
East Haddam, CT 06423-0281
Donna Lynn Cooper Hilton, Line Producer
Phone: (860) 873-8664
Fax: (860) 873-2329
www.goodspeed.org
info@goodspeed.org
Notes: Est. 1959.
Agent Only: Yes
Submission Materials: agent-only
Preferred Genre: Musical theatre
Preferred Length: Full-length
Submission Fee: No

Gorilla Theatre
PO Box 152225
Tampa, FL 33684
Phone: (813) 879-2914
www.gorillatheatre.com
info@gorillatheatre.com
Agent Only: No

Great Lakes Theater Festival
1501 Euclid Ave., # 300
Cleveland, OH 44115
Phone: (216) 241-5490
Fax: (216) 241-6315
www.greatlakestheater.org
mail@greatlakestheater.org
Notes: Est. 1961. Response: 3 months.
Agent Only: Yes
Submission Materials: professional referral
only
Preferred Genre: Plays (No Musicals)
Preferred Length: Full-length
Submission Fee: No

Green Light Arts
1819 JFK BLVD
#400
Philadelphia, PA 19103
Phone: (215) 681-0211
www.greenlightarts.org

alex@greenlightarts.org
Notes: Green Light Arts is a member-based
nonprofit organization that supports and unites
women artists of all disciplines to create art
that enriches our society.
Agent Only: No
Submission Materials: see website
Special interest: Women's Interest
Submission Fee: No

Greenbrier Valley Theatre
113 E. Washington St.
Lewisburg, WV 24901
Cathey Sawyer, Artistic Director
Phone: (304) 645-3838
Fax: (304) 645-3818
www.gvtheatre.org
cathey@gvtheatre.org
Notes: Est. 1967. Production: age 7 and
older, cast of 6–10, orchestra of 1–4, set
limit 1–2. Submit character descriptions,
scenic requirments, synopsis, and first ten
pages. Submissions not returned. Response: 6
months.
Agent Only: No
Preferred Genre: Plays or Musicals
Preferred Length: Full-length
Submission Fee: No

**Growing Stage—The Children's Theatre of
New Jersey**
P.O. Box 36
Netcong, NJ 07857
Phone: (973) 347-4946
Fax: (973) 691-7069
www.growingstage.com
info@growingstage.com
Notes: Est. 1982. We review submissions
between May through August only. Response
Time: 4 months
Agent Only: No
Special interest: Theatre for Young
Audiences
Submission Fee: No

Guthrie Theater
818 S. 2nd St.
Minneapolis, MN 55415
Jo Holcomb, Literary Specialist
Phone: (612) 225-6000
Fax: (612) 225-6004
www.guthrietheater.org
JoH@GuthrieTheater.org
Notes: Est. 1963. New 3-theater complex
opened 2006, includes 1100-seat thrust,

700-seat proscenium and 199-seat studio. The
Guthrie Theatre does not accept unsolicited
scripts from any source and does not request
scripts based on reading synopses or sample
dialogue. Any unsolicited scripts received will
be recycled.
Agent Only: Yes
Submission Fee: No

**Harlequin Productions of Cayuga
Community College**
197 Franklin St.
Auburn, NY 13021
Robert Frame, Director of Theater
Phone: (315) 255-1743
Fax: (315) 255-2117
www.cayuga-cc.edu
framer@cayuga-cc.edu
Notes: Est. 1958. 6 performances over 2
weekends (fall and spring) with college stu-
dents in high-quality extracurricular program.
Production: age 16–35, cast of 7–14. Response:
1 year.
Agent Only: No
Submission Materials: full script, S.A.S.E.
Preferred Genre: Plays (No Musicals)
Preferred Length: Any length
Submission Fee: No

Hartford Stage
50 Church St.
Hartford, CT 06103
Phone: (860) 525-5601
Fax: (860) 224-0183
www.hartfordstage.org
litman@hartfordstage.org
Notes: Est. 1963. Author must be a
Connecticut resident.
Agent Only: Yes
Submission Materials: agent-only
Preferred Genre: All genres
Preferred Length: Full-length
Submission Fee: No

**Harwich Junior Theatre (HJT; Harwich
Winter Theatre)**
105 Division St.
West Harwich, MA 02671
Phone: (508) 432-2002
Fax: (508) 432-0726
www.hjtcapecod.org
hjt@capecod.net
Notes: Est. 1951 New plays for intergenerational casts and audiences. Production: intergenerational, no fly. Response: 6 months.

Agent Only: No
Submission Materials: S.A.S.E., synopsis
Preferred Genre: All genres
Preferred Length: Any length
Special interest: Theatre for Young
Audiences
Submission Fee: No

Hedgerow Theatre
64 Rose Valley Rd.
Media, PA 19063
Phone: (610) 565-4211
Fax: (610) 565-1672
www.hedgerowtheatre.org
preed@hedgerowtheatre.org
Notes: Est. 1923. Readings of new plays by
Delaware Valley writers in readings and work-
shops. Production: cast of 2–8. Response: 2
months query, 4 months script.
Agent Only: No
Submission Materials: query letter, synopsis
Preferred Genre: All genres
Preferred Length: Any length
Submission Fee: No

Hip Pocket Theatre
Box 136758
Ft. Worth, TX 76136
Phone: (817) 246-9775
Fax: (817) 246-5651
www.hippocket.org
hippockettheatre@aol.com
Notes: Est. 1977. Production: simple set, out-
door amphitheater. Response: 2 months.
Agent Only: No
Submission Materials: audio CD, synopsis
Preferred Genre: Plays or Musicals
Preferred Length: Full-length
Submission Fee: No

Hobo Junction Productions
2526 West Argyle Avenue
Apt 2
Chicago, IL 60625
Phone: (773) 820-2732
www.hobojunctionproductions.com
hobojunction@sbcglobal.net
Notes: Established in 2008. Focus on innovative, imaginative and original approaches
to comedy. See website for details. Rolling
deadline.
Agent Only: No
Submission Materials: full script, query
letter, S.A.S.E., synopsis
Preferred Genre: Comedy

Preferred Length: Full-length
Submission Fee: No

Honolulu Theatre for Youth
1129 Bethel Street, Suite 700
Honolulu, HI 96813
Eric Johnson, Artistic Director
Phone: (808) 839-9885
Fax: (808) 839-7018
www.htyweb.org
artistic@htyweb.org
Notes: Est. 1955. Commissioning and pro-
ducing new plays, Sep–May. Production: cast
limit 5.
Agent Only: No
Submission Materials: query letter
Preferred Genre: Theatre for Young
Audiences
Preferred Length: 50–60 min.
Special interest: Theatre for Young
Audiences
Submission Fee: No

Horizon Theatre Rep [NY]
41 E. 67th St.
New York, NY 10021
Phone: (212) 737-3357
Fax: (212) 737-5103
www.htronline.org
info@htronline.org
Notes: Est. 2000. Unproduced/unoptioned
only. Submissions not returned. Production:
ages 16–75, cast size 4–15. Response: 1 month.
Agent Only: No
Submission Materials: synopsis
Preferred Genre: Plays (No Musicals)
Preferred Length: Any length
Submission Fee: No

Hubris Productions
2257 N Lincoln Ave
Chicago, IL 60614
Lorraine Freund
Phone: (773) 398-3273
www.hubrisproductions.com
lorraine@hubrisproductions.com
Notes: Looking for new work; unoptioned,
unproduced, unpublished. Email submissions
only. Play submissions should be sent with a
money order made out to: Hubris Productions.
Agent Only: No
Submission Materials: full script, query
letter, synopsis
Preferred Genre: Plays (No Musicals)
Preferred Length: Full-length

Special interest: LGBT
Submission Fee: Yes
Deadline(s): Ongoing

Hudson Theatres
6539 Santa Monica Blvd.
Los Angeles, CA 90038
Elizabeth Reilly, Artistic Director
Phone: (323) 856-4252
Fax: (323) 856-4316
www.hudsontheatre.com
ereilly@hudsontheatre.com
Notes: Est. 1991. Response: 6 months query, 1 year script.
Agent Only: No
Submission Materials: 10-pg sample, query letter, synopsis
Preferred Genre: All genres
Preferred Length: Full-length
Submission Fee: No

Huntington Theatre Company
264 Huntington Ave.
Boston, MA 02115
Phone: (617) 273-1503
Fax: (617) 353-8300
www.huntingtontheatre.org
chaugland@huntingtontheatre.bu.edu
Notes: Est. 1981. Massachusetts or Rhode Island writers send unsolicited. Others, must have agent submit. Response: 1 year.
Agent Only: No
Submission Materials: full script, S.A.S.E.
Preferred Genre: All genres
Preferred Length: Any length
Submission Fee: No

Hypothetical Theatre Company
P.O. Box 944
New York, NY 10009
Phone: (212) 780-0800
Fax: (212) 780-0859
www.hypotheticaltheatre.org
htc@hypotheticaltheatre.org
Notes: Est. 1986. Work must be unproduced in NYC. Response: 6 months.
Agent Only: Yes
Submission Materials: agent-only
Preferred Genre: Plays (No Musicals)
Preferred Length: Full-length
Submission Fee: No

IATI Theatre (Instituto Arte Teatral Internacional)
59-61 East 4th Street, 2nd Floor

New York, NY 10003
Haydn Diaz, Literary Associate
Phone: (212) 505-6757
www.iatitheater.org
info@iatitheater.org
Notes: Established in 1968, IATI Theater is dedicated to addressing contemporary issues of broad human interest. Our mission is to perform and promote our contemporary Latino heritage through programming that displays vibrant texts and explore the avant-garde, sometimes incorporating dance and music. Staged readings and workshops are also part of our creative output, thus serving as a bridge between artists and underserved communities nationwide from our New York home in the East Village.
Agent Only: No
Submission Materials: online only
Preferred Length: Full-length
Special interest: Latino
Submission Fee: No
Deadline(s): June 30, 2013

Idaho Repertory Theatre (IRT)
University of Idaho–Box 442008
Moscow, ID 83844
Phone: (208) 885-6465
Fax: (208) 885-2558
www.idahorep.org
theatre@uidaho.edu
Notes: Seeking work from new/emerging unpublished writer. Submit via email only. Production: ages 13–35, cast of 2–10. Response: 4 months.
Agent Only: No
Submission Materials: query letter
Preferred Genre: All genres
Preferred Length: Any length
Submission Fee: No

Illusion Theater
528 Hennepin Ave., #704
Minneapolis, MN 55403
Michael Robins, Executive Producing Director
Phone: (612) 339-4944
Fax: (612) 337-8042
www.illusiontheater.org
info@illusiontheater.org
Notes: Est. 1974. Submit via email. Response: 1 year.
Agent Only: No
Submission Materials: professional referral only

Preferred Genre: All genres
Preferred Length: Any length
Submission Fee: No

Imagination Stage
4908 Auburn Ave.
Bethesda, MD 20814
Phone: (301) 961-6060
Fax: (301) 718-9526
www.imaginationstage.org
kbryer@imaginationstage.org
Notes: Est. 1979. Production: cast of 4–10.
Agent Only: No
Submission Materials: 10-pg sample,
outline, query letter
Preferred Genre: All genres
Preferred Length: Any length
Submission Fee: No

Indiana Repertory Theatre
140 W. Washington St.
Indianapolis, IN 46204
Richard J. Roberts, Resident Dramaturg
Phone: (317) 635-5277
Fax: (317) 236-0767
www.irtlive.com
rroberts@irtlive.com
Notes: Est. 1972. Interested in material with
cross-generational appeal that also explore cul-
tural/ethical issues with a Midwestern voice.
Production: cast limit 10. Submit via email.
Response: 6 months
Agent Only: No
Submission Materials: query letter, resume,
synopsis
Preferred Genre: Plays (No Musicals)
Preferred Length: Any length
Submission Fee: No

INTAR (International Arts Relations) Theatre
500 West 52nd Street, 4th Floor
New York, NY 10019
Louis Moreno, Artistic Director
Phone: (212) 695-6134
www.intartheatre.org
lmoreno@intartheatre.org
Notes: Nurture the professional development
of Latino theater artists, produce bold, innovative, artistically significant plays that reflect
diverse perspectives. We are looking for full
length plays, solo shows, musicals, adaptations, or translations that fit INTAR's mission.
Pleae include full script, brief cover letter, a
short bio, development history of the play, and
current contact information.
Agent Only: No
Special interest: Latino
Submission Fee: No

InterAct Story Theatre
32 Pennydog Court
Silver Spring, MD 20902
Ali Oliver-Krueger, General Director
Phone: (301) 879-9305
Fax: (240) 491-9884
www.interactstory.com
info@interactstory.com
Agent Only: No
Submission Fee: No

InterAct Theatre Company [PA]
2030 Sansom St.
Philadelphia, PA 19103
Phone: (215) 568-8077
Fax: (215) 568-8095
www.interacttheatre.org
bwright@interacttheatre.org
Notes: Est. 1988. Looking for work that
explores specific social/political themes/issues.
Production: 1–8. Response: 6–12 months.
Agent Only: No
Submission Materials: 10-pg sample, query
letter, resume
Preferred Genre: Plays (No Musicals)
Preferred Length: Full-length
Submission Fee: No

Irish Arts Center
553 W. 51st St.
New York, NY 10019
Phone: (212) 757-3318
Fax: (212) 247-0930
www.irishartscenter.org
info@irishartscenter.org
Notes: Est. 1972.
Agent Only: No
Submission Materials: see website
Submission Fee: No

Irish Repertory Theatre
132 W. 22nd St.
New York, NY 10011
Kara Manning, Literary Manager
Phone: (212) 255-0270
Fax: (212) 255-0281
www.irishrep.org
kara@irishrep.org

Notes: Ongoing new works reading series reflecting the Irish and Irish American experience. Female playwrights and writers of color encouraged.
Agent Only: No
Submission Materials: see website
Preferred Genre: All genres
Preferred Length: Any length
Submission Fee: No

Itheatrics
628 W 52 St. Suite 1F
New York, NY 10019
Lindsay Weiner
Phone: (646) 467-8090
Fax: (646) 467-8096
www.itheatrics.com
info@itheatrics.com
Agent Only: No
Submission Fee: No

Jewish Theater of New York
Box 845, Times Sq. Sta.
New York, NY 10108
Phone: (212) 494-0050
Fax: (212) 494-0050
www.jewishtheater.org
thejtny@aol.com
Notes: Est. 1994. Seeking unproduced/unpublished/unoptioned work. Submissions not returned. Response: 3 months.
Agent Only: No
Submission Materials: synopsis
Preferred Genre: Musical theatre
Preferred Length: Full-length
Submission Fee: No

Jewish Women's Theatre
521 Latimer Road
Santa Monica, CA 90402
Ronda Spinak, Artistic Director
Fax: (310) 454-1858
www.jewishwomenstheatre.org
ronda@jewishwomenstheatre.org
Notes: Most interested in the stories of Jewish women in America today. Must have small casts (under 5). Prefer short (under 10 minutes) plays, poems, songs, stories, monologues, but please check the website to determine the current season's themes for the shows and submit accordingly.
Agent Only: No
Submission Materials: see website
Preferred Length: 10-min./10pgs.

Special interest: Women's Interest
Submission Fee: No

Josiah Theatre Works
345 Lenox Ave
New York, NY 10027
Nickolas L. Long, Playwright-at-large,
Artistic Director
Phone: (347) 291-6289
joshiahtheatre@gmail.com
Notes: Josiah Theatre Works welcomes playwrights and lyricists seeking productions in Manhattan and touring shows. We specialize in period drama and musicals.
Agent Only: No
Preferred Genre: Plays or Musicals
Preferred Length: Any length
Submission Fee: Yes

Judith Shakespeare Company NYC
367 Windsor Hwy., #409
New Windsor, NY 12553
Joanne Zipay, Artistic Director/Producer
Phone: (212) 592-1885
www.judithshakespeare.org
judithshakes@gmail.com
Notes: Est. 1995. Offers "Resurgence" concert reading series and full productions of new plays with heightened language and significant roles for women. Submit by US mail only.
Agent Only: No
Submission Materials: 10-pg sample, synopsis
Preferred Genre: Plays (No Musicals)
Preferred Length: Any length
Submission Fee: No

Kairos Italy Theater (KIT)
60 E. 8th Street, #12B
New York, NY 10003
Laura Caparrotti, Artistic Director
Phone: (212) 254-4025
Fax: (801) 749-6727
www.kitheater.com
info@kitheater.com
Notes: Est. 2002. Produces plays by and about Italian authors and Italian themes. Submit by email.
Agent Only: No
Submission Materials: 10-pg sample, synopsis
Preferred Genre: Plays (No Musicals)
Preferred Length: Any length
Submission Fee: No

Kansas City Repertory Theatre
4949 Cherry St.
Kansas City, MO 64110
Phone: (816) 235-2727
Fax: (816) 235-5367
www.kcrep.org
prestonem@kcrep.org
Notes: Est. 1964. Formerly Missouri
Repertory Theatre.
Agent Only: No
Preferred Genre: All genres
Preferred Length: Full-length
Submission Fee: No

Kids' Entertainment
500 St. Clair Ave
Ste 808
Toronto, ON M6C1A8
Phone: (416) 971-4836
Fax: (416) 971-4841
www.kidsentertainment.net
admin@kidsentertainment.net
Agent Only: No
Special interest: Theatre for Young
Audiences
Submission Fee: No

Kidworks Touring Theatre Co.
3524 N. Leavitt St.
2nd Floor
Chicago, IL 60618
Andrea Salloum, Artistic Director
Phone: (773) 907-9932
Fax: (773) 907-9933
www.kidworkstheatre.org
kidworkstheatre@aol.com
Notes: Est. 1987.
Agent Only: No
Special interest: Theatre for Young
Audiences
Submission Fee: No

Killing Kompany
21 Turn Ln.
Levittown, NY 11756
Phone: (212) 772-2590
Fax: (212) 202-6495
www.killingkompany.com
killingkompany@killingkompany.com
Notes: Interactive shows for dinner theater.
Agent Only: No
Preferred Genre: Interactive
Preferred Length: Full-length
Submission Fee: No

L.A. Theatre Works (LATW)
681 Venice Blvd.
Venice, CA 90291
Phone: (310) 827-0808
Fax: (310) 827-4949
www.latw.org
bfox@latw.org
Notes: Est. 1974. Live performances and studio recordings for broadcast over public radio. Response: 6 months.
Agent Only: Yes
Submission Materials: agent-only
Preferred Genre: Radio plays
Preferred Length: Any length
Submission Fee: No

La Centale Galerie Powerhouse
4296 St-Laurent Boulevard
Montreal, QC H2W 1Z3
Phone: (514) 871-0268
www.lacentrale.org
galerie@lacentrale.org
Notes: Growing out of the feminist art movement and founded in 1973, La Centrale Galerie Powerhouse is one of the oldest artist-run centers in Quebec. The center's mandate expands on a history of feminist art practices and engages a broader spectrum of underrepresented artists and their initiatives within established art institutions. The gallery aims to provide a platform for contemporary art informed by feminist and gender theory, as well as intercultural and transdisciplinary practices.
Agent Only: No
Submission Materials: see website
Special interest: Women's Interest
Submission Fee: No

La Jolla Playhouse
Box 12039
La Jolla, CA 92039
Phone: (858) 550-1070
Fax: (858) 550-1075
www.lajollaplayhouse.org
information@ljp.org
Notes: Est. 1947. Commissions playwrights and provides developmental support thru Page to Stage readings (est. 2001). Response: 2 months query, 1 year script.
Agent Only: No
Submission Materials: see website
Preferred Genre: Plays or Musicals
Preferred Length: Full-length
Submission Fee: No

La MaMa Experimental Theater Club
74-A E. 4th St.
New York, NY 10003
Phone: (212) 254-6468
Fax: (212) 254-7597
www.lamama.org
web@lamama.org
Notes: Est. 1961. Response: 6 months.
Agent Only: No
Submission Materials: professional referral only
Preferred Genre: Plays (No Musicals)
Preferred Length: Any length
Submission Fee: No

LAByrinth Theater Company
307 W. 38th Street, Suite 1605
New York, NY 10018
Philip S. Hoffman, Co-Artistic Dir.
Phone: (212) 513-1080
Fax: (212) 513-1123
www.labtheater.org
lab@labtheater.org
Agent Only: No
Preferred Genre: All genres
Preferred Length: Any length
Submission Fee: No

LaMicro Theater
Box 20019, London Terrace
New York, NY 10011
Berioska Ipinza, Executive Director
Phone: (212) 929-0332
www.lamicrotheater.org
info@lamicrotheater.org
Notes: Est. 2003. Bilingual productions of contemporary and emerging playwrights; explore new ideas and generate dialogue concerning the realities faced by our diverse communities.
Agent Only: No
Submission Materials: see website
Special interest: Latino
Submission Fee: No

Lark Theatre Company, The
939 8th Ave.
#301
New York, NY 10019
Phone: (212) 246-2676
Fax: (212) 246-2609
www.larktheatre.org
submissions@larktheatre.org
Agent Only: No
Submission Materials: see website

Preferred Genre: All genres
Preferred Length: Full-length
Submission Fee: No

Leaping Thespians
Karen White, Director
www.leapingthespians.ca
leapingthespians@hotmail.com
Notes: Leaping Thespians is a woman's theatre company bringing stories of lesbians' lives to Vancouver audiences. We want to present original work and nurture emerging talents on stage and behind the scenes. We accept new members for every production. We are always interested in reading scripts of at least one hour's length, where all parts can be played by women. If you would like us to consider producing your work, please send a production/workshop/dramaturge history of your script as well as a synopsis.
Agent Only: No
Submission Materials: synopsis
Special interest: Women's Interest
Submission Fee: No

Lewis Family Playhouse at the Victoria Gardens Center
12505 Culture Center Drive
Rancho Cucamonga, CA 91739
Susan Sluka-Kelly, Cultural Arts Supervisor
Phone: (909) 477-2775
Fax: (909) 477-2774
www.lewisfamilyplayhouse.com
susan.sluka-kelly@cityofrc.us
Agent Only: No
Submission Fee: No

Lexington Children's Theatre
418 West Short Street
Lexington, KY 40507
Phone: (859) 254-4546
Fax: (859) 254-9512
www.lctonstage.org
info@lctonstage.org
Agent Only: No
Special interest: Theatre for Young Audiences
Submission Fee: No

Lincoln Center Theater
150 W. 65th St.
New York, NY 10023
Phone: (212) 362-7600
www.lct.org
info@lct.org

Notes: Est. 1966. Response: 2 months.
Agent Only: Yes
Submission Materials: agent-only
Preferred Genre: All genres
Preferred Length: Full-length
Submission Fee: No

Literally Alive
The Players Theatre
115 MacDougal St.
New York, NY 10012
Phone: (212) 866-5170
www.literallyalive.com
brenda@literallyalive.com
Agent Only: No
Preferred Genre: Plays or Musicals
Preferred Length: Any length
Special interest: Theatre for Young
Audiences
Submission Fee: No

Little Fish Theatre (LFT)
777 Centre St.
San Pedro, CA 90731
Phone: (310) 512-6030
Fax: (310) 507-0269
www.littlefishtheatre.org
holly@littlefishtheatre.org
Notes: Est. 2002. No longer accepting full
length plays, see website for annual Pick of the
Vine short play festival.
Agent Only: No
Submission Materials: see website
Preferred Genre: Plays (No Musicals)
Preferred Length: 10-min./10pgs.
Submission Fee: No
Deadline(s): See website

Looking Glass Theatre [NY]
422 W. 57th St.
New York, NY 10019
Erica Nilson, Literary Manager
Phone: (212) 307-9467
www.lookingglasstheatrenyc.com
lgtlit@yahoo.com
Notes: Est. 1993. Submit work via US
mail AND email. Author must be female.
Production: minimal. Response: 6 months–1
year.
Agent Only: No
Submission Materials: full script
Preferred Genre: Plays (No Musicals)
Preferred Length: 10-min./10pgs.
Submission Fee: No
Deadline(s): February 1 (yearly); August 1
(yearly)

Lookingglass Theatre [IL]
2936 N. Southport Ave., Fl. 3
Chicago, IL 60657
Phone: (773) 477-9257
www.lookingglasstheatre.org
info@lookingglasstheatre.org
Notes: Ensemble-based theater producing pri-
marily company-developed projects. Shows
are highly physical with strong narrative. No
kitchen sink or talking heads.
Agent Only: No
Submission Materials: query letter, S.A.S.E.,
synopsis
Preferred Genre: Plays (No Musicals)
Preferred Length: Any length
Submission Fee: No

Los Angeles Women's Theatre Project
10061 Riverside Dr
Toluca Lake, CA 91602
Dee Jea Cox, Co-Founder/Artistic Director
Phone: (818) 471-9100
www.LAWomenstheatreproject.com
info@womenstheatreproject.com
Notes: A nonprofit 501(c)3 organization dedi-
cated to supporting, empowering and creating
opportunities for women in the performing
arts.
Agent Only: No
Submission Materials: see website
Special interest: Women's Interest
Submission Fee: No

Lost Nation Theater
City Hall
39 Main St.
Montpelier, VT 05602
Phone: (802) 229-0492
Fax: (802) 223-9608
www.lostnationtheater.org
info@lostnationtheater.org
Notes: Est. 1977. Production: cast limit 8,
unit set, no fly. Response: 2 months query, 4
months script.
Agent Only: No
Submission Materials: 10-pg sample, query
letter, resume, synopsis
Submission Fee: No
Deadline(s): November 1, 2012

Luna Stage
555 Valley Road
West Orange, NJ 07052
Cheryl Katz, Associate Artistic Director
Phone: (973) 395-5551
www.lunastage.org

cherylkatz.luna@gmail.com
Agent Only: No
Submission Materials: see website
Preferred Genre: All genres
Preferred Length: Full-length
Submission Fee: No
Deadline(s): Accepts scripts from 9/15–4/15

Magic Theatre
Ft. Mason Center., Bldg. D
San Francisco, CA 94123
Dori Jacob, Literary Manager
Phone: (415) 441-8822
Fax: (415) 771-5505
www.magictheatre.org
dorij@magictheatre.org
Notes: Magic produces world premieres
and 2nd and 3rd productions of new work.
Production: cast limit 8. Response: 3–9
months script.
Agent Only: No
Submission Materials: see website
Preferred Genre: Comedy
Preferred Length: Full-length
Submission Fee: No
Deadline(s): Rolling

Main Street Theater
2540 Times Blvd.
Houston, TX 77005
Rebecca Greene Udden, Artistic Director
Phone: (713) 524-3622
Fax: (713) 524-3977
www.mainstreettheater.com/
rudden@mainstreettheater.com
Notes: Est. 1975. Production: cast limit 9.
Plays by women.
Agent Only: No
Submission Materials: see website
Submission Fee: No

Marin Theater Company (MTC)
397 Miller Ave.
Mill Valley, CA 94941
Margot Melcon, Literary Manager
Phone: (415) 388-5200
Fax: (415) 388-1217
www.marintheatre.org
literarymanager@marintheatre.org
Notes: Est. 1966. Marin Theatre Company
accepts full scripts for season consideration
when submitted by an agent; playwrights
may submit a letter of inquiry. Response time
approximately 6–9 months. Marin Theatre
Company has an open script submission policy

for our two annual new play prizes. See web-
site for submission guidelines.
Agent Only: No
Submission Materials: see website
Preferred Genre: Plays (No Musicals)
Preferred Length: Full-length
Submission Fee: No
Deadline(s): August 31 for play prize
submission

Ma-Yi Theatre Company
520 8th Ave, #309
New York, NY 10018
Phone: (212) 971-4862
Fax: (212) 971-4862
www.ma-yitheatre.org
info@ma-yitheatre.org
Notes: Est. 1989. Submissions not returned.
Agent Only: No
Submission Materials: query letter, synopsis
Preferred Genre: Plays (No Musicals)
Preferred Length: Full-length
Special interest: Asian-American
Submission Fee: No

MCC Theater
311 W. 43rd St., #206
New York, NY 10036
Phone: (212) 727-7722
Fax: (212) 727-7780
www.mcctheater.org
literary@mcctheater.org
Notes: Est. 1986. Production: cast limit 10.
Response: 2 months.
Agent Only: No
Submission Materials: 10-pg sample, query
letter, S.A.S.E., synopsis
Preferred Genre: All genres
Preferred Length: Full-length
Submission Fee: No

McCarter Theater Center
91 University Pl.
Princeton, NJ 08540
Carrie Hughes, Literary Director
Phone: (609) 258-6500
Fax: (609) 497-0369
www.mccarter.org
chughes@mccarter.org
Notes: Response: 6 months.
Agent Only: Yes
Submission Materials: agent-only
Preferred Genre: Plays or Musicals
Preferred Length: Full-length
Submission Fee: No

Merrimack Repertory Theatre

132 Warren St.
Lowell, MA 01852
Phone: (978) 654-7550
Fax: (978) 654-7575
www.merrimackrep.org
info@merrimackrep.org
Notes: Est. 1979. Production: cast limit 8.
Prefer digital scripts. Response: 12 months.
Agent Only: Yes
Submission Materials: agent-only
Preferred Genre: Plays (No Musicals)
Preferred Length: Full-length
Submission Fee: No

Metro Theater Company

8308 Olive Blvd.
St. Louis, MO 63132
Carol North, Artistic Director
Phone: (314) 997-6777
Fax: (314) 997-1811
www.metrotheatercompany.org
carol@metrotheatercompany.org
Notes: Est. 1973. Mainstage shows, tours and
commissions of theater for children and family
audiences. Production: cast limit 10. Response:
3 months.
Agent Only: No
Submission Materials: 10-pg sample,
S.A.S.E., synopsis
Preferred Genre: Plays or Musicals
Preferred Length: 50–60 min.
Special interest: Theatre for Young
Audiences
Submission Fee: No

MetroStage

1201 N. Royal St.
Alexandria, VA 22314
Carolyn Griffin, Producing Artistic Director
Phone: (703) 548-9044
Fax: (703) 548-9089
www.metrostage.org
info@metrostage.org
Notes: Est. 1984. Production: cast limit 6–8,
orchestra limit 5, unit set. Musicals must
already be workshopped and have a demo cd.
Author should have an agent.
Agent Only: No
Submission Materials: 10-pg sample,
S.A.S.E., synopsis
Preferred Length: Full-length
Submission Fee: No

Milwaukee Chamber Theatre

158 N. Broadway
Milwaukee, WI 53202
C. Michael Wright, Producing Artistic
Director
Phone: (414) 276-8842
Fax: (414) 277-4477
www.chamber-theatre.com
michael@chamber-theatre.com
Notes: Est. 1975. Production: small cast, unit
set. Response: 6 months. Only interested in
Wisconsin writers or those writing about
Wisconsin locations and themes.
Agent Only: No
Submission Materials: 10-pg sample, query
letter, S.A.S.E., synopsis
Preferred Genre: All genres
Preferred Length: Full-length
Submission Fee: No
Deadline(s): Accepting all year round

Milwaukee Repertory Theater

108 E. Wells St.
Milwaukee, WI 53202
Phone: (414) 224-1761
Fax: (414) 224-9097
www.milwaukeerep.com
bhazelton@milwaukeerep.com
Notes: Est. 1954. minimum response time: 6
months.
Agent Only: No
Submission Materials: see website
Preferred Genre: Plays or Musicals
Preferred Length: Full-length & 10-min.
Submission Fee: No
Deadline(s): See website

Miracle Theatre Group

425 SE 6th Ave.
Portland, OR 97214
Olga Sanchez, Artistic Director
Phone: (503) 236-7253
Fax: (503) 236-4174
www.milagro.org
olga@milagro.org
Notes: Est. 1985. Author must be Hispanic.
Production: cast limit 10, no fly. Response: 1
year. Seeking plays but will consider musicals.
Agent Only: No
Submission Materials: full script
Preferred Genre: Plays (No Musicals)
Preferred Length: Full-length
Special interest: Latino
Submission Fee: No

Missouri Repertory Theatre
4949 Cherry St.
Kansas City, MO 64110
Phone: (816) 235-2727
Fax: (816) 235-6562
www.missourireptheatre.org
theatre@umkc.edu
Notes: Est. 1964.
Agent Only: Yes
Submission Materials: agent-only
Preferred Genre: Plays (No Musicals)
Preferred Length: Full-length
Submission Fee: No

Mixed Blood Theatre Company
1501 S. 4th St.
Minneapolis, MN 55454
Phone: (612) 338-0937
Fax: (612) 338-1851
www.mixedblood.com
literary@mixedblood.com
Notes: Est. 1976. Response: 4 months.
Agent Only: No
Submission Materials: see website
Preferred Genre: All genres
Preferred Length: Full-length
Submission Fee: No

Moving Arts
Box 481145
Los Angeles, CA 90048
Phone: (323) 666-3259
Fax: (323) 666-2841
www.movingarts.org
info@movingarts.org
Notes: Est. 1992. Currently not accepting
submissions.
Agent Only: No
Preferred Genre: Plays (No Musicals)
Preferred Length: Full-length
Submission Fee: No

National Theatre of the Deaf
325 Pequot Ave
New London, CT 06320
Betty Beekman
Phone: (860) 574-9063
Fax: (860) 574-9107
www.ntd.org
bbeekman@ntd.org
Notes: Est. 1967. Looking for work unproduced professionally. Production: cast limit
10, touring set. Response: 1 month query, 6
months script.
Agent Only: No

Submission Materials: 10-pg sample, query
letter, S.A.S.E., synopsis
Preferred Genre: Plays (No Musicals)
Preferred Length: Full-length
Special interest: Deaf
Submission Fee: No

National Yiddish Theater—Folksbiene
135 W. 29th St.
Room 504
New York, NY 10001
Phone: (212) 213-2120
Fax: (212) 213-2186
www.folksbiene.org
info@folksbiene.org
Notes: Seeking material in Yiddish or based
on Yiddish source material.
Agent Only: No
Submission Materials: see website
Preferred Genre: Plays or Musicals
Preferred Length: Any length
Submission Fee: No

Near West Theatre (NWT)
6514 Detroit Avenue
Cleveland, OH 44102
Carole L. Hedderson, Business Director
Phone: (216) 961-9750
Fax: (216) 961-6381
nearwesttheatre.org
LDoerr@nearwesttheatre.org
Agent Only: No
Submission Fee: No

New Conservatory Theatre Center
25 Van Ness Ave., Lower Lobby
San Francisco, CA 94102
Ed Decker, Artistic Director
Phone: (415) 861-4914
Fax: (415) 861-6988
www.nctcsf.org
ed@nctcsf.org
Notes: Est. 1981. Material must be unoptioned.
Response: 2–4 months.
Agent Only: No
Submission Materials: see website
Preferred Genre: No translation or
adaptation
Preferred Length: Any length
Submission Fee: No

New Federal Theatre
292 Henry St.
New York, NY 10002
Phone: (212) 353-1176

Fax: (212) 353-1088
www.newfederaltheatre.org
newfederal@aol.com
Notes: Est. 1970. Production: cast limit 5, unit set. Response: 6 months.
Agent Only: No
Submission Materials: full script, S.A.S.E.
Preferred Genre: Plays (No Musicals)
Preferred Length: Full-length
Submission Fee: No

New Georges
109 W. 27th St., #9-A
New York, NY 10001
Kara-Lynn Vaeni, Literary Manager
Phone: (646) 336-8077
Fax: (646) 336-8077
www.newgeorges.org
info@newgeorges.org
Notes: New Georges does not read submissions for production, but to discover compelling writers to bring into relationship with the company, with an eye to future collaboration.
Agent Only: No
Submission Materials: full script
Preferred Genre: Plays (No Musicals)
Preferred Length: Full-length
Special interest: Women's Interest
Submission Fee: No

New Ground Theatre
2113 E. 11th St.
Davenport, IA 52803
Chris Jansen, Artistic Director
Phone: (563) 326-7529
Fax: (563) 359-7576
www.newgroundtheatre.org
cjansen@hotmail.com
Notes: Est. 2001. Author must be resident of Iowa, Illinois or quad city area. Production: cast limit 6, unit set, no fly. Response: 6 months.
Agent Only: No
Submission Materials: full script
Preferred Genre: All genres
Preferred Length: Full-length
Submission Fee: No

New Group, The
410 W. 42nd St.
New York, NY 10036
Phone: (212) 244-3380
Fax: (212) 244-3438
www.thenewgroup.org
info@thenewgroup.org

Notes: Est. 1991. Workshops and readings. US mail submissions only. Response: 2 months for samples, 9 months for full scripts.
Agent Only: No
Submission Materials: see website
Preferred Genre: Plays (No Musicals)
Preferred Length: Full-length
Submission Fee: No

New Jersey Repertory Company
179 Broadway
Long Branch, NJ 07740
Phone: (732) 229-3166
Fax: (732) 229-3167
www.njrep.org
njrep@njrep.org
Notes: Est. 1997. Seeking unproduced/unpublished via email only. US mail submits not returned. Production: cast limit 4 for plays and musicals. 6–7 Full length plays produced each year. 15–20 readings produced each year.
Agent Only: No
Submission Materials: audio CD, character breakdown, full script, synopsis
Preferred Genre: Plays or Musicals
Preferred Length: Full-length
Submission Fee: No
Deadline(s): Ongoing

New Repertory Theatre
200 Dexter Ave.
Watertown, MA 02472
Bridget Kathleen O'Leary, Artistic Associate
Phone: (617) 923-7060
Fax: (617) 923-7625
www.newrep.org
bridgetoleary@newrep.org
Notes: Est. 1984. Author must have agent or be a local playwright. Production: cast limit 12.
Agent Only: No
Submission Materials: full script
Preferred Genre: Plays or Musicals
Preferred Length: Full-length
Submission Fee: No

New Theatre
4120 Laguna St.
Coral Gables, FL 33146
Phone: (305) 443-5373
Fax: (305) 443-1642
www.new-theatre.org
schambers@new-theatre.org
Notes: Est. 1986. New works and new adaptations of Shakespeare sought. Production: cast limit 6, minimal set. Response: 2–3 months.

Agent Only: No
Submission Materials: see website
Preferred Genre: All genres
Preferred Length: Full-length
Submission Fee: No
Deadline(s): See website

New Theatre Project, The
Keith Paul Medelis, Artistic Director
Phone: (810) 623-0909
www.thenewtheatreproject.org
keith@thenewtheatreproject.org
Notes: We do not accept snail mail scripts, please E-MAIL all submissions. Please include full script, synopsis, and character listing (including all possible doubling). We are interested in LGBT, young people, adaptations, or work based on classical texts, true stories, or nontraditional.
Agent Only: No
Submission Materials: E-mail only
Preferred Length: Full-length
Special interest: LGBT
Submission Fee: No

New Works/Vantage Theatres
1251 W. Muirlands Dr.
La Jolla, CA 92037
Dori Salois, Artistic Manager
Phone: (858) 456-9664
vantagetheatre.com
vantagetheatre@gmail.com
Notes: Seeking work with big political/spiritual ideas.
Agent Only: No
Submission Materials: full script, S.A.S.E., synopsis
Preferred Genre: Plays (No Musicals)
Preferred Length: Any length
Submission Fee: No

New World Theater (NWT)
100 Hicks Way, #16 Curry Hicks
Amherst, MA 01003
Phone: (413) 545-1972
Fax: (413) 545-4414
nwt@admin.umass.edu
Notes: Hosts "New Works for a New World" every summer & invite up to 4 artists for a development residency.
Agent Only: No
Submission Materials: query letter
Preferred Genre: All genres
Preferred Length: Any length
Submission Fee: No

New York Stage and Film (NYSAF)
214 West 29th Street, Suite 1001
New York, NY 10001
Phone: (212) 736-4240
Fax: (212) 736-4241
www.newyorkstageandfilm.org
info@newyorkstageandfilm.org
Notes: Est. 1985. Summer season (Jun–Aug) in residence as part of Powerhouse program at Vasser College. Response: 6 months.
Agent Only: No
Submission Materials: full script, S.A.S.E.
Preferred Genre: Plays (No Musicals)
Preferred Length: Full-length
Submission Fee: No

New York Theatre Workshop (NYTW)
83 E. 4th St.
New York, NY 10003
Phone: (212) 780-9037
Fax: (212) 460-8996
www.nytw.org
info@nytw.org
Notes: Est. 1979. Works of innovative form & language about socially relevant issues. Response: 3 months query, 8 months script.
Agent Only: No
Submission Materials: 10-pg sample, query letter, resume, S.A.S.E., synopsis
Preferred Genre: Plays (No Musicals)
Preferred Length: Full-length
Submission Fee: No

Next Theater Company
927 Noyes St.
Suite 108
Evanston, IL 60201
Jenny Avery, Artistic Director
Phone: (847) 475-1875
Fax: (847) 475-6767
www.nexttheatre.org
info@nexttheatre.org
Notes: Est. 1981. Commissions 1 world premiere per season. Production: cast limit 10
Agent Only: No
Submission Materials: 10-pg sample, query letter, S.A.S.E., synopsis
Preferred Genre: Plays (No Musicals)
Preferred Length: Full-length
Submission Fee: No

Nightwood Theatre
55 Mill Street
Suite 301
Case Goods Warehouse, Bldg. No. 71

Toronto, ON M5A 3C4
Phone: (416) 944-1740
Fax: (416) 944-1739
www.nightwoodtheatre.net
info@nightwoodtheatre.net
Notes: The oldest professional women's the-
atre company in Canada. Founded in 1979 by
Cynthia Grant, Kim Renders, Mary Vingoe
and Maureen White, Nightwood has produced,
developed and toured landmark, award-win-
ning plays by and about Canadian women.
Agent Only: No
Special interest: Women's Interest
Submission Fee: No

Nora Theatre Company, The
450 Massachusetts Ave
Cambridge, MA 02139
Phone: (617) 576-9278
www.thenora.org
info@thenora.org
Notes: The Nora Theatre Company produces
illuminating contemporary and modern classic
theater and champions the voice of women.
Agent Only: No
Submission Materials: see website
Special interest: Women's Interest
Submission Fee: No

North Carolina Theatre for Young People
406 Tate Street
PO Box 26170
Greensboro, NC 27402-6170
Jody Kaizen, UNCG Theatre Manager
Phone: (336) 334-4601
Fax: (336) 334-5100
performingarts.uncg.edu/theatre
jtcauthe@uncg.edu
Agent Only: No
Special interest: Theatre for Young
Audiences
Submission Fee: No

Northern Stage
Box 4287
White River Junction, VT 05001
Phone: (802) 291-9009
www.northernstage.org
info@northernstage.org
Notes: Est. 1997.
Agent Only: No
Submission Materials: query letter, S.A.S.E.
Preferred Genre: All genres
Preferred Length: Full-length
Submission Fee: No

Northlight Theatre
9501 N. Skokie Blvd.
Skokie, IL 60077
Kristin Leahey, Resident Dramaturg
Phone: (847) 679-9501
Fax: (847) 679-1879
www.northlight.org
kleahey@northlight.org
Notes: Est. 1975. Preference given to writers
from Illinois.
Agent Only: No
Submission Materials: see website
Preferred Genre: All genres
Preferred Length: 10-min./10pgs.
Submission Fee: No

Obsidian Theatre Company
1089 Dundas Street East
Toronto, ON M4M-1R9, Canada
Phone: (416) 463-8444
www.obsidiantheatre.com
obsidiantheatre@bellnet.ca
Notes: Check website for submission details.
Agent Only: No
Submission Materials: see website
Preferred Genre: Plays (No Musicals)
Preferred Length: Full-length
Submission Fee: No

Omaha Theater Company at The Rose
2001 Farnam St.
Omaha, NE 68102
Michael Miller, Literary Manager
Phone: (402) 502-4624
Fax: (402) 344-7255
www.rosetheater.org
michaelm@rosetheater.org
Notes: Est. 1949. Production: cast limit 10,
unit set. Response: 6 months. Please submit
a cover letter with contact information and a
script sample.
Agent Only: No
Submission Materials: see website
Preferred Genre: Plays (No Musicals)
Preferred Length: One-Act
Special interest: Theatre for Young
Audiences
Submission Fee: No

Open Eye Theater
PO Box 959
Margaretville, NY 12455
Amie Brockway, Producing Artistic Director
Phone: (845) 586-1660
Fax: (845) 586-1660

www.theopeneye.org
openeye@catskill.net
Notes: Est. 1972. Readings and productions
for a multigenerational audience. Production:
small cast, modest set. Response: 6 months.
Agent Only: No
Submission Materials: query letter, synopsis
Preferred Genre: All genres
Preferred Length: Any length
Special interest: Theatre for Young
Audiences
Submission Fee: No

Opera Cleveland
1422 Euclid Ave, #1052
Cleveland, OH 44115
Phone: (216) 575-0903
Fax: (216) 575-1918
www.operacleveland.org
williamson@operacleveland.org
Notes: Est. 2006 (merger of Lyric Opera
Cleveland, Cleveland Opera). Spring-fall
season and summer festival of 3 full-length
operas. Response: 1 month.
Agent Only: No
Submission Materials: audio CD, full script,
query letter, S.A.S.E., synopsis
Preferred Genre: Opera
Preferred Length: Full-length
Submission Fee: No

Oregon Shakespeare Festival
Box 158
Ashland, OR 97520
Phone: (541) 482-2111
Fax: (541) 482-0446
www.osfashland.org
literary@osfashland.org
Notes: Est. 1935. Response: 6 months.
Agent Only: No
Submission Materials: query letter
Preferred Genre: Plays (No Musicals)
Preferred Length: Full-length
Submission Fee: No

Orlando Repertory Theatre
1001 East Princton St
Orlando, FL 32803
Brian Diaz, Company Manager
Phone: (407) 896-7365
Fax: (407) 897-3284
www.orlandorep.com
briand@orlandorep.com
Notes: The Rep is a professional theatre for
young audiences with a mission to enlighten,

entertain and enrich children and adults by
producing theatre of exceptional quality. The
award winning Rep Youth Academy provides
classes, camps and workshops for children
along with professional development opportunities to local classroom teachers. Housed in
a three-theatre complex in Loch Haven Park.
The Rep is also home to the University of
Central Florida's MFA in Theatre for Young
Audiences graduate programs.
Agent Only: No
Submission Fee: No

Passage Theatre
P.O. Box 967
Trenton, NJ 08605
Phone: (609) 392-0766
Fax: (609) 392-0318
www.passagetheatre.org
info@passagetheatre.org
Notes: Est. 1985. Seeks boundary-pushing
& stylistically adventurous new works.
Production: Modest cast size 4–6 actors, no
fly. Response: 5 months.
Agent Only: No
Submission Materials: see website
Preferred Genre: Plays or Musicals
Preferred Length: Any length
Submission Fee: No
Deadline(s): Ongoing

Patrick's Cabaret
3010 Minnesota Ave.
Minneapolis, MN 55406
Phone: (612) 724-6273
www.patrickscabaret.org
amy@patrickscabaret.org
Notes: Est. 1986. Primarily a rental house for
shared evenings of short works (up to 15 min-
utes). Production: all ages,cast 2–20, minimal
sets. Response: 1 month
Agent Only: No
Submission Materials: query letter
Preferred Genre: All genres
Preferred Length: 15 min.
Submission Fee: Yes

PCPA Theatrefest
800 S. College Dr.
Santa Maria, CA 93454
Phone: (805) 928-7731
Fax: (805) 928-7506
www.pcpa.org
literary@pcpa.org

Notes: Est. 1964. Response: 3 months query, 6 months script.
Agent Only: No
Submission Materials: query letter, synopsis
Preferred Genre: Plays (No Musicals)
Preferred Length: Full-length
Submission Fee: No

Pearl Theatre Company, Inc.
307 West 38th St.
Suite 1805
New York, NY 10018
Phone: (212) 505-3401
Fax: (212) 505-3404
www.pearltheatre.org
kfarrington@pearltheatre.org
Notes: Est. 1982. Focusing on classical adaptations/translations or based on classical themes/characters only. Production: age 18–75, cast size 6–13, 1 set. Response: 4–6 months.
Agent Only: No
Submission Materials: character breakdown, synopsis
Preferred Genre: Adaptation
Preferred Length: Any length
Submission Fee: No

Pegasus Theater Company
Box 942
Monte Rio, CA 95462
Phone: (707) 522-9043
www.pegasustheater.com
director@pegasustheater.com
Notes: Est. 1998.
Agent Only: No
Submission Materials: see website
Submission Fee: No

Penguin Repertory Company
Box 91
Stony Point, NY 10980
Phone: (845) 786-2873
Fax: (845) 786-3638
www.penguinrep.org
Andrew@penguinrep.org
Notes: Est. 1977. Full length plays, small sets, five characters or fewer. No electronic submissions, no calls please. Response: Up To One Year.
Agent Only: No
Submission Materials: full script
Preferred Genre: Plays (No Musicals)
Preferred Length: Full-length
Submission Fee: No

Pennsylvania Youth Theatre
25 W 3rd St
Bethlehem, PA 18015
Phone: (610) 332-1400
Fax: (610) 332-1405
www.123pyt.org
office@123pyt.org
Agent Only: No
Special interest: Theatre for Young Audiences
Submission Fee: No

Penumbra Theatre Company
270 N. Kent St.
St. Paul, MN 55102
Phone: (651) 288-6795
Fax: (651) 224-3180
www.penumbratheatre.org
sarah.bellamy@penumbratheatre.org
Notes: Est. 1976. Response: 9 months.
Agent Only: No
Submission Materials: see website
Preferred Genre: Plays (No Musicals)
Preferred Length: Any length
Submission Fee: No

People's Light and Theatre Company
39 Conestoga Rd.
Malvern, PA 19355
Phone: (610) 647-1900
www.peopleslight.org
Notes: Est. 1974. We are currently not accepting unsolicited scripts.
Agent Only: No
Submission Materials: 10-pg sample, full script, query letter, synopsis
Preferred Genre: Plays (No Musicals)
Preferred Length: Full-length
Submission Fee: No

Performance Network Theatre
120 E. Huron St.
Ann Arbor, MI 48104
Phone: (734) 663-0696
Fax: (734) 663-7396
www.performancenetwork.org
david@performancenetwork.org
Notes: Est. 1981. Production: cast limit 10, no fly. Response: 6 months.
Agent Only: No
Submission Materials: 10-pg sample, S.A.S.E., synopsis
Preferred Genre: Plays (No Musicals)
Preferred Length: Full-length
Submission Fee: No

Philadelphia Theatre Company (PTC)
230 S. Broad St.
Ste. 1105
Philadelphia, PA 19102
Carrie Chapter, Literary Manager
Phone: (215) 985-1400
Fax: (215) 985-5800
www.philadelphiatheatrecompany.org
literary@philadelphiatheatrecompany.org
Notes: Est. 1974. Agent submissions or local writers only. 4 contemporary US plays/season (Sep–July). Production: cast limit 8. Response: an e-letter of acknowledgement only; 6 months to 1 year. No phone calls, please.
Agent Only: No
Submission Materials: see website
Preferred Genre: Plays (No Musicals)
Preferred Length: Full-length
Submission Fee: No

Phoenix Arts Association Theatre [CA]
414 Mason St. #601
San Francisco, CA 94102
Linda Ayres-Frederick, Executive Artistic Director
Phone: (415) 336-1020
Fax: (415) 664-5001
www.phoenixtheatresf.org
Lbaf23@aol.com
Notes: Est. 1985. NOTE: Due to economics, we have taken a hiatus from receiving new scripts. Production: cast limit 7, unit set. Response: 6 weeks query, 6 months script.
Agent Only: No
Submission Materials: see website
Preferred Genre: Plays (No Musicals)
Submission Fee: No

Phoenix Theatre [IN]
749 N. Park Ave.
Indianapolis, IN 46202
Bryan Fonseca, Literary Manager
Phone: (317) 635-7529
www.phoenixtheatre.org
bfonseca@phoenixtheatre.org
Notes: Est. 1983. Production: cast limit 6. Response: 6 months.
Agent Only: Yes
Submission Materials: 10-pg sample, query letter, S.A.S.E., synopsis
Preferred Length: Any length
Submission Fee: No

Pier One Theatre
Box 894

Homer, AK 99603
Lance Petersen, Artistic Director
Phone: (907) 235-7333
Fax: (907) 235-7333
www.pieronetheatre.org
info@pieronetheatre.net
Notes: Est. 1973. Non-Equity community theater. Response: 6 months.
Agent Only: No
Submission Materials: full script, S.A.S.E.
Preferred Genre: Plays or Musicals
Preferred Length: Full-length
Submission Fee: No

Pillsbury House Theatre
3501 Chicago Ave. S.
Minneapolis, MN 55407
Phone: (612) 825-0459
Fax: (612) 827-5818
www.pillsburyhousetheatre.org
raymondn@pillsburyhousetheatre.org
Notes: Est. 1992. Submit by invitation only. Production: cast limit 10. Response: 5 months query, 6 months script.
Agent Only: Yes
Submission Materials: agent-only
Preferred Genre: Plays (No Musicals)
Preferred Length: Full-length
Submission Fee: No

Pioneer Theatre Company
300 South 1400 East, #205
Salt Lake City, UT 84112
Karen Azenberg, Artistic Director
Phone: (801) 581-6356
Fax: (801) 581-5472
www.pioneertheatre.org
karen.azenberg@PTC.utah.edu
Notes: Est. 1962. Response: 6 months.
Agent Only: Yes
Submission Materials: agent-only
Preferred Genre: All genres
Preferred Length: Full-length
Submission Fee: No

Pittsburgh Public Theater
621 Penn Ave.
Pittsburgh, PA 15222
Phone: (412) 316-8200
Fax: (412) 316-8216
www.ppt.org
Notes: Est. 1975. Not accepting submissions at this time.
Agent Only: No
Submission Fee: No

Plan-B Theatre Company
138 W. 300 S.
Salt Lake City, UT 84101
Jerry Rapier, Producing Director
Phone: (801) 297-4200
www.planbtheatre.org
jerry@planbtheatre.org
Notes: Est. 1995. Submit script via email in PDF format. Focused on work by Utah-based playwrights (playwrights with ties to Utah will also be considered). Production: cast limit 5, minimal set. Response: 3 months.
Agent Only: No
Submission Materials: full script, S.A.S.E.
Preferred Genre: Plays (No Musicals)
Preferred Length: 90 min./no intermission
Special interest: LGBT
Submission Fee: No

Play With Your Food
PO Box 2161
Westport, CT 06880
Phone: (203) 247-4083
www.jibproductions.org
carole@jibproductions.org
Notes: Looking for first rate one-act plays for Connecticut's popular lunchtime play-reading series, Play With Your Food.
Agent Only: No
Submission Materials: full script
Preferred Genre: Plays (No Musicals)
Preferred Length: One-Act
Submission Fee: No

Playhouse on the Square
51 S. Cooper St.
Memphis, TN 38104
Phone: (901) 725-0776
www.playhouseonthesquare.org
info@playhouseonthesquare.org
Notes: Est. 1968. No longer accepting submissions.
Agent Only: No
Submission Fee: No

Playmakers of Baton Rouge
Reilly Theatre Tower Drive, LSU
Baton Rouge, LA 70803
Karli Henderson
Phone: (225) 578-6996
www.playmakers.net
karli@playmakers.net
Agent Only: No
Submission Fee: No

Plays for Young Audiences
c/o The Children's Theatre Co,
2400 3rd Ave S
Minneapolis, MN 55404
Phone: (612) 872-5108
Fax: (612) 874-8119
www.playsforyoungaudiences.org
mwright@playsforyoungaudiences.org
Agent Only: No
Special interest: Theatre for Young Audiences
Submission Fee: No

Playwrights Horizons
416 W. 42nd St.
New York, NY 10036
Adam Greenfield, Director, New Play Development
Phone: (212) 564-1235
Fax: (212) 594-0926
www.playwrightshorizons.org
literary@playwrightshorizons.org
Notes: Est. 1971. Offering 6 productions/season and numerous readings to new American voices. See website for material preferences. Production: cast limit 10. Response: 6 months for plays; 9 months for musicals. Hard copy, full manuscripts only. No synopses, samples, or electronic submissions.
Agent Only: No
Submission Materials: audio CD, bio, full script, S.A.S.E.
Preferred Genre: Plays or Musicals
Preferred Length: Full-length
Submission Fee: No

Playwrights Theatre of New Jersey
Box 1295
Madison, NJ 07940
Phone: (973) 514-1787
Fax: (973) 514-2060
www.ptnj.org
jpietrowski@ptnj.org
Notes: Est. 1986. Works accepted through New Play Development Program. Production: ages 10 and above; casts up to 6. Response: 1 year.
Agent Only: No
Submission Materials: 10-pg sample, S.A.S.E., synopsis
Preferred Genre: Plays (No Musicals)
Preferred Length: Full-length
Submission Fee: No

Playwrights/Actors Contemporary Theatre (PACT)
105 W. 13th St., #5-G
New York, NY 10011
Juel Wiese, Managing Director
Phone: (212) 242-5888
Fax: (212) 242-5888
juelwiese@msn.com
Notes: Production: cast of up to 8, unit set. Query letter or E-Mail only.
Agent Only: No
Preferred Genre: Drama
Preferred Length: Full-length & 10-min.
Special interest: American
Submission Fee: No

Polarity Ensemble Theatre
135 Asbury Ave.
Evanston, IL 60202
Phone: (847) 475-1139
www.petheatre.com
richard@petheatre.com
Notes: Visit our website and register on our auditions list to be notified when we accept/ read scripts. We work exclusively with Chicago-Area playwrights.
Agent Only: No
Submission Materials: full script
Preferred Genre: Plays or Musicals
Preferred Length: Full-length
Submission Fee: No

Poplar Pike Playhouse (PPP)
7653 Old Poplar Pike
Germantown, TN 38138
Frank Bluestein, Director
Phone: (901) 755-7775
Fax: (901) 755-6951
www.ppp.org
PopPikePlayhouse@aol.com
Notes: Est. 1976. Occasionally produce original work. Production: ages 14–19, full orchestra. Response: 3 months.
Agent Only: No
Submission Materials: full script, S.A.S.E.
Preferred Genre: Plays or Musicals
Preferred Length: Any length
Special interest: Theatre for Young Audiences
Submission Fee: No

Porchlight Music Theatre
4200 W. Diversey Ave.
Chicago, IL 60639
Phone: (773) 777-9884
Fax: (773) 777-9886
www.porchlightmusictheatre.org
info@porchlightmusictheatre.org
Notes: Est. 1994. Response: 6 months.
Agent Only: No
Submission Materials: audio CD, bio, S.A.S.E., synopsis
Preferred Genre: Musical theatre
Preferred Length: Full-length
Submission Fee: No

Portland Center Stage [OR]
128 NW 11th Ave.
Portland, OR 97209
Phone: (503) 445-3793
Fax: (503) 445-3721
www.pcs.org
kelseyt@pcs.org
Notes: Est. 1988. At this time, not accepting unsolicited script submission for general season consideration. If you are interested in submitting a script for JAW: A Playwrights Festival, visit the JAW Script Submission page: http://www.pcs.org/jaw/#scripts
Agent Only: No
Submission Materials: 10-pg sample, query letter, resume
Preferred Genre: All genres
Preferred Length: Full-length
Submission Fee: No

Portland Stage Company [ME]
PO Box 1458
Portland, ME 04104
Phone: (207) 774-1043
Fax: (207) 774-0576
www.portlandstage.com
dburson@portlandstage.com
Notes: Est. 1974. Response: 2 months query, 6 months script.
Agent Only: Yes
Submission Materials: full script, synopsis
Preferred Genre: Plays (No Musicals)
Preferred Length: Full-length
Submission Fee: No
Deadline(s): Rolling

Prairie Fire Children's Theatre
PO Box 82
Barrett, MN 56311
Phone: (320) 528-2596
www.prairiefirechildrenstheatre.com
prairiefirechildrenstheatre@gmail.com
Agent Only: No

Special interest: Theatre for Young Audiences
Submission Fee: No

Pregones Theater
571-575 Walton Ave.
Bronx, NY 10451
Rosalba Rolon, Artistic Director
Phone: (718) 585-1202
Fax: (718) 585-1608
www.pregones.org
rrolon@pregones.org
Notes: Create and perform original musical theatre and plays rooted in Puerto Rican/Latino cultures.
Agent Only: No
Submission Materials: 10-pg sample
Special interest: Latino
Submission Fee: No

Premiere Stages at Kean University
Hutchinson Hall, 1000 Morris Ave.,
Union, NJ 07083
Clare Drobot, Producing Associate
Phone: (908) 737-4092
Fax: (908) 737-4636
www.kean.edu/premierestages
premiere@kean.edu
Agent Only: No
Submission Materials: see website
Submission Fee: No

Present Company
520 Eighth Ave., #311
New York, NY 10018
Phone: (212) 279-4488
Fax: (212) 279-4466
www.fringenyc.org
info@presentcompany.org
Notes: Creators and producers of the New York International Fringe Festival featuring 200+ shows every August in New York City.
Agent Only: No
Submission Materials: see website
Preferred Genre: All genres
Preferred Length: Any length
Submission Fee: Yes
Deadline(s): See website

Primary Stages
307 W. 38th St, #1510
New York, NY 10018
Phone: (212) 840-9705
Fax: (212) 840-9725
www.primarystages.org

info@primarystages.org
Notes: Est. 1984. Founded to produce new plays and develop playwrights. Response: 1 year.
Agent Only: Yes
Submission Materials: agent-only
Preferred Genre: All genres
Preferred Length: Full-length
Submission Fee: No

Prime Stage Theatre
Box 99446
Pittsburgh, PA 15233
Wayne Brinda, Artistic Director
Phone: (724) 773-0700
www.primestage.com
wbrinda@primestage.com
Notes: Literature based youth and adult theatre. Production: age 12–senior citizen
Agent Only: No
Submission Materials: 30-pg sample, query letter, S.A.S.E., synopsis
Preferred Genre: Adaptation
Preferred Length: Full-length
Special interest: Theatre for Young Audiences
Submission Fee: No

Public Theater [NY]
425 Lafayette St.
New York, NY 10003
Liz Frankel, Literary Manager
Phone: (212) 539-8530
Fax: (212) 539-8505
www.publictheater.org
submissions@publictheatre.org
Notes: Est. 1954. Response: 6 months.
Agent Only: No
Submission Materials: 10-pg sample, query letter, synopsis
Preferred Genre: Plays or Musicals
Preferred Length: Full-length
Submission Fee: No

Puerto Rican Traveling Theatre (PRTT)
304 W. 47th St.
New York, NY 10036
Miriam Colon Valle, Artistic Director
Phone: (212) 354-1293
Fax: (212) 307-6769
www.prtt.org
miriam@prtt.org
Notes: Est. 1977. Present and produce truly bilingual professional theater. Offer artistic

development to emerging and established artists.
Agent Only: No
Special interest: Latino
Submission Fee: No

Pulse Ensemble Theatre
248 W 35th Street, 15th Fl.
New York, NY 10018
Alexa Kelly, Artistic Director
Phone: (212) 695-1596
Fax: (212) 594-4208
www.pulseensembletheatre.org
theatre@pulseensembletheatre.org
Notes: Est. 1989. Only developing new works in Playwrights' Lab. Response: up to 1 year.
Agent Only: No
Submission Materials: 10-pg sample, S.A.S.E., synopsis
Preferred Genre: Plays (No Musicals)
Preferred Length: Full-length
Submission Fee: No

Purple Rose Theatre Company
137 Park St.
Chelsea, MI 48118
Phone: (734) 433-7782
Fax: (734) 475-0802
www.purplerosetheatre.org
info@purplerosetheatre.org
Notes: Est. 1991. Prefer comedy. Must be unoptioned/unpublished/unproduced. Production: ages 18–80, cast of 2–10. Response: 8 months.
Agent Only: No
Submission Materials: 15-pg sample, character breakdown, S.A.S.E., synopsis
Preferred Genre: Plays (No Musicals)
Preferred Length: Full-length
Submission Fee: No

Queens Theatre in the Park
Box 520069
Flushing, NY 11352
Rob Urbinati, Director, New Play Development
Phone: (718) 760-0064
Fax: (718) 760-1972
www.queenstheatre.org
roburbinati@gmail.com
Notes: Est. 2001. New play development series. Production: cast limit 6. Response: 1 year.
Agent Only: No
Submission Materials: see website

Preferred Genre: All genres
Preferred Length: Full-length
Submission Fee: No

Rainbow Dinner Theatre
3065 Lincoln Hwy East
Box 56
Paradise, PA 17562
David DiSavino, Executive Producer
Phone: (717) 687-4300
Fax: (717) 687-8280
www.rainbowdinnertheatre.com
david@rainbowdinnertheatre.com
Notes: Est. 1984. Professional non-Equity dinner theater. Production: ages 18 and older, cast of 2–12, set limit 2. Response: 6 months.
Agent Only: No
Submission Materials: 10-pg sample, S.A.S.E., synopsis
Preferred Genre: Plays (No Musicals)
Preferred Length: Full-length
Submission Fee: No

Rattlestick Playwrights Theatre
244 Waverly Pl.
New York, NY 10014
Phone: (212) 627-2556
Fax: (630) 839-8352
www.rattlestick.org
info@rattlestick.org
Notes: Yearlong development program, culminating in annual spring Exposure Festival. Production: cast of up to 8.
Agent Only: No
Submission Materials: see website
Preferred Genre: All genres
Preferred Length: Full-length
Submission Fee: No

Raven Theatre New Play Workshop
6157 North Clark Street
Chicago, IL 60660
Susan Lieberman, Literary Manager
Phone: (773) 338-2177
Fax: (773) 338-6547
www.RavenTheatre.com
susan@RavenTheatre.com
Notes: Est. 1992. Annual New Play Workshop. Script must be previously unproduced.
Agent Only: No
Submission Materials: see website
Preferred Genre: No musicals or adaptations
Preferred Length: Full-length
Submission Fee: No
Deadline(s): See website

Red Bull Theater
Literary Submission
P.O. Box 250863
New York, NY 10025
Phone: (212) 414-5168
www.redbulltheater.com
info@redbulltheater.com
Notes: Est. 2003. Interested in new full-length plays and adaptations that relate to our mission of exploring Jacobean themes/heightened language. US mail only. Response: six months.
Agent Only: Yes
Submission Materials: see website
Preferred Genre: Plays or Musicals
Preferred Length: Any length
Submission Fee: No

Repertorio Espanol
138 E. 27th St.
New York, NY 10016
Robert Federico, Executive Director
Phone: (212) 225-9999
Fax: (212) 225-9085
www.repertorio.org
r.federico@repertorio.org
Notes: Est. 1968. Introduce the best of Latin American, Spanish, and Hispanic-American theatre in distinctive, quality productions, and bring theatre to a broad audience.
Agent Only: No
Submission Materials: see website
Preferred Length: Full-length
Special interest: Latino
Submission Fee: No

Rivendell Theatre Ensemble
5775 N Ridge Ave
#1
Chicago, IL 60660
Rachel Walshe, Literary Manager
Phone: (773) 334-7728
rivendelltheatre.org/
rachel@rivendelltheatre.net
Notes: Committed to cultivating the talents of women theatre artists and to seeking out innovative plays that explore the unique female experience in an intimate, salon environment. You may submit your play through a literary agent or accompanied by a letter of recommendation by a theater professional (i.e. an artistic director or literary manager at a professional theater). If neither of these apply to you, you may write a letter of inquiry and submit it, along with a brief synopsis and your resume.

Agent Only: No
Submission Materials: query letter, resume, synopsis
Special interest: Women's Interest
Submission Fee: No

Riverside Theatre [FL]
3250 Riverside Park Dr.
Vero Beach, FL 32963
Allen D. Cornell, Artistic Director
Phone: (772) 231-5860
Fax: (772) 234-5298
www.riversidetheatre.com
info@riversidetheatre.com
Notes: Est. 1985. Production: cast limit 10.
Agent Only: No
Submission Materials: query letter, synopsis
Preferred Genre: Plays or Musicals
Preferred Length: Full-length
Special interest: Theatre for Young Audiences
Submission Fee: No

Riverside Theatre [IA]
213 N. Gilbert St.
Iowa City, IA 52245
Jody Hovland, Artistic Director
Phone: (319) 887-1360
Fax: (319) 887-1362
www.riversidetheatre.org
artistic@riversidetheatre.org
Notes: Est. 1981. Open submissions for Riverside Theatre's annual monologue festival, Walking The Wire. Due to staff limitations, we unfortnately cannot accept unsolicited scripts directly from playwrights. Scripts may be submitted by agents & professional representatives as well as all NNPN member theatres. Some unsolicited work may be considered based on the strength of a professional recommendation. See website for annual deadline and complete guidelines.
Agent Only: Yes
Submission Materials: agent-only
Preferred Length: 10-min./10pgs.
Submission Fee: No

RoaN Productions
30-43 41st St.
Ste. 1
Astoria, NY 11103
C. Abeydeera, Literary Manager
Phone: (646) 415-8206
www.roanproductions.com
corina@roanproductions.com

Notes: RoaN Productions is dedicated in producing works with a strong feminine perspective in a collaborative environment, with non-traditional casting. Presently accepting submissions for reading series.
Agent Only: No
Submission Materials: see website
Preferred Length: Full-length
Special interest: Women's Interest
Submission Fee: No

Rosalind Productions
P.O. Box 480820
Los Angeles, CA 90048
Phone: (310) 422-1636
www.rosalindproductions.com
abigail@rosalindproductions.com
Notes: Rosalind Productions explores stories in which the female characters are as vital, complex and influential as the male characters.
Agent Only: No
Special interest: Women's Interest
Submission Fee: No

Round House Theatre
Box 30688
Bethesda, MD 20824
Phone: (240) 644-1099
Fax: (240) 644-1090
www.roundhousetheatre.org
productionstaff@roundhousetheatre.org
Notes: Est. 1978. Literary Works Project in Bethesda, and New Works Series in Silver Spring. Production: cast limit 8, piano only, unit set. Response: 2 months query, 1 year script.
Agent Only: No
Submission Materials: query letter
Preferred Genre: All genres
Preferred Length: Any length
Submission Fee: No

Royal Court Theatre
Sloane Sq.
London SW1W 8AS, United Kingdom
www.royalcourttheatre.com
infor@royalcourttheater.com
Notes: Est. 1956. Production/development for both international writers and young writers. See website for details. US mail material only.
Agent Only: No
Submission Materials: S.A.S.E., synopsis
Preferred Genre: All genres
Preferred Length: Full-length
Submission Fee: No

Salt Lake Acting Company
168 West 500 North
Salt Lake City, UT 84103
Phone: (801) 363-7522
Fax: (801) 532-8513
www.saltlakeactingcompany.org
andra@saltlakeactingcompany.org
Notes: Est. 1970. SLAC works with writers to workshop new pieces and produces new works (plays/musicals/adaptations).
Agent Only: No
Submission Materials: 20-pg sample, bio, query letter, synopsis
Preferred Genre: Plays or Musicals
Preferred Length: Any length
Submission Fee: No

San Diego Repertory Theatre
79 Horton Plz.
San Diego, CA 92101-6144
Phone: (619) 231-3586
Fax: (619) 235-0939
www.sdrep.org
arasbeary@sdrep.org
Notes: Est. 1976. We no longer accept unsolicited scripts from unrepresented writers. However, given our commitment to supporting new work, writers who reside in the Southern California area may submit a query letter that includes a current email contact and brief biography of your writing history, noting awards and production history, a paragraph about why your play is a good match for the San Diego Rep, a one-page synopsis of the play including number of cast, genre, and run-time for musicals, please also include a CD with sample songs from the score.
Agent Only: Yes
Submission Materials: full script
Preferred Genre: All genres
Preferred Length: Full-length
Submission Fee: No

Santa Monica Playhouse
1211 4th St.
Suite #201
Santa Monica, CA 90401
Cydne Moore, Dramaturg
Phone: (310) 394-9779
Fax: (310) 393-5573
www.santamonicaplayhouse.com
theatre@SantaMonicaPlayhouse.com
Notes: Est. 1960. Production: cast limit 10. Response: 9 months query, 12 months script.
Agent Only: No

Submission Materials: 10-pg sample, query letter, resume
Preferred Genre: Plays (No Musicals)
Preferred Length: Full-length
Submission Fee: No

Seacoast Repertory Theatre
125 Bow St.
Portsmouth, NH 03801
Phone: (603) 433-4793
Fax: (603) 431-7818
www.seacoastrep.org
craig@seacoastrep.org
Notes: Est. 1986. Offers 8 mainstage and 6 youth works each year. Submissions must be unoptioned. Response: 6 months.
Agent Only: No
Submission Materials: 10-pg sample, S.A.S.E., synopsis
Preferred Genre: All genres
Preferred Length: Any length
Special interest: Theatre for Young Audiences
Submission Fee: No

Seattle Children's Theatre
201 Thomas St.
Seattle, WA 98109
Phone: (206) 443-0807
Fax: (206) 443-0442
www.sct.org
info@sct.org
Notes: Est. 1975.
Agent Only: No
Special interest: Theatre for Young Audiences
Submission Fee: No

Seattle Jewish Theater Company
5225 50th Avenue NE, #203
Seattle, WA 98105
Phone: (212) 581-8655
www.seattlejewishtheater.com
seattlejewishtheatercompany@gmail.com
Agent Only: No
Submission Materials: 10-pg sample, query letter, S.A.S.E., synopsis
Preferred Genre: Plays (No Musicals)
Preferred Length: Any length
Special interest: Jewish
Submission Fee: No

Seattle Repertory Theatre
155 Mercer St.
Box 900923

Seattle, WA 98109
Phone: (206) 443-2210
Fax: (206) 443-2379
www.seattlerep.org
bradena@seattlerep.org
Notes: Est. 1963. 8–9 plays/year on 2 proscenium stages: 850-seat Bagley Wright; 300-seat Leo K. Staff: Response: 6 months.
Agent Only: No
Submission Materials: full script, S.A.S.E.
Preferred Genre: Plays (No Musicals)
Preferred Length: Any length
Submission Fee: No

Second Stage Theatre
305 W. 43rd St.
New York, NY 10036
Kyle Frisina, Director of Play Development
Phone: (212) 787-8302
Fax: (212) 397-7066
www.2st.com
kfrisina@2st.com
Notes: Est. 1979. 2 Off-Broadway theaters, 6 shows per season; work featuring heightened realism and sociopolitical issues.
Agent Only: Yes
Submission Materials: agent-only
Preferred Genre: Plays or Musicals
Preferred Length: Full-length
Submission Fee: No

Seventh Street Playhouse, LLC
PO Box 15414
Washington, DC 20003
Phone: (202) 544-6973
mysite.verizon.net/vzer9r4g/
seventhstreetplayhouse/index.html
aegallo2368@verizon.net
Notes: Email unpublished submissions only. Prior professional recommendations only.
Agent Only: No
Submission Materials: 10-pg sample, synopsis
Preferred Genre: Plays (No Musicals)
Preferred Length: Any length
Submission Fee: No

Shadowlight Productions
22 Chattanooga St.
San Francisco, CA 94114
Phone: (415) 648-4461
Fax: (415) 641-9734
www.shadowlight.org
info@shadowlight.org

Notes: Est. 1972. Production: cast limit 15.
Response: 1 month.
Agent Only: No
Submission Materials: see website
Preferred Genre: Plays (No Musicals)
Preferred Length: Full-length
Submission Fee: No

Shakespeare & Company
70 Kemble St.
Lenox, MA 01240
Phone: (413) 637-1199 Ext 111
Fax: (413) 637-4274
www.shakespeare.org
tsimotes@shakespeare.org
Notes: Est. 1978. Not accepting submissions at
this time. Production: cast of 2–8. Response:
3 months.
Agent Only: No
Submission Materials: 10-pg sample, query
letter, S.A.S.E., synopsis
Preferred Genre: Plays (No Musicals)
Preferred Length: Full-length
Submission Fee: No

Shakespeare Theatre Company
516 8th St. SE
Washington, DC 20003-2834
Phone: (202) 547-3230
Fax: (202) 547-0226
www.shakespearetheatre.org
afox@shakespearetheatre.org
Notes: Est. 1986. Classical theatre dedicated
to works of Shakespeare and other classical
writers in new translations and adaptations.
Agent Only: No
Submission Materials: query letter, S.A.S.E.
Preferred Genre: Plays (No Musicals)
Preferred Length: Full-length
Submission Fee: No

She Said Yes! Theatre
64 Quidi Vidi Rd
St. John, NL A1A 1C1, Canada
Phone: (709) 739-0702
www.shesaidyestheatre.ca
sara@shesaidyestheatre.ca
Notes: She Said Yes! is an unincorporated,
non-profit, artist-driven feminist theatre company based in St. John's, Newfoundland.
She Said Yes! endeavours to push the artistic
boundaries of its artists by introducing challenging, well-developed scripts, new methods
of creation and new acting techniques to the
creative community of St. John's. Through

developmental programming such as the Mail-
Order Dramaturgy program and the Women's
Work Festival, we also aim to provide a secure
and open environment for female playwrights
to hone and perfect their works in progress.
Agent Only: No
Submission Materials: see website
Special interest: Women's Interest
Submission Fee: No

Shotgun Productions Inc.
165 E. 35 St., #7-J
New York, NY 10016
Patricia Klausner, Managing Director
Phone: (212) 689-2322
Fax: (212) 689-2322
www.shotgunproductions.org
literary@shotgun-productions.org
Notes: Est. 1989. 3-step development, includes
staged readings, workshops and full pro-
ductions for unoptioned/unproduced work.
Response: 1 year.
Agent Only: No
Submission Materials: query letter, synopsis
Preferred Genre: Plays (No Musicals)
Preferred Length: Full-length
Submission Fee: No

Signature Theatre Company [NY]
630 9th Ave., #1106
New York, NY 10036
Phone: (212) 967-1913
Fax: (212) 967-2957
www.signaturetheatre.org
kbowen@signaturetheatre.org
Notes: Est. 1990. Premieres and revivals pro-
duced in a season of work by current and past
playwrights in residence.
Agent Only: Yes
Submission Materials: see website
Submission Fee: No

SignStage
11635 Euclid Ave.
Cleveland, OH 44106
William Morgan, Artistic Manager/Producer
Phone: (216) 325-7559
Fax: (216) 325-7659
www.chsc.org
wmorgan@chsc.org
Notes: Est. 1975. In-school residencies, edu-
cational performances about deaf awareness.
Response only if interested.
Agent Only: No
Submission Materials: S.A.S.E., synopsis

Special interest: Deaf
Submission Fee: No

Silk Road Theatre Project
680 S. Federal
Ste 301
Chicago, IL 60605
Phone: (312) 857-1234 Ext 202
Fax: (312) 577-0849
www.srtp.org
jamil@srtp.org
Notes: We are currently not accepting unsolicited scripts. We accept full-length scripts only by US mail. Work must be from playwrights and about protagonists of Asian, MIddle Eastern, and Mediterranean descent.
Agent Only: No
Submission Materials: 15-pg sample, query letter, synopsis
Preferred Genre: Plays (No Musicals)
Preferred Length: One-Act
Special interest: Multi-Ethnic
Submission Fee: No

Six Figures Theatre Company
Box 88, Planetarium Sta.
New York, NY 10024
Phone: (212) 946-1737
www.sixfigures.com
info@sixfigures.com
Notes: Not accepting submissions at this time.
Agent Only: No
Submission Materials: see website
Preferred Genre: Musical theatre
Preferred Length: Full-length
Submission Fee: No

Society Hill Playhouse
507 S. 8th St.
Philadelphia, PA 19147
Deen Kogan
Phone: (215) 923-0210
Fax: (215) 923-1789
www.societyhillplayhouse.org
shp@erols.com
Notes: Submit by US mail only. Production: cast of up to 8. Response: 3 months.
Agent Only: No
Submission Materials: query letter, S.A.S.E.
Preferred Genre: Plays or Musicals
Preferred Length: Full-length
Submission Fee: No

SoHo Repertory Theatre Inc.
401 Broadway, Suite 300
New York, NY 10013
Phone: (212) 941-8632
Fax: (212) 941-7148
www.sohorep.org
sohorep@sohorep.org
Notes: Est. 1975.
Agent Only: No
Submission Materials: see website
Preferred Genre: All genres
Preferred Length: Any length
Submission Fee: No

South Camden Theatre Company
Waterfront South Theatre
400 Jasper Street
Camden, NJ 08104
Joseph M. Paprzycki, Artistic Director
Phone: (856) 409-0365
www.southcamdentheatre.org
info@southcamdentheatre.org
Notes: Est. 2005. No unsolicited material. The South Camden Theatre Company is a nonprofit organization dedicated to helping revitalize the City of Camden, New Jersey by producing meaningful, professional theater in the City's Waterfront South District. We are here to serve the community; its adults, children, and we exist to provide hope for the rebirth of our city, while providing a voice and stage for those who live, work and dream here.
Agent Only: Yes
Submission Fee: No

South Coast Repertory Theatre
PO Box 2197
Costa Mesa, CA 92628
Kimberly Colburn, Assistant Literary Manager
Phone: (714) 708-5500
Fax: (714) 545-0391
www.scr.org
kimberly@scr.org
Notes: Est. 1964. Mainstage programming, family programming, reading series, playwrights new work fest. Response: 2 months query; 6 months script.
Agent Only: No
Submission Materials: 10-pg sample, query letter, S.A.S.E., synopsis
Preferred Genre: Plays or Musicals
Preferred Length: Full-length
Special interest: Theatre for Young Audiences
Submission Fee: No

Stage 773
1225 W. Belmont Ave.
Chicago, IL 60657
Phone: (773) 929-7367
Fax: (773) 327-1404
www.stage773.com
info@stage773.com
Agent Only: No
Submission Materials: see website
Submission Fee: No

Stage One: The Louisville Children's Theater
323 W. Broadway
Suite #609
Louisville, KY 40202
Phone: (502) 498-2436
Fax: (502) 588-4344
www.stageone.org
stageone@stageone.org
Notes: Est. 1946. Classic and contemporary tales of childhood with strong social and emotional content. Production: cast limit 12, touring set. Response: 3 months.
Agent Only: No
Submission Materials: 10-pg sample, query letter
Preferred Genre: Plays or Musicals
Preferred Length: Any length
Special interest: Theatre for Young Audiences
Submission Fee: No

Stages Repertory Theatre [TX]
3201 Allen Pkwy., #101
Houston, TX 77019
Phone: (713) 527-0220
Fax: (713) 527-8669
www.stagestheatre.com
Notes: Est. 1978. Production cast limit: 6. Response: 9 months.
Agent Only: No
Submission Materials: full script
Preferred Genre: Plays (No Musicals)
Preferred Length: Full-length
Submission Fee: No

Stages Theatre Company [MN]
1111 Main St.
Hopkins, MN 55343
Phone: (952) 979-1120
Fax: (952) 979-1124
www.stagestheatre.org
brow@stagestheatre.org

Notes: Est. 1984. Material must be 60–70 min. Production: ages 10–21 in primary roles. Response: 3 months.
Agent Only: No
Submission Materials: full script, query letter, S.A.S.E., synopsis
Preferred Genre: Plays (No Musicals)
Preferred Length: One-Act
Special interest: Theatre for Young Audiences
Submission Fee: No

Stageworks/Hudson [NY]
41-A Cross St.
Hudson, NY 12534
Phone: (518) 828-7843
Fax: (518) 828-4026
www.stageworkstheatre.org
contact@stageworkstheater.org
Notes: Est. 1993. Production: cast limit 8, unit set, no fly. Response: 8 months.
Agent Only: No
Submission Materials: query letter, synopsis
Preferred Genre: Adaptation
Preferred Length: Full-length
Submission Fee: No

Statement Productions
Box 496
Kittredge, CO 80457
Phone: (303) 670-8397
Fax: (303) 670-1897
freerobbie@aol.com
Notes: Not accepting work at this time. Usually, productions mostly of 2-women plays. Production: age 30–50, cast of up to 10. Response: 90 days.
Agent Only: No
Submission Materials: full script, S.A.S.E.
Preferred Genre: Musical theatre
Preferred Length: Any length
Submission Fee: No

Steppenwolf Theatre Company
758 W. North Ave., 4th Fl.
Chicago, IL 60610
Phone: (312) 335-1888
Fax: (312) 335-0808
www.steppenwolf.org
acarter@steppenwolf.org
Notes: Est. 1976. Actor's collective performing in three spaces. Production: cast limit 10. Response: 6–8 months.
Agent Only: No

Submission Materials: 10-pg sample, query letter, resume, synopsis
Preferred Genre: Plays (No Musicals)
Preferred Length: Full-length
Submission Fee: No

Steppingstone Theatre
55 Victoria Street N
Saint Paul, MN 55104
Phone: (651) 225-9265
Fax: (651) 225-1225
www.steppingstonetheatre.org
info@steppingstonetheatre.org
Agent Only: No
Submission Fee: No

Strand Theater Company
1823 North Charles
Baltimore, MD 21201
Phone: (443) 874-4917
www.strand-theater.org
info@strand-theatre.org
Notes: The Strand accepts new play submissions year round! We need new and interesting works to wow Baltimore. We like plays that use magical realism, tell stories about real people, and focus on relevant issues. We love plays by women and want to tell their stories.
Agent Only: No
Special interest: Women's Interest
Submission Fee: No

Sundance Institute Theatre
180 Varick St, Suite 1330
New York, NY 10014
Christopher Hibma, Associate Director
Phone: (646) 822-9563
Fax: (310) 360-1975
www.sundance.org/programs/theatre
theatre@sundance.org
Notes: Est. 2003. Equity Special Agreement. 2-week developmental workshop focusing on musical theater and ensemble-created work. Assistance: stipend, room/board, travel. Frequency: annual. By invitation only.
Agent Only: No
Submission Fee: No

Sundog Theatre
Box 10183
Staten Island, NY 10301
Susan Fenley, Artistic Director
Phone: (718) 816-5453
www.SundogTheatre.org
info@sundogtheatre.org

Notes: Ferry Plays: looking for six 10–25 minute unproduced/unoptioned plays with Staten Island Ferry as setting. Full length work: cast of 2–10, orchestra limit 4, minimal set.
Agent Only: No
Submission Materials: see website
Preferred Genre: Plays or Musicals
Preferred Length: Any length
Submission Fee: No
Deadline(s): None for full length works; December 1 for Ferry Plays

Sweetwood Productions
3406 Riva Ridge Rd.
Austin, TX 78746
Pat Hazell, Chief Creative Officer
Phone: (512) 383-9498
Fax: (512) 383-1680
www.sweetwoodproductions.com
pat@sweetwoodproductions.com
Notes: Not accepting submissions at this time.
Agent Only: No
Preferred Genre: Comedy
Preferred Length: Full-length
Submission Fee: No

Synchronicity Performance Group
Box 6012
Atlanta, GA 31107
Phone: (404) 523-1009
Fax: (404) 325-5168
www.synchrotheatre.com
info@synchrotheatre.com
Notes: Est. 1997. Dedicated to strong women characters, scripts with depth, meaning and social content and powerful stories. Production: cast limit 12, no fly. Response only if interested.
Agent Only: No
Submission Materials: 10-pg sample, query letter, S.A.S.E., synopsis
Preferred Genre: Plays (No Musicals)
Preferred Length: Full-length
Submission Fee: No

Syracuse Stage
820 E. Genesee St.
Syracuse, NY 13210
Phone: (315) 443-4008
Fax: (315) 443-9846
www.syracusestage.org
kebass@syr.edu
Notes: Est. 1974. Production: small cast. Syracuse Stage is not accepting usolicited scripts at this time.

Agent Only: Yes
Submission Materials: agent-only
Preferred Genre: Plays (No Musicals)
Preferred Length: Full-length
Submission Fee: No

TADA! Youth Theater
15 W 28th St, Fl. 3
New York, NY 10001
Phone: (212) 252-1619
Fax: (212) 252-8763
www.tadatheater.com
jgreer@tadatheater.com
Notes: Est. 1984. Production: teenage cast
(limit 2 adults). Response: 6 months.
Agent Only: No
Submission Materials: see website
Preferred Genre: Musical theatre
Preferred Length: Full-length
Special interest: Theatre for Young
Audiences
Submission Fee: No

Teatro Circulo
65 East 4th Street
New York, NY 10003
Jose Oliveras, Artistic Director
Phone: (212) 505-1808
Fax: (212) 505-1806
www.teatrocirculo.org
joliveras@teatrocirculo.org
Notes: Illustrate works of Spanish and Latin
American playwrights.
Agent Only: No
Special interest: Latino
Submission Fee: No

Teatro Dallas
1331 Record Crossing Rd.
Dallas, TX 75235
Cora Cordona, Artistic Director
Phone: (214) 689-6492
Fax: (214) 670-3243
www.teatrodallas.org
teatro@airmail.net
Notes: Est. 1985. Work (in English or Spanish)
about Latino issues; priority given to Latino or
Iberian playwrights. US mail. Production: cast
limit 6, unit set. Response if interested.
Agent Only: No
Submission Materials: query letter, S.A.S.E.,
synopsis
Preferred Genre: Plays (No Musicals)
Preferred Length: Any length
Special interest: Latino

Submission Fee: Yes

**Teatro Latea Latin American Theater
Experiment & Associates**
Clemente Soto Velez Cultural & Education
Center
107 Suffolk St.
New York, NY 10002
Nelson Landrieu, Executive Director
Phone: (212) 529-1948
Fax: (212) 529-7362
www.teatrolatea.com
nelson@teatrolatea.com
Notes: Est. 1982. Provide opportunities to
New York's emerging and professional artists.
Agent Only: No
Special interest: Latino
Submission Fee: No

Teatro SEA
Clemente Soto Velez Cultural & Education
Center
107 Suffolk Street, 2nd floor
New York, NY 10002
Manuel Moran, Founder, CEO & Artistic
Director
Phone: (212) 529-1545
Fax: (212) 529-1567
www.teatrosea.org
mmoran@sea-ny.org
Notes: Gives a voice to young people through
theater and the arts, facilitates learning, pro-
vides training and motivates and challenges
young people to stay in school. Also special-
izes in puppeteering and works for children.
Agent Only: No
Submission Fee: No

Teatro Vista
3712 N Broadway
#275
Chicago, IL 60613
Phone: (312) 666-4659
Fax: (312) 666-4659
www.teatrovista.org
info@teatrovista.org
Notes: We focus on works by, about or for
Latinos.
Agent Only: No
Submission Materials: character breakdown,
synopsis
Preferred Genre: Plays or Musicals
Preferred Length: Full-length
Special interest: Latino
Submission Fee: No

Tectonic Theater Project
204 W 84th St
New York, NY 10024
Phone: (212) 579-6111
Fax: (212) 579-6112
www.tectonictheaterproject.org
literary@tectonictheaterproject.org
Notes: Est. 1992. Lab led by Moises Kaufman.
Response: 1 month.
Agent Only: No
Submission Materials: full script, S.A.S.E.,
synopsis
Preferred Genre: All genres
Preferred Length: Full-length
Submission Fee: No

Ten Grand Productions
123 E 24th Street
New York, NY 10010
Phone: (212) 253-2058
Fax: (917) 591-9398
jhewitt@tengrand.org
Notes: Est. 2003.
Agent Only: No
Submission Materials: 20-pg sample,
S.A.S.E.
Preferred Genre: Drama
Preferred Length: Full-length
Submission Fee: No

Tennessee Repertory Theatre
161 Rains Ave.
Nashville, TN 37203
Phone: (615) 244-4878
Fax: (615) 782-4001
www.tennesseerep.org
represervations@gmail.com
Notes: Est. 1985. Production: small cast, small
orchestra. Response: 1 year.
Agent Only: No
Submission Materials: see website
Preferred Genre: Plays or Musicals
Preferred Length: Full-length
Submission Fee: No

Tennessee Women's Theatre Project
Z. Alexander Looby Theatre
2301 Rosa L. Parks Blvd
Nashville, TN 37228
Phone: (615) 681-7220
www.twtp.org
maryanna@twtp.org
Notes: Giving voice to women through theater
arts.

Agent Only: No
Submission Materials: see website
Special interest: Women's Interest
Submission Fee: No

Thalia Spanish Theatre
41-17 Greenpoint Ave.
Sunnyside, NY 11104
Angel Gil Orrios, Artistic/Executive Director
Phone: (718) 729-3880
www.thaliatheatre.org
agil@thaliatheatre.org
Notes: Est. 1977. First and only bilingual
Hispanic theatre in Queens. Unique produc-
tions of plays, musicals and dance of Spanish
and Latin American culture.
Agent Only: No
Special interest: Latino
Submission Fee: No

The PlayGround Theatre
9806 NE 2nd Ave
Miami Shores, FL 33138
Elaiza Irizarry, Executive Director
Phone: (305) 751-9550
Fax: (605) 751-9556
www.theplaygroundtheatre.com
elaiza@theplaygroundtheatre.com
Agent Only: No
Submission Fee: No

Theater 2020, Inc.
Theater 2020, Inc.
57 Montague Street, Suite 7-I
New York, NY 11201
Judith Jarosz, Producing Artistic Director
www.theater2020.com
theater2020@gmail.com
Notes: We prefer shows with casts with 10 or
under roles (doubling parts is fine) and that
require one unit set, or sets that can be suggested with limited set pieces and props. As
part of our mission to create more opportunities for women in the arts, the cast must contain equal number of parts for men and women
or more for women!
Agent Only: No
Submission Materials: character breakdown,
synopsis
Preferred Genre: All genres
Preferred Length: Any length
Special interest: Women's Interest
Submission Fee: No
Deadline(s): Ongoing

Theater at Monmouth
Box 385
Monmouth, ME 04259
Phone: (207) 933-2952
Fax: (207) 933-2952
www.theateratmonmouth.org
TAMOffice@TheaterAtMonmouth.org
Notes: Est. 1970. Only adaptations of popular classics for adults and children. Response: 2 months.
Agent Only: No
Submission Materials: query letter, synopsis
Preferred Genre: Plays (No Musicals)
Preferred Length: Any length
Special interest: Theatre for Young Audiences
Submission Fee: No

Theater Breaking Through Barriers
306 W. 18th St. #3A
New York, NY 10011
Ike Schambelan, Artistic Director
Phone: (212) 243-4337
Fax: (212) 243-4337
www.tbtb.org
ischambelan@nyc.rr.com
Notes: Est. 1979. Work must be about disability or by a disabled writer. Production: cast of 1–6. Either US Mail or Electronic submissions are accepted. Response: 2 months.
Agent Only: No
Submission Materials: full script, S.A.S.E.
Preferred Genre: All genres
Preferred Length: Any length
Special interest: Disabled
Submission Fee: No

Theater for the New City (TFNC)
155 1st Ave.
New York, NY 10003
Phone: (212) 254-1109
Fax: (212) 979-6570
www.theaterforthenewcity.net
crystalfield@theaterforthenewcity.net
Notes: Est. 1970. Experimental new works.
Agent Only: No
Submission Materials: 10-pg sample, S.A.S.E., synopsis
Preferred Genre: Experimental
Preferred Length: Any length
Submission Fee: No

Theater IV
114 Broad St.
Richmond, VA 23220
Phone: (804) 783-1688
www.theatreiv.org
TheatreIVandBarksdale@gmail.com
Notes: Est. 1975. Fairy tales, folk tales, fables, history, African American history, safety, outreach, science. Production: cast of 3–5, touring set. Audience: Grades K–12. Response: 2 months query, 2 years script.
Agent Only: No
Submission Materials: query letter, synopsis
Preferred Genre: Plays or Musicals
Preferred Length: One-Act
Special interest: Theatre for Young Audiences
Submission Fee: No

Theater J
1529 16th St. NW
Washington, DC 20036
Phone: (202) 777-3228
Fax: (202) 518-9421
www.theaterj.org
shirleys@washingtondcjcc.org
Notes: Est. 1991. Offers readings, workshops, and productions of work that celebrates the distinctive urban voice and social vision of the Jewish culture. Response: 6 months.
Agent Only: No
Submission Materials: 10-pg sample, synopsis
Preferred Genre: Plays or Musicals
Preferred Length: Full-length
Submission Fee: No

Theatre at the Center / Lawrence Arts Center
940 New Hampshire St.
Lawrence, KS 66044
Phone: (785) 843-2787
Fax: (785) 843-6629
www.lawrenceartscenter.com
ricaverill@lawrenceartscenter.org
Notes: Est. 1973. Submit by email. Production: cast limit 6 adults or 30 youth. Response: 6 weeks query, 3 months script.
Agent Only: No
Submission Materials: 10-pg sample, synopsis
Preferred Genre: Plays or Musicals
Preferred Length: Full-length
Special interest: Theatre for Young Audiences
Submission Fee: No

Theatre for a New Audience
154 Christopher St. #3-D
New York, NY 10014
Phone: (212) 229-2819
Fax: (212) 229-2911
www.tfana.org
info@tfana.org
Agent Only: No
Submission Materials: see website
Submission Fee: No

Theatre of Yugen
2840 Mariposa St.
San Francisco, CA 94110
Jubilith Moore, Artistic Director
Phone: (415) 621-0507
Fax: (415) 621-0223
www.theatreofyugen.org
info@theatreofyugen.org
Notes: Est. 1978. Traditional and new works
of East-West fusion primarily based on Noh
and Kyogen. Our plays tend to incorporate
music and dance and as such we prefer short
poetic scripts with minimal dialogue.
Agent Only: No
Submission Materials: query letter, S.A.S.E.
Preferred Genre: Experimental
Preferred Length: One-Act
Submission Fee: No

Theatre Rhinoceros
1360 Mission St. Ste #200
San Francisco, CA 94103
Phone: (415) 552-4100
Fax: (415) 552-2615
www.therhino.org
info@therhino.org
Notes: Est. 1977. Response: 6 months
Agent Only: Yes
Submission Materials: agent-only
Preferred Genre: Plays or Musicals
Preferred Length: Full-length
Special interest: LGBT
Submission Fee: No

Theatre Three [NY]
Box 512/412 Main St.
Port Jefferson, NY 11777
Jeffrey Sanzel, Executive Director
Phone: (631) 928-9202
Fax: (631) 928-9120
www.theatrethree.com
scrooooge@aol.com

Notes: Est. 1969. Theatre Three Production
Inc. Each season, festival presents 5 to 6 world
premieres on the second stage.
Agent Only: No
Submission Materials: see website
Preferred Genre: All genres
Submission Fee: No

Theatre Unbound
P.O. Box 6134
Minneapolis, MN 55406
Phone: (612) 721-1186
www.theatreunbound.com
ntallen@theatreunbound.com
Notes: Since 1999, Theatre Unbound has been
a force for creating live theatre wholly and
unabashedly about the lives of women. Theatre
written by women, directed by women, with
challenging, engaging roles for women.
Unleashing the energy of great female artists
working together.
Agent Only: No
Submission Materials: see website
Special interest: Women's Interest
Submission Fee: No

Theatreworks/USA [NY]
151 W. 26th St., Fl. 7
New York, NY 10001
Phone: (212) 647-1100
Fax: (212) 924-5377
www.theatreworksusa.org
info@theatreworksusa.org
Notes: Est. 1961. Production: age 20–50, cast
of up to 6, piano only, touring set.
Agent Only: Yes
Submission Materials: agent-only
Preferred Genre: All genres
Preferred Length: Full-length
Special interest: Theatre for Young
Audiences
Submission Fee: No

Thunderclap Productions
5248 Arboles Drive
Houston, TX 77035
Phone: (281) 954-4399
www.thunderclapproductions.com
info@thunderclapproductions.com
Notes: Est. 2011. Dedicated to developing and
performing new and underrepresented works
of theatre.No children's or liturgical plays.
Please see website for further details. In addition to our rolling call, we often post specific
calls for submissions on our site. Join our

writers and/or composers mailing lists to stay informed.
Agent Only: No
Submission Materials: see website
Preferred Genre: Plays or Musicals
Preferred Length: Any length
Submission Fee: No

Touchstone Theatre
321 E. 4th St.
Bethlehem, PA 18015
James P. Jordan, Producing Director
Phone: (610) 867-1689
www.touchstone.org
jp@touchstone.org
Notes: Est. 1981. We only accept proposals for collaborative work with movement-based company ensemble. Response: 8 months.
Agent Only: No
Submission Materials: query letter
Submission Fee: No

Transport Group
520 Eighth Ave.
Ste. 305
New York, NY 10018
Jack Cummings, Artistic Director
Phone: (212) 564-0333
Fax: (212) 564-0331
www.transportgroup.org
info@transportgroup.org
Agent Only: No
Submission Materials: see website
Preferred Genre: All genres
Preferred Length: Full-length
Special interest: American
Submission Fee: No

TriArts at the Sharon Playhouse
Box 1187
Sharon, CT 06069
Phone: (860) 364-7469
Fax: (860) 364-8043
www.triarts.net
info@triarts.net
Notes: Est. 1989. Submit between January–July. Production: no fly. Response: 2 months query, 6 months.
Agent Only: No
Submission Materials: audio CD, query letter, synopsis
Preferred Genre: Plays or Musicals
Preferred Length: Any length
Submission Fee: No

Deadline(s): January–July is best submission period

Trinity Repertory Company
201 Washington St.
Providence, RI 02903
Tyler Dobrowsky, Associate Artistic Director
Phone: (401) 351-4242
www.trinityrep.com
tdobrowsky@trinityrep.com
Notes: Trinity Rep is committed to the development and production of new theater works. Each season, we seek to produce at least one premiere production, as well as readings and workshops of plays in development. Our Mabel T. Woolley Literary Department reads and reviews hundreds of scripts, looking for new plays which support our aesthetic vision and our resident acting company. We are no longer accepting unsolicited scripts from playwrights without representation. Please see our website for further guidelines.
Agent Only: Yes
Submission Materials: 10-pg sample, query letter, synopsis
Preferred Genre: Plays (No Musicals)
Preferred Length: Full-length
Submission Fee: No

Trustus Theatre
Box 11721
Columbia, SC 29211
Sarah Hammond, Literary Manager
Phone: (803) 254-9732
Fax: (803) 771-9153
www.trustus.org
trustus@trustus.org
Notes: Est. 1985. See website
Agent Only: No
Submission Materials: see website
Preferred Genre: Plays (No Musicals)
Submission Fee: Yes
Deadline(s): See website

Turtle Shell Productions
300 W. 43rd St.
#403
New York, NY 10036
Phone: (646) 765-7670
www.turtleshellproductions.com
jcooper@TurtleShellProductions.com
Agent Only: No
Submission Materials: full script
Preferred Genre: All genres
Preferred Length: Any length

Submission Fee: No
Deadline(s): See website

Two River Theatre Company (TRTC)
21 Bridge Ave.
Red Bank, NJ 07701
Phone: (732) 345-1400
Fax: (732) 345-1414
www.trtc.org
info@trtc.org
Notes: Est. 1994. Does not accept unsolicited material.
Agent Only: Yes
Preferred Genre: Adaptation

Urban Stages
555 8th Ave. Room 1800
New York, NY 10018
Phone: (212) 421-1380
Fax: (212) 421-1387
www.urbanstages.org
urbanstage@aol.com
Notes: Production: cast size 5 or less, minimal sets. Response: 8 months. Submission: e-mailed submissions will not be accepted. ALL plays should be mailed.
Agent Only: No
Submission Materials: full script
Preferred Genre: Plays (No Musicals)
Preferred Length: Full-length
Submission Fee: No

Valley Youth Theatre (VYT)
807 N. 3rd St.
Phoenix, AZ 85004
Phone: (602) 253-8188 Ext 305
Fax: (602) 253-8282
www.vyt.com
bobb@vyt.com
Notes: Est. 1989. Response: 2 weeks query, 2 months script.
Agent Only: No
Submission Materials: audio CD, query letter, synopsis
Preferred Genre: Plays or Musicals
Preferred Length: Full-length
Special interest: Theatre for Young Audiences
Submission Fee: No

Venture Theatre (MT)
PO Box 112
Billings, MT 59103
www.venturetheatre.org/
venture@venturetheatre.org

Notes: See website for submission guidelines.
Agent Only: No
Submission Materials: full script, resume, synopsis
Preferred Genre: All genres
Preferred Length: One-Act
Submission Fee: Yes

Venus Theatre
The Venus Theatre Play Shack
21 C St
Laurel, MD 20707
Phone: (202) 236-4078
www.venustheatre.org
Notes: A women's theatre company that perform plays by talented women playwrights and employs talented female actors, directors, designers and others.
Agent Only: No
Submission Materials: see website
Special interest: Women's Interest
Submission Fee: No

Victory Gardens Theater
2433 N. Lincoln Ave.
Chicago, IL 60614
Aaron Carter, Literary Manager
Phone: (773) 549-5788
Fax: (773) 549-2779
www.victorygardens.org
acarter@victorygardens.org
Notes: Est. 1974. 5 productions/season.
Agent Only: No
Submission Materials: see website
Preferred Genre: All genres
Preferred Length: Full-length
Submission Fee: No
Deadline(s): agent submissions year-round

Victory Theatre Center
3326 W. Victory Blvd.
Burbank, CA 91505
Maria Gobetti, Artistic Director
Phone: (818) 841-4404
Fax: (818) 841-6328
www.thevictorytheatrecenter.org
thevictory@mindspring.com
Notes: Est. 1979. Includes 99-seat Big Victory and 50-seat Little Victory theaters. Production: unit set. Response: 1 year.
Agent Only: No
Submission Materials: full script, S.A.S.E.
Preferred Genre: Plays or Musicals
Preferred Length: Full-length
Submission Fee: No

Village Theatre
303 Front St. N.
Issaquah, WA 98027
Robb Hunt, Executive Producer
Phone: (425) 392-1942 Ext 113
Fax: (425) 391-3242
www.villagetheatre.org
rhunt@villagetheatre.org
Notes: Est. 1979. Readings, workshops and
productions of new musicals. Production: cast
limit 20. Response: 6 months.
Agent Only: No
Submission Materials: audio CD, full script,
S.A.S.E.
Preferred Genre: Musical theatre
Preferred Length: Full-length
Submission Fee: No

Vineyard Theatre
108 E. 15th St..
New York, NY 10003
Phone: (212) 353-3366
Fax: (212) 353-3803
www.vineyardtheatre.org
literary@vineyardtheatre.org
Notes: Est. 1981. Response: 1 year query.
Submissions not returned.
Agent Only: No
Submission Materials: 10-pg sample, audio
CD, query letter, resume, synopsis
Preferred Genre: All genres
Preferred Length: Full-length
Submission Fee: No

Virginia Stage Company (VSC)
Box 3770
Norfolk, VA 23514
Patrick Mullins, Associate Artistic Director
Phone: (757) 627-6988
Fax: (757) 628-5958
www.vastage.com
pmullins@vastage.com
Notes: Est. 1979. Production: cast limit 8.
Response: 1 month query, 6 months script.
Agent Only: No
Submission Materials: query letter, synopsis
Preferred Genre: All genres
Submission Fee: No

Vital Theatre Company
2162 Broadway, Fl. 4
New York, NY 10024
Karron Karr, General Manager
Phone: (212) 579-0528
Fax: (212) 579-0646

www.vitaltheatre.org
office@vitaltheatre.org
Notes: Not accepting unsolicited scripts at this
time.
Agent Only: Yes
Submission Fee: No

VS. Theatre Company
Box 2293
Los Angeles, CA 91610
Phone: (323) 816-2471
Fax: (323) 850-6045
www.vstheatre.org
info@vstheatre.org
Notes: Est. 2003. Production: cast limit 6.
Response: 6 months.
Agent Only: Yes
Submission Materials: agent-only
Preferred Genre: Plays (No Musicals)
Preferred Length: Full-length
Submission Fee: No

Walnut Street Theatre
825 Walnut St.
Philadelphia, PA 19103
Phone: (215) 574-3550
Fax: (215) 574-3598
www.walnutstreettheatre.org
literary@walnutstreettheatre.org
Notes: As America's oldest theatre, the Walnut
has been in existance as a theatre since 1809.
We are actively looking for new scripts for
possible production in our 2 theatre venues:
Our Studio space has a cast limit of 4–5, and
our mainstage has a cast limit of 14 (plays) and
20 (musicals). As one of the few theatres in the
country to accept unsolicited material, please
allow greater response time: 3 months query, 6
months script.
Agent Only: No
Submission Materials: see website
Preferred Genre: Plays or Musicals
Preferred Length: Full-length
Submission Fee: No

Weird Sisters Women's Theatre Collective
www.weirdsisterscollective.com
ally@weirdsisterscollective.com
Notes: A group of women in Austin, Texas
dedicated to promoting women in the arts. The
Collective embraces the feminist ideology of
collaboration; each participant is encouraged
to use her voice. The collaborative approach,
in an all-female and so more risk-free setting, empowers women. The Weirds explore

feminism and theater through theater productions, readings, lectures, salons, and parties throughout the year. Our process has been one of continual exploration.
Agent Only: No
Submission Materials: see website
Special interest: Women's Interest
Submission Fee: No

Wellfleet Harbor Actors Theater
Box 797
Wellfleet, MA 02667
Daniel Lombardo, Artistic Director
Phone: (508) 349-3011 Ext 107
Fax: (508) 349-9082
www.what.org
lombardo.what@gmail.com
Notes: Est. 1985. Cast size: 6 maximum. Response: 3 months query, 6 months script.
Agent Only: No
Submission Materials: 10-pg sample, bio, synopsis
Preferred Genre: All genres
Preferred Length: Full-length
Submission Fee: No

West End Studio Theatre
402 Ingalls St, Ste 3
Santa Cruz, CA 95060
Phone: (831) 425-9378
Fax: (831) 425-3333
westperformingarts.com
admin@westperformingarts.com
Agent Only: No
Submission Fee: No

Western Stage
411 Central Ave.
Salinas, CA 93901
Jon Selover, Artistic Director
Phone: (831) 755-6987
Fax: (831) 755-6954
www.westernstage.com
jselover@hartnell.edu
Agent Only: No
Submission Materials: audio CD, query letter, synopsis
Preferred Genre: All genres
Preferred Length: Full-length
Special interest: Theatre for Young Audiences
Submission Fee: No

Westport Arts Center
51 Riverside Ave.

Westport, CT 06880
Phone: (203) 222-7070
Fax: (203) 222-7999
www.westportartscenter.org
cara@westportartscenter.org
Notes: Programs in visual and performing arts.
Agent Only: No
Submission Materials: see website
Preferred Genre: All genres
Preferred Length: Any length
Submission Fee: No

Wet, Inc.
441 Lexington Ave, PH
New York, NY 10017
Phone: (212) 682-0265
wetweb.org/index.htm
info@wetweb.org
Notes: A non-for-profit production company that produces theater and film projects, events, panels, and workshops with challenging female stereotypes while celebrating women's diversity and strengths.
Agent Only: No
Submission Materials: see website
Special interest: Women's Interest
Submission Fee: No

What Girls Know
www.whatgirlsknow.com
info@whatgirlsknow.com
Notes: Theater program for adolescent girls in NYC from different ethnic and economic backgrounds.
Agent Only: No
Submission Materials: see website
Special interest: Women's Interest
Submission Fee: No

White Horse Theater Company
205 3rd Ave., #6-N
New York, NY 10003
Cyndy A. Marion, Producing Artistic Director
Phone: (212) 592-3706
www.whitehorsetheater.com
cymarion@whitehorsetheater.com
Notes: Est. 2002. Work must be unproduced. Response: 4 months.
Agent Only: No
Submission Materials: see website
Preferred Genre: Plays (No Musicals)
Preferred Length: Full-length
Special interest: Women's Interest
Submission Fee: No

Wilma Theater
265 S. Broad St.
Philadelphia, PA 19107
Walter Bilderback, Dramaturg/Literary
Manager
Phone: (215) 893-9456
Fax: (215) 893-0895
www.wilmatheater.org
WBilderback@wilmatheater.org
Notes: Est. 1979. Highly theatrical, poetic,
imaginative, politically evocative (not pro-
vocative), arousing, artful, bold, inventive.
Production: cast limit 8. Response: 1 year.
Agent Only: No
Submission Materials: see website
Preferred Genre: All genres
Preferred Length: Full-length
Submission Fee: No

Woman Made Gallery
685 North Milwaukee Ave
Chicago, IL 60642
Phone: (312) 738-0400
Fax: (312) 738-0404
www.womanmade.org
gallery@womanmade.org
Notes: The goal of Woman Made Gallery is
to support all women in the arts by providing
opportunities, awareness, and advocacy while
building an alternative community where
artistic values and criteria are determined by
women, for women.
Agent Only: No
Submission Materials: see website
Special interest: Women's Interest
Submission Fee: No

WomenArts
1442A Walnut Street #67
Berkeley, CA 94709
Martha Richards, Executive Director
Phone: (510) 868-5096
Fax: (650) 244-9136
www.womenarts.org
info@womenarts.org
Notes: A worldwide community of artists
and allies that work for empowerment, opportunity, and visibility for women artists. We
provide a variety of free online networking,
fundraising and advocacy services, and we
organize Support Women Artists Now Day
(SWAN Day), an annual international holiday
celebrating women's creativity in all its forms.
We believe in the power of women artists to
create, connect, and change the world.

Agent Only: No
Submission Materials: see website
Special interest: Women's Interest
Submission Fee: No

Women's Project and Production, Inc.
55 West End Ave.
New York, NY 10023
Megan Carter, Associate Artistic Director
Phone: (212) 765-1706
Fax: (212) 765-2024
www.womensproject.org
info@womensproject.org
Notes: As the nation's oldest and largest com-
pany dedicated to producing and promoting
theater created by women, Women's Project is
the magnetic force field for innovative artists
and adventurous theater-goers from around the
world.
Agent Only: No
Submission Materials: see website
Special interest: Women's Interest
Submission Fee: No

Women's Theatre Company
P.O. Box 5924
Parsippany, NJ 07054
Phone: (973) 316-3033
www.womenstheater.org
womenstheater@gmail.com
Notes: A professional theatre company dedi-
cated to the development, promotion and
inclusion of women in all aspects of theatre
production.
Agent Only: No
Submission Materials: see website
Special interest: Women's Interest
Submission Fee: No

Women's Theatre Project
1314 E. Las Olas Blvd
#31
Lauderdale, FL 33301
Phone: (954) 462-2334
www.womenstheatreproject.com
twtp@bellsouth.net
Notes: A company of professional female theatre artists dedicated to producing theatrical
works exploring the female voice, TWTP was
founded from a need for women's voices to be
heard and a desire to break down the stereotypes of women propelled by the media and to
create more professional theatrical opportunities for women of all shapes, sizes, races, and
ages. Produces 4 productions each calendar

year. Royalties paid to playwrights/publishing companies. TWTP seeks full-length plays with all-female casts by female playwrights for their intimate black box theatre.
Agent Only: No
Submission Materials: see website
Preferred Length: Full-length
Special interest: Women's Interest
Submission Fee: No

Woolly Mammoth Theatre Company
641 D St. NW
Washington, DC 20004
Phone: (202) 289-2443
www.woollymammoth.net
submissions@woollymammoth.net
Notes: Est. 1980. Production: cast limit 6. Response: 1 year., electronic submissions only, only accepts unsolicited submissions from dramatists in the Washington D.C. area.
Agent Only: No
Submission Materials: 10-pg sample, query letter, synopsis
Preferred Genre: Plays (No Musicals)
Preferred Length: Full-length
Submission Fee: No

WOW Cafe
59-61 E 4th St
New York, NY 10003
Phone: (212) 777-4280
www.wowcafe.org
wowcafetheatre@gmail.com
Notes: WOW Café Theater is a women's theater collective in NYC's East Village, which promotes the empowerment of women through the performing arts. Historically, WOW has been a majority lesbian woman's space. WOW welcomes the full participation of all women and transpeople in solidarity with women. WOW especially welcomes women and transpeople of color, and women and transpeople who identify as lesbians, bisexual and queer. We provide a working theater space to our members & the technical support to create and produce works, regardless of economic status. Attend a Tuesday night meeting, 6:30 at our space.
Agent Only: No
Submission Materials: see website
Special interest: Women's Interest
Submission Fee: No

Writers' Theatre
376 Park Ave.

Glencoe, IL 60022
Stuart Carden, Associate Artistic Director
Phone: (847) 242-6001
Fax: (847) 242-6011
www.writerstheatre.org
literary@writerstheatre.org
Notes: Est. 1992. Response: 6 months.
Agent Only: No
Submission Materials: 10-pg sample, S.A.S.E., synopsis
Preferred Genre: Plays or Musicals
Preferred Length: Full-length
Submission Fee: No

Yale Repertory Theatre
Box 208244
New Haven, CT 06520
Amy Boratko, Literary Manager
Phone: (203) 436-9098
www.yalerep.org
literary.office@yale.edu
Notes: Est. 1965. Response: 2 months query, 4 months script.
Agent Only: Yes
Submission Materials: agent-only
Preferred Genre: Plays or Musicals
Preferred Length: Full-length
Submission Fee: No

Yangtze Repertory Theatre of America
22 Howard St., #3-B
New York, NY 10013
Dr. Joanna Chan, Artistic Director
Phone: (212) 732-2799
Fax: (914) 923-0733
www.yangtze-rep-theatre.org
joannawychan@juno.com
Notes: Founded in 1992; welcomes submission of multi-lingual (English and Chinese) dramatic works with an Asian theme for a large (18–20) multi-ethnic cast; and usually responds in less than a month.
Agent Only: No
Submission Materials: see website
Preferred Length: Full-length
Special interest: Asian-American
Submission Fee: No

York Shakespeare Company
1852 West 4th Street, #2R
Brooklyn, NY 11223
Seth Duerr, Artistic Director
Phone: (646) 623-7117
Fax: (646) 964-6575
www.yorkshakespeare.org

info@yorkshakespeare.org
Notes: Est. 2001. Seeking Classical-oriented, unoptioned work. Need professional recommendation.
Agent Only: No
Submission Materials: full script
Preferred Genre: Plays or Musicals
Preferred Length: Full-length
Submission Fee: No

York Theatre Company
619 Lexington Ave.
New York, NY 10022
Phone: (212) 935-5820
Fax: (212) 832-0037
www.yorktheatre.org
mail@yorktheatre.org
Notes: Est. 1985. Opportunities include developmental reading series. Production: cast of 3–6, piano only. Submit via US mail. Response: 6 months.
Agent Only: No
Submission Materials: audio CD, full script, S.A.S.E.
Preferred Genre: Musical theatre
Preferred Length: Full-length
Submission Fee: No

Youth Performance Co
3338 University Ave SE
Minneapolis, MN 55414
Sherilyn Howes, Associate Director
Phone: (612) 623-9180
Fax: (612) 623-1020
www.youthperformanceco.com
showes@youthperformanceco.org
Agent Only: No
Special interest: Theatre for Young Audiences
Submission Fee: No

Youth Stages
287 Walnut Lane
Princeton, NJ 08540-3459
Jean P. Rosolino, Founder
Phone: (609) 430-9000
www.youthstages.com
manager@youthstages.com
Agent Only: No
Preferred Genre: Theatre for Young Audiences
Submission Fee: No

Educational Opportunities

Colleges and Universities

Academy of Art University
79 New Montgomery Street
San Francisco, CA 94105
Phone: (800) 544-2787
Fax: (415) 618-6287
www.academyart.edu
info@academyart.edu
Notes: Est. 1929. Rolling admissions.
Undergraduate and Graduate degree programs.
Certificates, Continuing Art Education, and
Pre-college programs available online and on
campus. Fees: $765/unit (undergrad), $865/
unit (grad)

Adelphi University
P.O. Box 701
Garden City, NY 11530
Phone: (516) 877-4044
academics.adelphi.edu/artsci/creativewriting
mfa@adelphi.edu
Notes: MFA in Creative Writing. The English
Department offers the Master of Fine Arts
(M.F.A.) program in Creative Writing, with
advanced workshops in fiction, poetry, creative
non-fiction, and dramatic writing, and courses
in literature, language, and theory. The M.F.A.
in Creative Writing offers students the opportunity to specialize in three major genres: fiction, poetry, and dramatic writing.
Submission Fee: Yes

Angelo State University (ASU)
Box 10895, ASU Station
San Angelo, TX 76909
Bill Doll, Director of University Theater
Phone: (325) 942-2146 Ext 6191
Fax: (325) 942-2033
www.angelo.edu
bill.doll@angelo.edu
Notes: BA in Theatre Arts.
Submission Materials: full script
Preferred Genre: Plays or Musicals
Preferred Length: Full-length
Submission Fee: No

Arizona State University (ASU)
School of Theatre and Film
Box 872002
Tempe, AZ 85287
Guillermo Reyes, Professor
Phone: (480) 965-0519
Fax: (480) 965-5351
www.theatrefilm.asu.edu/degrees/grad/mfa_
theatre/dramatic_writing.php

Guillermo.Reyes@asu.edu
Notes: BA, MFA, PHD in Theatre. Available
concentrations: directing, dramatic writing,
interdisciplinary digital media and performance, interdisciplinary concentration with
the School of Arts, Media and Engineering),
performance, performance design and theatre
for youth.
Submission Fee: Yes
Deadline(s): February 1 of every year (for
application materials)

Artistic New Directions
250 W. 90th St. #15-G
New York, NY 10024
Janice Goldberg, Artistic Co-Director
Phone: (212) 875-1857
Fax: (212) 875-1857
www.artisticnewdirections.org
artnewdir@aol.com
Notes: Ongoing Wednesday night devel-
opment lab, Anything Goes, open to all
from which we cull material. We produce
works-in-progress, workshops, and Equity
Showcases. No unsolicited material. We spon-
sor Playwrights Retreat and Masters Improv
Retreat every summer. Also, annual Eclectic
Evening of Shorts. Workshops/Classes in solo
work and improv to develop character and
script, among others. Also, Jeffery Sweet's
From Improv To Script.
Submission Materials: see website
Preferred Genre: All genres
Submission Fee: No

Bard College
Box 5000
Annandale-on-Hudson, NY 12504
JoAnne Akalaitis, Chair, Theater Department
Phone: (845) 758-7957
www.bard.edu
rbangiola@bard.edu
Notes: BA in Theatre. MFA in music.
Submission Fee: No

Bates College
Schaeffer Theater, #302
Lewiston, ME 04238
Phone: (207) 786-8294
www.bates.edu
mreidy@bates.edu
Submission Fee: No

Boston Playwrights' Theatre at Boston University
949 Commonwealth Ave.
Boston, MA 02215
Michael Duncan Smith, Program Coordinator
Phone: (617) 353-5443
Fax: (617) 353-6196
www.bu.edu/bpt/playwriting-program.html
newplays@bu.edu
Notes: We offer an MFA in Playwriting, accepting four to six playwrights annually into this program. While some Playwriting programs are part of the Theatre Department, ours is different–we are part of the English Department in the College of Arts and Sciences, though our work as a professional theatre keeps us firmly in the theatre world.
Submission Materials: query letter, S.A.S.E.
Preferred Genre: All genres
Preferred Length: Any length
Submission Fee: No

Bowling Green State University (BGSU)
338 South Hall
Bowling Green, OH 43403
Phone: (419) 372-2222
Fax: (419) 372-7186
www.bgsu.edu/theatrefilm
theatrefilm@bgsu.edu
Notes: BA, MA, PHD in Theatre.
Submission Fee: Yes

Brigham Young University
Dept. of Theatre and Media Arts
D-581 HFAC
Provo, UT 84602
Phone: (801) 422-7768
Fax: (801) 422-0654
www.byu.edu
tmaweb@byu.edu
Submission Fee: Yes

Brooklyn College—CUNY
English Dept.
2900 Bedford Ave.
Brooklyn, NY 11210
Eliza Hornig, MFA Administrator
Phone: (718) 951-5197
depthome.brooklyn.cuny.edu/english/graduate/mfa/pwriting.htm
EHornig@brooklyn.cuny.edu
Notes: MFA in Playwriting. The playwriting program is dedicated to the proposition that writing for the theater is not a business of finished thought and dead rules. Rather,

we endeavor to pursue kinds of writing that involve an ongoing conversation with theater of the past and (hopefully) the future.
Submission Fee: Yes

Brown University
Box 1852, Waterman St.
Providence, RI 02912
Rebecca Schneider, Department Chair
Phone: (401) 863-3283
www.brown.edu/Departments/Theatre_Speech_Dance/grad/playwritingmfa.html
erik_ehn@brown.edu
Notes: MFA in Playwriting. Brown is a chief and storied site for the formation of playwrights, established to grant broad inventive license while offering close mentorship and profound resources (in the department, the university, and the greater community, locally to internationally). Alumni distinguish themselves by their professional credits, and by their collegial élan.
Submission Materials: see website
Submission Fee: Yes

California College of the Arts
1111 8th Street
San Francisco, CA 94107
Joseph Lease, Department Chair
Phone: (415) 703-9523
www.cca.edu/academics/graduate/writing
eblack2@cca.edu
Notes: MFA in Writing. The MFA Program in Writing at California College of the Arts is a two-year course of study. Our program offers workshops in fiction, poetry, creative nonfiction, cross-genre writing, playwriting, and screenwriting. Rather than require you to declare a specific genre, we instead leave open the option to take workshops in various genres.
Submission Fee: No

California Institute of the Arts
24700 McBean Pkwy.
Valencia, CA 91355
Phone: (661) 253-7716
theater.calarts.edu/programs/writing
jrutzmoser@calarts.edu
Notes: MFA in Writing. A Writing Program located in an Art School offers different opportunities than those found in the more traditional habitat of an English department. Not only do writers benefit from taking courses and collaborating with others in different metiers, the pedagogical ethos of art schools

is different.The program is non-tracking, and all faculty have multi-disciplinary practices, with experience in publishing, editing, reviewing, criticism, scholarship, collaboration and translation.
Submission Materials: see website
Submission Fee: Yes

Campbell University
Box 128
Buries Creek, NC 27506
Phone: (910) 893-1507
www.campbell.edu/artsandsciences/theater/
buildyourfuture@campbell.edu
Notes: Degree offered: B.A.
Submission Materials: see website
Submission Fee: Yes

Carnegie Mellon University
Purnell Center A32
Pittsburgh, PA 15213
Rob Handel, Coordinator, Graduate
Admissions
Phone: (412) 268-2398
www.drama.cmu.edu/
rhandel@andrew.cmu.edu
Notes: Carnegie Mellon is uniquely positioned to offer an intense experience that combines training in playwriting, screenwriting, television writing, and theatrical entrepreneurship. As an integral part of the Carnegie Mellon School of Drama, the oldest degree-granting theatre program in the United States, the Dramatic Writing program provides ongoing collaboration with the next generation of important actors, directors, and designers. Dramatic Writing MFA candidates have the opportunity to see their thesis play fully produced in the New Works Series and have two teleplays fully produced in studio conditions. Interested students have the opportunity to teach undergraduate playwriting and screenwriting classes.
Submission Materials: see website
Submission Fee: Yes
Deadline(s): January 1, 2013

Catholic University of America
Catholic University, Dept. of Drama
620 Michigan Ave. NE
Washington, DC 20064
Jon Klein, Head of MFA Writing Program
Phone: (202) 319-5351
drama.cua.edu/graduate/mfa-playwriting.cfm
kleinj@cua.edu

Notes: MFA in Playwriting. In this three year program, playwrights collaborate with actors and directors to shape and reshape their works in classrooms, readings and workshops. They will come in contact with a variety of dramaturgical techniques for the development of dramatic action, character, language and structure. The focus is on a professional and practical approach to scriptwriting, culminating in the writing of five or more stage plays, a screenplay and a television script.
Submission Materials: see website
Submission Fee: Yes
Deadline(s): January 31, 2013

Central Washington University (CWU)
CWU Theater Dept.
400 E. University Way
MS: 7460
Ellensburg, WA 98926
Scott Robinson, Department Chair
Phone: (509) 963-2020
www.cwu.edu/~theatre
scott.robinson@cwu.edu
Notes: BA and MA in Theatre.
Submission Materials: see website
Preferred Genre: Theatre for Young
Audiences
Preferred Length: Any length
Special interest: Multi-Ethnic
Submission Fee: No

Chapman University
1 University Dr.
Orange, CA 92866
Phone: (714) 997-6711
www.chapman.edu/wilkinson/graduate-
studies/ma-mfa-english.aspx
pjquinn@chapman.edu
Notes: MFA in Creative Writing. The M.F.A. program at Chapman fosters the growth of fiction writers and poets through workshops, technique courses, literature courses, the John Fowles Literary Forum Core, and the literary journal Elephant Tree. The culmination of each M.F.A. student's work is a book-length thesis project in fiction or poetry. (Students may complete a thesis in creative nonfiction, stage drama, or screenplay, with the approval of the graduate program director.)
Submission Fee: No

College of Charleston (CofC)
66 George St.
Charleston, SC 29424

Phone: (843) 849-8287
Fax: (843) 953-8210
www.cofc.edu
ashleyf@cofc.edu
Submission Materials: see website
Submission Fee: Yes

College of the Holy Cross
1 College St.
Worcester, MA 01610
Phone: (508) 793-3490
www.holycross.edu
eisser@holycross.edu
Submission Materials: see website
Submission Fee: Yes

Columbia College [IL]
72 E. 11th St.
Chicago, IL 60605
John Green, Allen and Lynn Turner Theatre
Chair
Phone: (312) 344-6100
www.colum.edu/theatre
theatre@colum.edu
Submission Materials: see website
Submission Fee: Yes

Columbia University School of the Arts Theatre Program
2960 Broadway MC 1807, 601 Dodge Hall
New York, NY 10027-7021
Julie Rossi, Director of Academic
Administration
Phone: (212) 854-3408
Fax: (212) 854-3344
www.arts.columbia.edu/mfa-playwriting-concentration
theatre@columbia.edu
Notes: MFA in Playwriting. The playwriting program takes a pragmatic approach, stressing the process and development of a writer's skills, with the understanding that there is not one way to write a wonderful play but many ways, as Aeschylus and Shakespeare and Chekhov have proven. The philosophy of the program is based on the idea that the work must come from within the playwright.
Submission Materials: see website
Submission Fee: Yes

DePaul University
2135 N. Kenmore Ave.
Chicago, IL 60614
Phone: (773) 325-7932

theatreschool.depaul.edu
dcorrin@depaul.edu
Submission Fee: Yes

Drexel University, Westphal College
3141 Chestnut St.
Philadelphia, PA 19104
Phone: (215) 895-1920
Fax: (215) 895-2452
www.drexel.edu/westphal
nick.anselmo@drexel.edu
Submission Materials: see website
Submission Fee: Yes

Duke University
Box 90680
Durham, NC 27708
Jody McAuliffe, Chair, Theater Studies
Phone: (919) 660-3343
Fax: (919) 684-8906
www.theaterstudies.duke.edu/
theater@duke.edu
Notes: We do not accept unsolicited scripts of any kind.
Submission Fee: Yes

Eastern Michigan Univ. Applied Drama & Theatre for Young
103 Quirk Street
Ypsilanti, MI 48197
Patricia Zimmer, Professor
Phone: (734) 487-0033
Fax: (734) 487-3443
www.emich.edu/cta/dtfyindex.htm
pzimmer@emich.edu
Submission Fee: No

Emerson College
10 Boylston Pl., 5th Floor
Department of Performing Arts
Boston, MA 02116
Phone: (617) 824-8780
www.emerson.edu/academics/departments/performing-arts
stagedoor@emerson.edu
Notes: Degree offered: BA
Submission Materials: see website
Submission Fee: Yes

Florida State University
239 Fine Arts Bldg.
Tallahassee, FL 32306
Barbara Thomas, Program Assistant
Phone: (850) 644-7257
Fax: (850) 644-7246

www.theatre.fsu.edu/Graduate/MFA/Stage-and-Screen-Writing
bgthomas@admin.fsu.edu
Notes: MFA in Stage and Screen Writing. The course of study in Writing for the Stage & Screen is offered jointly by the College of Motion Picture, Television and Recording Arts, and The School of Theatre. Only six writing students are admitted each fall. The program is comprised of six consecutive semesters (61 hours of completed coursework) that lead to a Master of Fine Arts Degree.
Submission Materials: application
Submission Fee: Yes

Goddard College (Plainfield)
123 Pitkin Road
Plainfield, VT 05667
Phone: (802) 322-1693
www.goddard.edu/mfa-creative-writing
paul.selig@goddard.edu
Notes: The low-residency Master of Fine Arts in Creative Writing Program is a 48-credit, rigorous, student-centered program for writers who choose to live their lives and hone their writing skills at the same time. The MFA in Creative Writing Program is ideal for people with commitments to family, work, or other personal obligations, or for people who simply want to improve their writing in the way that most writers end up working on their own.
Submission Fee: No

Hollins University
PO Box 9603
Roanoke, VA 24020
Todd Ristau, Program Director
Phone: (540) 362-6386
www.hollins.edu/grad/playwriting/index.html
tristau@hollins.edu
Notes: Summer Intensive in MFA program in Playwriting: Hollins' M.F.A. program in playwriting is designed for those interested in playwriting as well as those who want an academic study of theatre with the playscript as the central foundation.
Submission Materials: see website
Submission Fee: Yes

Hunter College—CUNY
695 Park Ave
New York, NY 10065
Mark Bly, MFA Graduate Advisor
Phone: (713) 448-0079
mbly@hunter.cuny.edu

Notes: The Rita and Burton Goldberg MFA in Playwriting is a selective two year program with a strong emphasis on production. Under the guidance of award wining playwright Tina Howe, Playwright in Residence, and internationally known new play dramaturg and playwriting professor Mark Bly, you will study the craft of playwriting, theater history, dramatic literature, and play analysis in Hunter's Department of Theatre as well as be encouraged to take electives. The second year students also participate in the unique Hunter Playwrights Festival where they receive an Equity Showcase production featuring professional directors, actors, designers and student actors in support of their work presented before an invited industry audience of theatre professionals.
Submission Fee: No

Indiana University
257 N. Jordan Ave., Rm. A300U
Bloomington, IN 47405
Ken Weitzman, Head of Playwriting
Phone: (812) 855-4535
Fax: (812) 856-0698
www.indiana.edu/~thtr/academics/MFA_playwriting.shtml
kweitzma@indiana.edu
Notes: The M.F.A. in playwriting is a three-year program designed for writers with original voices who are committed to making an impact on the profession. The training is comprised of coursework, productions, and professional engagement. Classes are designed to give the writer a broad education in dramatic writing, in order to explore and develop multiple ways to tell a story as well as multiple ways to make a living.
Submission Materials: see website
Submission Fee: Yes
Deadline(s): February 1, 2013

Johnson County Community College
12345 College Blvd.
Overland Park, KS 66210
Phone: (913) 469-8500
Fax: (913) 469-2585
www.jccc.net
bpettigr@jccc.net
Notes: No original play submissions accepted.
Submission Fee: Yes

Kansas State Univ. (KSU)
129 Nichols Hall

Manhattan, KS 66506
Phone: (785) 532-6875
Fax: (785) 532-3714
www.k-state.edu/theatre
jsutd@ksu.edu
Notes: BA/BS in Theatre MA in Theatre MA in Theatre with a Concentration in Drama Therapy NAST Accredited

Lesley University
29 Everett Street
Cambridge, MA 02138
Jana M. Van der Veer
www.lesley.edu/gsass/creative_writing
jvanderv@lesley.edu
Notes: The MFA Program in Creative Writing at Lesley University takes your writing as seriously as you do, working with you to turn your promise into settled accomplishment. Students may choose one of five program concentrations: fiction, nonfiction, poetry, writing for stage and screen, writing for young people. The residency includes workshops, seminars, lectures, and readings, providing a forum for collaboration and for constructive critique of students' work.
Submission Fee: No

Louisiana Tech University
PO Box 8608
Ruston, LA 71272
Phone: (318) 257-2711
Fax: (318) 257-4571
performingarts.latech.edu
lulu@latech.edu
Notes: Degree offered: BA, MA
Submission Materials: see website
Submission Fee: Yes

Loyola Marymount University
1 LMU Dr.
MS 8210
Los Angeles, CA 90045
Stephen Shepherd, Program Director
Phone: (310) 568-6225
www.lmu.edu
sshephe1@lmu.edu
Notes: MFA in Creative Writing—The Creative Writing Emphasis offers a range of coursework in several genres and modes of writing. In addition to strong fiction and poetry workshops, the Emphasis offers innovative classes including The Novella, Prose Poetry, The Memoir, Constraint Based Writing, Playwriting, and more. Students may also work with faculty in other departments, including film and theatre.
Submission Materials: see website
Preferred Genre: All genres
Preferred Length: Any length
Submission Fee: No

Loyola University New Orleans
6363 St. Charles Ave., Box 155
New Orleans, LA 70118
Phone: (504) 865-3840
Fax: (504) 865-2284
www.loyno.edu/theatrearts
theatre@loyno.edu
Notes: Degree offered: BA.
Submission Materials: see website
Submission Fee: Yes

Minnesota State University Moorhead
1104 7th Avenue
Moorhead, MN 56563
Phone: (218) 477-2134
graduate@mnstate.edu
Notes: The Master of Fine Arts (MFA) in Creative Writing is a degree for students who wish to improve their creative writing abilities on the graduate level. The program is designed to be completed on either a full-time or a part-time basis. Students usually complete the program in two and a half to five years. The MFA is a terminal degree. Most of the student's work will be in actual writing courses, in tutorials, and in thesis preparation.
Submission Fee: No

Montclair State University
1 Normal Ave., MSU LI-126G
Montclair, NJ 07043
Randy Mugleston, Department Chair
Phone: (973) 655-7343
www.montclair.edu/Pages/theatredance
muglestonr@mail.montclair.edu
Notes: Degrees offered: BA, BFA, MA.
Submission Materials: see website
Submission Fee: Yes
Deadline(s): See website

Mount Holyoke College
50 College St.
South Hadley, MA 01075
Phone: (413) 538-2118
Fax: (413) 538-2838
www.mtholyoke.edu/acad/theatre
theatre@mtholyoke.edu
Notes: Degree offered: BA.

Submission Materials: see website
Submission Fee: Yes

Murray State Univ. (MSU)
MSU, FA 106
Murray, KY 42071
David Balthrop, Chair, Theater/Dance Dept.
Phone: (270) 762-4421
Fax: (270) 809-4422
www.murraystate.edu/theatre
dbalthrop@murraystate.edu
Notes: BA/BS. The department is very hands-on with work required on productions by all theatre majors and minors. The student-faculty radio is currently 12:1. We produce shows from all genres and from all major time frames in three different theatre spaces. An interview/audition or portfolio review is required if scholarship money is requested. Dramatic and comedic monologue of 60–90 seconds, or portfolio (CD, DVD, any format).
Deadline(s): January 1 for students wishing to apply for scholarsihp funds

Nebraska Wesleyan University
500 St. Paul Ave.
Lincoln, NE 68504
Phone: (402) 465-2386
www.nebrwesleyan.edu
jsc@nebrwesleyan.edu
Notes: Degrees offered: BA in Theatre Education; BFA in Acting, Directing, Musical Theatre, Theatre Design and Technology, Theatre Studies.
Submission Materials: see website
Submission Fee: Yes

New School For Drama
151 Bank Street
New York, NY 10014
Phone: (212) 229-5859
Fax: (212) 242-5018
www.newschool.edu/drama/
hoytr@newschool.edu
Notes: MFA in Playwriting. The New School for Drama's playwriting program prepares a select group of students for professional careers as skilled dramatic writers in theater, film and television. We believe that a complete playwriting education requires rigorous attention to craft and artistic exploration as well as consistent opportunities to apply one's developing skills through presentations and productions.
Submission Fee: No

New York University, Goldberg Department of Dramatic Writing
721 Broadway, Fl. 7
New York, NY 10003
Phone: (212) 998-1940
Fax: (212) 998-4069
ddw.tisch.nyu.edu/page/graduate.html
tisch.ddw@nyu.edu
Notes: MFA in Dramatic Writing. Acceptance into the Department enrolls all students in the Division of Playwriting and the Division of Film and TV Writing. Students study in both divisions, concentrating in at least one medium as their studies advance. During the first year, the graduate seminars in theatre will require an original ten-minute play, a one-act play, and a full-length play. Students also start study in either film or television, completing either a full-length screenplay or a half hour television script. In the spring, individual workshops give students the opportunity to continue their exploration and assess their suitability for one or more of the mediums.
Submission Materials: see website
Submission Fee: No

New York University, Musical Theater Writing
113-A 2nd Ave., Fl. 1
New York, NY 10003
Phone: (212) 998-1830
Fax: (212) 995-4873
gmtw.tisch.nyu.edu/page/home.html
muscial.theatre@nyu.edu
Notes: Est. 1981. MFA for composers, lyricists and bookwriters from Institution of Performing Arts at Tisch School of the Arts. Response: Decisions are made in April for class starting in September.
Submission Materials: see website
Preferred Genre: Musical theatre
Submission Fee: Yes
Deadline(s): April

Northern Kentucky University
NKU, FA 205-A
Highland Heights, KY 41099
Phone: (859) 572-6362
Fax: (859) 572-6057
www.nku.edu/~theatre
davissa@nku.edu
Notes: Degrees offered: BA, BFA.
Submission Materials: application
Submission Fee: Yes

Northwest Children's Theater & School
1819 NW Everett St., Suite 216
Portland, OR 97209
Phone: (503) 222-2190
Fax: (503) 222-4130
nwcts.org
Notes: NA
Submission Materials: see website
Submission Fee: No

Northwestern University
Theatre Interpertation Building
1949 Campus Drive
Evanston, IL 60208
Phone: (847) 467-1157
Fax: (847) 467-2019
www.communication.northwestern.edu/
programs/mfa_writing_screen_stage/intro
write@northwestern.edu
Notes: MFA in Writing for the Screen and
Stage. We've designed our MFA Program
around six core courses, which introduce you
to a set of 'transportable' media writing con-
cepts, as well as specific idioms/genres. You'll
build a significant portfolio— at least a short
screenplay, play, TV episode, and full-length
thesis project of your choosing. You'll understand not just the art and craft of media writing, but also the business of media writing as
we'll practice pitching, taking meetings, writing query letters, and understanding contracts.
Submission Materials: application
Submission Fee: Yes

Oakland University
Music, Theater, Dance
Rochester, MI 48309
Phone: (248) 370-2030
Fax: (248) 370-2041
www.oakland.edu/mtd
knox@oakland.edu
Notes: BA, BFA. Meadow Brook Theater is on
campus.
Submission Materials: application
Submission Fee: No

Ohio University
Kantner Hall 307
Athens, OH 45701
Charles Smith, Head, Playwriting Program
Phone: (740) 593-4818
Fax: (740) 593-4817
www.ohioplaywriting.org
ohioplaywriting@gmail.com

Notes: MFA in Playwriting. The Professional
Playwriting Program seeks to train playwrights to become craftspeople and artists
who contribute to the culture. The basic and
advanced principles of the craft can be learned
through earnest study of our dramatic literary
heritage and intensive practical application of
the craft.
Submission Fee: No

Ohio Wesleyan University (OWU)
Chappelear Drama Ctr.
Delaware, OH 43015
Elane Denny-Todd
Phone: (740) 368-3851
theatre.owu.edu
eedennyt@owu.edu
Notes: BA in Theatre.

Pace University
551 5th Ave
New York, NY 10176
Phone: (212) 346-1531
www.pace.edu/dysocademic-departments-
and-programs/asds
actorsstudiomfa@pace.edu
Notes: MFA in Playwriting. Founded in 1947
by Elia Kazan, Robert Lewis, and Cheryl
Crawford, the Actors Studio is a private space
where actors, directors, and playwrights can
practice their craft free from the pressures of
the public world. Over the years it has provided a unique opportunity for artists to grow
by offering a safe, closed, protected environment where they can experiment and stretch
their creativity beyond all boundaries. All students—actors, directors, playwrights—train
side-by-side as actors.
Submission Fee: No

Palm Beach Atlantic University
Box 24708
West Palm Beach, FL 33416
Phone: (561) 803-2000
www.pba.edu
Jofeue_leon@pba.edu
Submission Materials: see website
Submission Fee: Yes

Purdue University
552 W. Wood Street
West Lafayette, IN 47907
Phone: (765) 494-3074
Fax: (765) 496-1766
www.purdue.edu/theatre

theatre@purdue.edu
Notes: Degree offered: BA, MA, MFA.
Submission Materials: see website
Submission Fee: Yes

Queens College—CUNY
6530 Kissena Boulevard
Flushing, NY 11367
Nicole Cooley, Director
Phone: (718) 997-4671
www.qc.cuny.edu/creative_writing
nicole.cooley@qc.cuny.edu
Notes: MFA in Creative Writing and Literary Translation. Our program is new—We are now entering its fourth year-and has galvanized the energies of students and faculty alike. We are proud to be the latest MFA program in the City University of New York system and the only one in the borough of Queens. We offer degrees in poetry, prose, playwriting and literary translation.
Submission Fee: No

Radford University
Dance and Theatre
RU Station
Radford, VA 24142
Phone: (540) 831-5207
Fax: (540) 831-6313
theatre.asp.radford.edu
clefko@radford.edu
Notes: Degree offered: BA.
Submission Materials: see website
Submission Fee: Yes

Rutgers University (Camden)
406 Penn Street
Camden, NJ 08102
Lisa Zeidner, interim MFA Director
Phone: (856) 225-6121
mfa.camden.rutgers.edu/
mfa@comden.rutger.edu
Notes: MFA in Creative Writing. The Rutgers-Camden Master of Fine Arts in creative writing is a 42-credit terminal degree in the theory and practice of writing—the first of its kind in the Philadelphia/South Jersey area. Rutgers-Camden think writers in one genre can learn from writers in another—poets from fiction writers, fiction writers from memoirists, and memoirists from poets. Our unique multi-genre approach prepares our students not only to write poetry and prose but to teach at the college level.
Submission Fee: No

Rutgers University (Newark)
249 University Avenue
New Brunswick, NJ 07102
Jayne A. Phillips, Director
Phone: (973) 353-1107
www.ncas.rutgers.edu/mfa
rnmfa@newark.rutgers.edu
Notes: MFA in Creative Writing. MFA Program is a Nationally ranked, 48 credit hour, studio/research program, which means that our writers study literature as they endeavor to write it. The Program focuses strongly on 20 credit hours of Writing Workshop in a declared genre (one workshop, with permission of the department, may be cross-genre), and requires 7 thesis hours in which students work one-on-one with their mentor professors.
Submission Fee: No

Rutgers University (State University of New Jersey)
Rutgers University/Mason Gross School of the Arts,
Theatre Arts Department
2 Chapel Drive
New Brunswick, NJ 08901
Phone: (732) 932-9891
Fax: (732) 932-1409
www.masongross.rutgers.edu/
theatre@masongross.rutgers.edu
Notes: MFA program in playwrighting. Applications accepted Fall through March. See website for application, fees, submission requirements.
Submission Materials: see website
Submission Fee: Yes

San Francisco State University
Creative Writing Dept.
1600 Holloway Ave.
San Francisco, CA 94132
Phone: (415) 338-1891
online.sfsu.edu/~rconboy
cwriting@sfsu.edu
Notes: MFA in Playwriting—Surviving and thriving is the hallmark of this program, which has grown in the last ten years from a program centered on the classroom to one that continues to value intense classroom experiences while building active and spirited "on its feet" components powered by the communal efforts of faculty, students and alumni.
Submission Materials: application
Submission Fee: Yes

Sarah Lawrence College
1 Mead Way
Bronxville, NY 10708
Emanuel Lomax, Director of Graduate
Admissions
Phone: (914) 395-2371
Fax: (914) 395-2666
www.slc.edu/graduate/programs/writing/
index.html
elomax@sarahlawrence.edu
Notes: MFA in Writing. One of the largest programs of its kind in the country, Sarah Lawrence's nationally recognized Graduate Writing Program brings students into close mentoring relationships with active, successful writers. Students concentrate in fiction, creative nonfiction, or poetry, developing a personal voice while honing their writing and critical abilities. In addition to workshops, students benefit from one-on-one biweekly conferences with faculty.
Submission Fee: No

Smith College
Theatre Dept., Mendenhall Ctr.
Northampton, MA 01063
Len Berkman, Graduate Adviser
Phone: (413) 585-3206
www.smith.edu/gradstudy/degrees_playwrite.
php
lberkman@email.smith.edu
Notes: MFA in Playwriting—This program, offered by the Department of Theatre, provides specialized training to candidates who have given evidence of professional promise in playwriting. The Department of Theatre places great emphasis on collaborative work among designers, performers, directors and writers, thus offering a unique opportunity for playwrights to have their work nurtured and supported by others who work with it at various levels.
Submission Materials: see website
Submission Fee: Yes

Southern Methodist University (SMU)
Box 750369
Dallas, TX 75275
Phone: (214) 768-2937
www.smu.edu
gesmith@mail.smu.edu
Notes: Degrees offered: BFA, MFA.
Submission Materials: see website
Submission Fee: No

Spalding University's Brief-Residency MFA in Writing
851 S. Fourth Street
Louisville, KY 40203
Karen J. Mann, Administrative Director
Phone: (502) 873-4400
Fax: (502) 992-2409
www.spalding.edu/mfa
kmann@spalding.edu

SUNY Purchase
735 Anderson Hill Rd.
Purchase, NY 10577
Howard Enders, Chair, Dramatic Writing Program
Phone: (914) 251-6833
www.purchase.edu
howard.enders@purchase.edu
Submission Materials: see website
Submission Fee: Yes

Texas A&M University, Commerce (TAMU)
Pac 103
P.O. Box 3011
Commerce, TX 75429
Jim Tyler Anderson, KCACTF Vice Chair, Region VI
Phone: (903) 886-5346
Fax: (903) 468-3250
www.tamu-commerce.edu
jim.anderson@tamu-commerce.edu
Notes: BA, MA.

Texas State University, San Marcos
601 University Dr.
San Marcos, TX 78666
Phone: (512) 245-2147
Fax: (512) 245-8440
www.theatreanddance.txstate.edu
jf18@txstate.edu
Notes: Degrees offered: BA, BFA.
Submission Materials: see website
Submission Fee: Yes

Texas Tech Univ. (TTU)
Box 42061
Lubbock, TX 79409
Norman Bert, Head of Playwriting
Phone: (806) 742-3601
www.depts.ttu.edu/theatreanddance/
norman.bert@ttu.edu
Notes: BA, BFA, MA, MFA, PhD.
Submission Fee: No

The Juilliard School
Playwrights Program
60 Lincoln Center Plaza
New York, NY 10023
Tanya Barfield
Phone: (212) 799-5000 Ext 223
Fax: (212) 875-8437
www.juilliard.edu/degrees-programs/drama/
playwrights.php
admissions@juilliard.edu
Notes: MFA in Playwriting—The Lila
Acheson Wallace American Playwrights
Program encourages and aids the development
of new and diverse voices in the American
theater. Students may take any class in the
Drama Division and are encouraged to see
productions around the city by receiving free
or discounted tickets to many events on- and
off-Broadway. The essence of the Playwrights
Program lies in the weekly master class with
the playwright heads focusing on dramatic
structure and the cultivation of each writer's
individual voice.
Submission Materials: see website
Submission Fee: Yes

**The Little Theatre of Alexandria
Playwriting Class**
600 Wolfe Street
Alexandria, VA 22314
Phone: (703) 683-5578
Fax: (703) 683-1378
www.thelittletheatre.com/
virginia@thelittletheatre.com
Notes: Application Fee: $190. Eight week class
focusing on the art and craft of writing plays.

**University of California, Los Angeles
(UCLA)**
10920 Wilshire Blvd 5th Floor
Los Angeles, CA 90024-6502
Natasha Levy, Graduate Counselor for
Theater
www.tft.ucla.edu/programs/theater-
department/graduate-degrees/playwriting-
mfa/
theatergrad@tft.ucla.edu
Notes: MFA in Playwriting is a three year
program that trains and nurtures dramatists
whose purpose is to transform the way we see
and understand the world. Playwriting faculty
includes successful writers whose work has
been professionally produced throughout the
country. In the first year, playwrights complete
two short plays and a full length play. In the

second year, playwrights complete a second
full length play, a one person play, and an
additional writing project such as an adaptation for the stage or a screenplay. The third
year typically includes an internship with a
professional theater or film studio, or compara-
tive environment.
Submission Fee: No

University of California, Riverside (UCR)
The Department of Theatre
900 University Ave., ARTS 121
University of California, Riverside
Riverside, CA 92521
Michelle Harding, Program Manager
Phone: (951) 827-5568
theatre.ucr.edu
michelle.harding@ucr.edu
Notes: MFA in Creative Writing, Writing for
the Performing Arts. Our low residency program is unique in that it unites your academic
pursuits with a real world emphasis on the next
stage of your writing career–production and
publication. The program was designed and is
taught by writers for writers and is open to all
genres of writing, including fiction, nonfiction,
screenwriting and poetry, and all forms within
those genres including crime and science fiction; memoir, essay and single topic nonfiction;
commercial Hollywood films and television.
Submission Materials: see website
Preferred Genre: All genres
Preferred Length: Any length
Submission Fee: Yes

University of California, San Diego (UCSD)
9500 Gilman Dr., MC0344
La Jolla, CA 92093
Marybeth Ward, Graduate Program
Coordinator
Phone: (858) 534-1046
Fax: (858) 534-1080
theatre.ucsd.edu/academics/
graduatePrograms/playwriting.html
meward@ucsd.edu
Notes: MFA in Playwriting. Each year we
admit one or two individuals who will be nurtured by the close individual attention and
extensive production opportunities that are
unique to this program. We believe that the
theatre itself is a valuable teacher of playwrights and so playwrights work collaboratively with their colleagues in the MFA acting,
directing, design, and stage management programs to create stimulating and meaningful

works of art. The year-long development process includes a series of readings and a workshop week culminating in the New Play Festival, produced each April.
Submission Materials: see website
Submission Fee: Yes

University of California, Santa Barbara (UCSB)
552 University Rd.
Santa Barbara, CA 93106
Erin Creseda Wilson, Playwriting Program Chair
Phone: (805) 893-8303
www.theaterdance.ucsb.edu
ellena@silcom.com
Notes: Degrees offered: BA., BFA, MA, PhD.
Submission Materials: see website
Submission Fee: Yes

University of Idaho (UI)
Box 442008
Moscow, ID 83844
Phone: (208) 885-6465
www.uitheatre.com
rcaisley@uidaho.edu
Notes: Home of Idaho Repertory Theater. MFA in Dramatic Writing offered.
Submission Materials: see website
Submission Fee: Yes

University of Iowa
200 N. Riverside Dr., #107 TB
Iowa City, IA 52242
Art Borreca, Head, Playwrights Workshop
Phone: (319) 353-2401
Fax: (319) 335-3568
www.uiowa.edu/~theatre/programs/grad-playwriting.html
art-borreca@uiowa.edu
Notes: The Iowa Playwrights Workshop-The University of Iowa's MFA Program in Playwriting-is an intensive three-year program dedicated to educating playwrights for the professional theatre. The Playwrights Workshop seeks to create conditions in which writers can develop their unique voices while freely experimenting with a variety of creative processes and theatrical forms.
Submission Materials: see website
Submission Fee: Yes

University of Michigan (UM)
1226 Murfin Ave.
2230 Walgreen Drama Center
Ann Arbor, MI 48109
Phone: (734) 764-5350
Fax: (734) 647-2297
www.music.umich.edu/departments/theatre
theatre.info@umich.edu
Submission Materials: see website
Submission Fee: Yes

University of Minnesota Duluth (UMD)
Dept. of Theatre
141 MPAC
1215 Ordean Ct.
Duluth, MN 55812
Phone: (218) 726-8778
www.d.umn.edu/theatre/
pdennis@d.umn.edu
Notes: Degrees offered: BFA, BA.
Submission Materials: see website
Submission Fee: Yes

University of Missouri
129 Fine Arts Bldg.
Columbia, MO 65211
Phone: (573) 882-2021
Fax: (573) 884-4034
theatre.missouri.edu
ruffinc@missouri.edu
Notes: Degrees offered: BA, MA, PhD.
Submission Materials: see website
Submission Fee: Yes

University of Missouri, Kansas City
4949 Cherry St.
Kansas City, MO 64110
Phone: (816) 235-2702
cas.umkc.edu/theatre/
fhwriter@aol.com
Submission Materials: see website
Submission Fee: Yes

University of Nevada, Las Vegas (UNLV)
Department of Theatre
4505 Maryland Pkwy., Box 455036
Las Vegas, NV 89154
Phone: (702) 895-3666
Fax: (702) 895-0833
theatre.unlv.edu
theatre@unlv.edu
Notes: Est. 1967. Home of Nevada Conservatory Theatre.
Submission Materials: see website
Submission Fee: Yes

University of New Mexico (UNM)
1 UNM, MSC04-2570

Department of Theatre & Dance
Albuquerque, NM 87131
Phone: (505) 277-4332
Fax: (505) 277-8921
www.unm.edu/
wliotta@unm.edu
Notes: University established 1892. Theater
Deptartment established 1930. Degree offered:
MFA, dramatic writing.
Submission Materials: see website
Submission Fee: Yes

University of New Orleans (UNO)
Film, Theatre and Communication Arts
2000 Lake Shore Drive-PAC 307
New Orleans, LA 70148
Phone: (504) 280-6317
Fax: (504) 280-6318
www.uno.edu
dhoover@uno.edu
Notes: Degrees offered: BA, MFA.
Submission Materials: see website
Submission Fee: Yes

University of South Florida (USF)
4202 E. Fowler Ave., FAH 110
Tampa, FL 33620
Phone: (813) 974-2701
theatreanddance.arts.usf.edu/theatre
mpowers@arts.usf.edu
Notes: Degree offered: BA.
Submission Materials: see website
Submission Fee: Yes

University of Southern California
University Park, DRC 107
Los Angeles, CA 90089
Phone: (213) 740-1286
theatre.usc.edu/graduate-programs/graduate-
degrees/mfa-dramatic-writing.aspx
thtrinfo@usc.edu
Notes: The MFA in Dramatic Writing is an
intimate, dynamic three-year program that
approaches the craft through its critical roots
in playwriting and extends this exploration
into other genre of dramatic writing. The program encompasses stage, film and television
studies for today's dramatic writer.
Submission Materials: see website
Submission Fee: Yes

University of Texas, Austin
Department of Theate and Dance
The Unversity of Texas At Austin
1 University Station, D3900

Austin, TX 78712
Pamela Christian, Director of Graduate
Studies
Phone: (512) 232-5325
Fax: (512) 471-0824
www.utexas.edu/finearts/tad/
suzanz@mail.utexas.edu
Notes: The MFA in Playwriting Program at
the University of Texas at Austin is a demand-
ing, three-year course of study designed for
artists committed to professional dramatic
writing and its teaching. The curriculum
emphasizes the generation and revision of new
work, both by the individual playwright and in
progressive collaborations with other writers
and artists within the department.
Submission Materials: see website
Submission Fee: Yes

University of Texas, El Paso (UTEP)
Fox Fine Arts, Rm. 371
500 W. Univ. Ave.
El Paso, TX 79968
Phone: (915) 747-5746
Fax: (915) 747-5438
www.theatredance.utep.edu
jmurray@utep.edu
Submission Materials: see website
Preferred Genre: Plays (No Musicals)
Preferred Length: Any length
Submission Fee: No
Deadline(s): Open

University of Toledo
2801 W. Bancroft Ave.
Toledo, OH 43606
James S. Hill
Phone: (419) 530-2855
Fax: (419) 530-5439
www.utoledo.edu/as/theatrefilm
james.hill@utoledo.edu
Notes: PhD.

University of Tulsa (TU)
Kendall Hall, 600 S. College Ave. Tucker
Drive
Tulsa, OK 74104
Michael Wright, Director, Creative Writing
Phone: (918) 631-2566
Fax: (918) 631-5155
www.cas.utulsa.edu/writing
michael-wright@utulsa.edu
Notes: Degree offered: BA.
Submission Materials: see website
Submission Fee: Yes

University of Wyoming
1000 E. University Ave.
Dept. 3951
Laramie, WY 82071
Phone: (307) 766-2198
www.uwyo.edu/th&d
jchapman@uwyo.edu
Notes: Degrees offered: BA, BFA.
Submission Materials: see website
Submission Fee: Yes

Villanova Theatre
800 Lancaster Ave., Vasey 5
Villanova, PA 19085
Phone: (610) 519-4897
Fax: (610) 519-6803
theatre.villanova.edu
elisa.hibbs@villanova.edu
Submission Materials: see website
Submission Fee: Yes

Virginia Tech (VT)
250 E. Henderson Hall
Blacksburg, VA 24061
Phone: (540) 231-5335
Fax: (540) 231-7321
www.theatrecinema.vt.edu
praun@vt.edu
Notes: Degrees offered: BA, MFA.
Submission Materials: see website
Submission Fee: Yes

Wayne State University
4841 Cass Ave.
Detroit, MI 48201
Phone: (313) 577-6508
www.wayne.edu
d_magidson@wayne.edu
Notes: Degrees offered: BA, BFA, MFA, MFA, PhD.
Submission Materials: see website
Submission Fee: Yes

Wellesley College
106 Central St.
Wellesley, MA 02181
Nora Hussey, Director, Theater Studies
Phone: (781) 283-2029
Fax: (781) 283-3654
theatre.wellesley.edu
nhussey@wellesley.edu
Notes: BA.

Wright State University
Department of Theatre, Dance & Motion Pictures
3640 Col. Glenn Hwy.
Dayton, OH 45435
Phone: (937) 775-3702
www.wright.edu/tdmp
victoria.oleen@wright.edu
Notes: Stuart McDowell, Chair. BA, BFA.

Yale University School of Drama
Box 208325
New Haven, CT 06520
Maria Leveton, Admissions Administrator
Phone: (203) 432-0254
drama.yale.edu/program/playwriting
maria.leveton@yale.edu
Notes: MFA in Playwriting–Yale School of Drama's Playwriting department is designed to guide the writer in finding honest and vivid strategies that articulate the personal and cultural impulses for writing and making theatre. Yale School of Drama's playwriting program believes that every voice is unique: by intense submersion into a spectrum of aesthetics, literature and theory, the writer's singular voice is strengthened.
Submission Materials: see website
Submission Fee: Yes
Deadline(s): See website

Workshops

Academy for New Musical Theatre (ANMT)
5628 Vineland Ave.
North Hollywood, CA 91601
Elise Dewsberry, Artistic Director
Phone: (818) 506-8500
Fax: (818) 506-8500
www.anmt.org
academy@anmt.org

Notes: Est. 1981. Commercial development (readings, workshops, contest) of new musicals. Additional programs include online curriculum, mentoring/development/feedback. Submit via website.
Submission Materials: query letter
Preferred Genre: Musical theatre
Preferred Length: Any length
Submission Fee: Yes

Deadline(s): December 15 for New Musicals; August 1 for ANMT Core Curriculum

ASCAP Musical Theatre Workshop [NY]
1 Lincoln Plaza, Fl. 7
New York, NY 10023
Michael A. Kerker, Director Musical Theatre
Phone: (212) 621-6234
Fax: (212) 621-6558
www.ascap.com
mkerker@ascap.com
Notes: Directed by Stephen Schwartz, program of 50-minutes from works-in-progress before a panel of professional directors, musical directors, producers, critics and fellow writers. All sessions begin 7pm, May–Jun.
Submission Materials: audio CD (4 songs), bio, song descriptions, synopsis
Preferred Genre: Musical theatre
Preferred Length: 50–60 min.
Submission Fee: No

ASCAP/Disney Musical Theatre Workshop [CA]
7920 W. Sunset Blvd., Fl. 3
Los Angeles, CA 90046
Michael Kerker, Director Musical Theatre
Phone: (323) 883-1000
Fax: (323) 883-1049
www.ascap.com
mkerker@ascap.com
Notes: Directed by Stephen Schwartz, 50-min presentation of works-in-development before a professional panel. All sessions begin 7pm, Jan–Feb.
Submission Materials: audio CD (4 songs), bio, song descriptions, synopsis
Preferred Genre: Musical theatre
Preferred Length: 50–60 min.
Submission Fee: No

Asian American Theater Company NewWorks Incubator Project
1695 18th Street, C101
San Francisco, CA 94577
Duy Nguyen, Artistic Director
Phone: (415) 913-7366
Fax: (415) 543-5638
www.asianamericantheater.org
duy@asianamericantheater.org
Notes: Est. 2003. Combines San Francisco's best emerging playwrights and actors to create original new plays. Lead by Sean Lim and mentored by Philip Kan Gotanda, the group meets twice monthly to test new material and ideas. After six months, four new plays are presented.

BMI Lehman Engel Musical Theatre Workshop
BMI
7 World Trade Center
250 Greenwich Street
New York, NY 10007
Patrick Cook, Director
Phone: (212) 220-3181
Fax: (212) 220-4450
www.bmi.com/genres/theatre
pcook@bmi.com
Notes: Weekly 2-hr sessions (Sept–May) Monday evenings (First Year) or Tuesday evenings (Second Year) in NYC. No housing available.
Submission Materials: application, audio CD
Preferred Genre: Musical theatre
Preferred Length: Any length
Submission Fee: Yes
Deadline(s): August 1, 2013

BMI Lehman Engel Musical Theatre Workshop—Librettists
BMI
7 World Trade Center
250 Greenwich Street
New York, NY 10007
Phone: (212) 830-2508
Fax: (212) 262-2508
www.bmi.com
jbanks@bmi.com
Notes: Weekly 2-hour sessions (Monday eves, Sep–May) in NYC. Occasional special events. No housing available. Download application from website.
Submission Materials: 10-pg sample, application
Preferred Genre: Musical theatre
Preferred Length: Any length
Submission Fee: Yes
Deadline(s): See website

Broadway Tomorrow Musical Theatre
191 Claremont Ave., #53
New York, NY 10027
Elyse Curtis, Artistic Director
Phone: (212) 531-2447
Fax: (212) 532-2447
www.solministry.com/bway_tom.html
solministry@earthlink.net
Notes: Est. 1983. New musicals with new age, transformative, spiritual themes. Concert

readings with writer/composer involvement.
Response time: 6 months.
Submission Materials: audio CD (3 songs),
S.A.S.E., synopsis
Preferred Genre: Adaptation
Preferred Length: Any length
Submission Fee: No

Cherry Lane Theatre Mentor Project
38 Commerce St.
New York, NY 10014
Phone: (212) 989-2020
Fax: (212) 989-2867
www.cherrylanetheatre.org
company@cherrylanetheatre.org
Notes: Est. 1997. Pairs young writers by pro-
fessional recommendation with master to work
on scripts for full season, ending with Equity
Showcase. Production: medium cast size, no
orchestra. Submissions not returned.
Submission Materials: see website
Preferred Genre: All genres
Preferred Length: Any length
Submission Fee: No

Chesterfield Writer's Film Project
1158 26th St., Box 544
Santa Monica, CA 90401
Phone: (213) 683-3977
Fax: (310) 260-6116
www.chesterfield-co.com
Notes: Based at Paramount Pictures, Writer's
Film Project began with support of Steven
Spielberg's Amblin Entertainment. Currently
on hiatus, please see our website for the most
updated information.
Submission Fee: No

Colorado New Play Summit
1101 13th St.
Denver, CO 80204
Phone: (303) 893-4000
Fax: (303) 825-2117
www.dcpa.org
bsevy@dcpa.org
Notes: Est. 1979. Yearly play festival seeks
unproduced scripts. Agent submissions
only, except for the Rocky Mountain states
(Arizona,Colorado,Idaho,Montana,New
Mexico,Utah,Wyoming). Response time: 6
months.
Submission Materials: agent-only
Preferred Genre: Plays (No Musicals)
Preferred Length: Full-length
Submission Fee: No

David Henry Hwang Writers Institute
120 N. Judge John Aiso St.
Los Angeles, CA 90012
Jeff Liu, Literary Manager
Phone: (213) 625-7000
Fax: (213) 625-7111
www.eastwestplayers.org
jliu@eastwestplayers.org
Notes: Est. 1991. 2 workshops per year (fall,
spring).
Submission Materials: query letter
Submission Fee: Yes

Fieldwork
161 6th Ave, Fl. 14
New York, NY 10013
Pele Bauch, Associate Director, Programming
Phone: (212) 691-6969
Fax: (212) 255-2053
www.thefield.org
pele@thefield.org
Notes: Est. 1986. Fieldwork is a unique forum
for artists to share developing works and
exchange feedback, peer to peer. As a method
for giving feedback, Fieldwork reveals how
each piece is perceived by others and fosters
a detailed information exchange. Incisive and
stimulating critiques are guided by an experienced facilitator. Participants meet weekly to
share their developing works.
Preferred Genre: All genres
Submission Fee: Yes

Florida Playwrights' Process
736 Scotland St.
Dunedin, FL 34698
Phone: (727) 734-0880
Fax: (727) 734-0880
flplaypro@yahoo.com
Notes: Unproduced/unoptioned musical
development with technical support. Request
application via email. Production: cast up
to 6, simple set, simple props & costumes.
Response: 3 months.
Submission Materials: 30-pg sample, full
script, S.A.S.E., synopsis
Preferred Genre: Musical theatre
Preferred Length: Any length
Submission Fee: No

Frank Silvera Writers' Workshop
P.O. Box 1791
Manhattanville Station
New York, NY 10027

Garland Lee Thompson, Founding Executive
Director
Phone: (212) 281-8832
Fax: (212) 281-8839
www.fsww.org
playrite@earthlink.net
Notes: Est. 1973. Playwright development
program. Submit via US mail or hand deliver.
Work must be unoptioned/unproduced/
unpublished.
Submission Materials: full script, S.A.S.E.
Preferred Genre: All genres
Submission Fee: No

Hangar Theatre
Box 205
Ithaca, NY 14851
Nick Saldivar, Literary Manager
Phone: (607) 273-8588
www.hangartheatre.org
literary@hangartheatre.org
Notes: The Hangar Theatre welcomes script
submissions to our Mainstage season, as well
as the Hangar Pilot Reading Series. The Pilot
Reading Series offers new and established
playwrights a chance to work with Hangar
alumni directors and actors on new plays.
During the Fall and Spring, the series takes
place in New York City. In the Summer, the
series returns to Ithaca where the playwright is
offered a week to workshop the play with the
Lab Compay, our resident apprentice company
of bourgeoning actors and directors.
Submission Materials: see website
Preferred Genre: All genres
Preferred Length: Any length
Submission Fee: Yes
Deadline(s): March 15, 2013

Harold Prince Musical Theatre Program
311 W. 43rd St., #307
New York, NY 10036
Phone: (212) 246-5877
Fax: (212) 246-5882
www.directorscompany.org
directorscompany@gmail.com
Submission Materials: see website
Preferred Genre: Musical theatre
Preferred Length: Full-length
Submission Fee: Yes

Horse Trade Theater Group
85 E. 4th St.
New York, NY 10003
Hedi Grumelot, Associate Producer

Phone: (212) 777-6088
Fax: (212) 777-6120
www.horsetrade.info
submissions@horsetrade.info
Notes: Horse Trade is a self-sustaining theater development group; with a focus on new
work featuring a resident artist program.
The Horse Trade Playwriting Workshop
brings together a playwright cohort that work
together to develop and polish completed full
length drafts of plays. The workshop sessions
are designed to clarify storytelling, develop
craft, and provide resources for professional
playwright development. Each playwright
will have the opportunity to receive feedback
from professional dramaturges and directors,
submit revisions for critique, and use writing
tactics that strategically develop their scripts.
The workshop will culminate in the presentation of 10 minutes of each script directed and
performed by The Drafts Ensemble. Based on
audience feedback and the input of workshop
facilitators, one script will be choses for a full
length reading in the Red Room.
Submission Materials: full script
Preferred Genre: All genres
Preferred Length: Any length
Submission Fee: No

Jeffrey Sweet's Improv for Playwrights
250 W. 90th St., #15-G
New York, NY 10024
Kristine Niven, Artistic Co-Director
Phone: (212) 875-1857
www.artisticnewdirections.org
artnewdir@aol.com
Notes: Est. 1986. Jeffrey Sweet teaches
technique for setting up scenes to improvise
toward first drafts of one-acts, plus revising,
introducing characters, and using improv for
full-lengths. Monthly sessions. Fees: vary per
length of session

Manhattan Playwrights Unit (MPU)
338 W. 19th St., #6-B
New York, NY 10011
Saul Zachary, Artistic Director
Phone: (212) 989-0948
Fax: (212) 823-0084
saulzachary@yahoo.com
Notes: Est. 1979. Ongoing biweekly in-house
workshop for professional-level playwrights
and screenwriters. Informal and intense.
Submissions not returned.
Submission Materials: query letter, resume

Preferred Genre: All genres
Preferred Length: Any length
Submission Fee: No

Missouri Playwrights Workshop (MPW)
129 Fine Arts Bldg.
Columbia, MO 65211
David Crespy, Artistic Director
Phone: (573) 882-0535
Fax: (573) 884-4034
www.theatre.missouri.edu/mpw/index.htm
crespyd@missouri.edu
Notes: Est. 1998. Weekly salon for developing work by playwrights residing in Missouri as well as MU theatre alumni, faculty, and staff who can attend workshop. Submissions not returned.
Submission Materials: query letter, synopsis
Preferred Genre: All genres
Preferred Length: Any length
Submission Fee: No

New Directors/New Works (ND/NW)
Drama League
520 8th Ave., #320
New York, NY 10018
Roger Danforth, Artistic Director
Phone: (212) 244-9494
Fax: (212) 244-9191
www.dramaleague.org
directorsproject@dramaleague.org
Notes: Directors Project program to support new works by directors and collaborating artists.
Submission Materials: see website
Preferred Genre: Plays or Musicals
Preferred Length: Any length
Submission Fee: Yes
Deadline(s): See website

Pataphysics
41 White St.
New York, NY 10013
The Flea
Phone: (212) 226-0051
Fax: (212) 965-1808
www.theflea.org
garyw@theflea.org
Notes: Pataphysics workshops are scheduled sporadically and occur unexpectedly. To receive notification of upcoming classes, please email.
Submission Materials: see website
Submission Fee: No

PlayGround
268 Bush Street #2912
San Francisco, CA 94104
Jim Kleinmann, Artistic Director
Phone: (415) 992-6677
Fax: (415) 704-3177
playground-sf.org
jim@playground-sf.org
Notes: PlayGround offers playwriting master classes with leading Bay Area playwrights, dramaturgs and producers. These classes are open to the public and take place at A.C.T. Studios on the first Monday of the month. Advance registration required.
Submission Fee: No

Playwrights' Center of San Francisco Staged Readings
588 Sutter St., #403
San Francisco, CA 94102
Phone: (415) 820-3206
playwrightscentersf.org
Submission Materials: see website
Preferred Genre: All genres
Preferred Length: Any length
Submission Fee: No
Deadline(s): See website

Playwrights Foundation
1616 16th Street, Suite 350
San Francisco, CA 94103
Phone: (415) 626-2176
Fax: (415) 575-1355
www.playwrightsfoundation.org
jill@playwrightsfoundation.org
Notes: Every year Playwrights Foundation produces the Bay Area Playwrights Festival (BAPF) in July. For submission information and deadlines please refer to our website.

Playwrights Gallery
119 W. 72nd St., #2700
New York, NY 10023
Deborah Savadge, Literary Manager
Phone: (212) 595-4597
www.playwrightsgallery.com
playwrightsgallery@gmail.com
Notes: Est. 1989. Ongoing workshop. Company of professional actors reads new work by NYC-based playwrights twice monthly. Sept-June. Public readings 2–3 times/year. Meet Sep-June. Two sessions: Tuesdays, Wednesdays, noon–2pm. Response Time: 9 months.
Submission Materials: 10-pg sample

Preferred Length: Full-length
Submission Fee: No
Deadline(s): January 1, 2013; 7/1/2013

Playwrights' Platform
9 Cutter Lane
Quincy, MA 02171
www.playwrightsplatform.org
membership@playwrightsplatform.org
Notes: Est. 1976. Monthly developmental
readings in Boston area and annual festival in
Boston, Massachusetts. Response: 3 months.
Submission Materials: see website
Preferred Genre: All genres
Preferred Length: Any length
Submission Fee: Yes

Primary Stages Playwriting Workshops
307 W. 38th St., #1510
New York, NY 10018
Phone: (212) 840-9705
Fax: (212) 840-9725
www.primarystages.org
info@primarystages.org
Notes: Est. 2002. Each week, 8 writers bring
10–15 pages for instructor feedback and group
discussion, completing first draft of new full-
length in 10 weeks.
Submission Materials: application
Preferred Genre: Plays (No Musicals)
Preferred Length: Full-length
Submission Fee: Yes

Pulse Ensemble Theatre's Playwrights' Lab
248 W. 35th St., 15th Floor
New York, NY 10001
Brian Richardson, Company manager
Phone: (212) 695-1596
www.pulseensembletheatre.org
brian@pulseensembletheatre.org
Notes: Develops work of each playwright in
4-month workshop. Group (limit 10) meets
3 hours/week to read scenes, with discussion
afterward. Presents two showcases of 3 works/
year. Some plays selected for further development. Group is under the leadership of Award
winning playwright Lezley Steele. Fees $100/
month.
Preferred Genre: All genres

**Remembrance Through the Performing
Arts New Play Development**
P.O. Box 162446
Austin, TX 78716
Rosalyn Rosen, Artistic Director

Phone: (512) 329-9118
Fax: (512) 329-9118
remperarts@aol.com
Notes: Est. 1988. New plays (unoptioned/
unproduced/unpublished) in workshop through
work in progress productions. Production: cast
limit 8. Response: 2 months.
Submission Materials: 10-pg sample, query
letter, S.A.S.E., synopsis
Preferred Genre: Plays (No Musicals)
Preferred Length: Any length
Submission Fee: No

Sewanee Writers' Conference
735 University Ave., 123-D Gailor H
Sewanee, TN 37383
Phone: (931) 598-1141
Fax: (931) 598-1145
www.sewaneewriters.org
cpeters@sewanee.edu
Notes: Est. 1990. Workshop in late July led
by two noted playwrights. Limited number of
scholarships and fellowships available on a
competitive basis.
Submission Materials: see website
Preferred Genre: All genres
Preferred Length: Any length
Submission Fee: Yes
Deadline(s): See website

Soho Rep Writer/Director Lab
Soho Repertory
401 Broadway, Suite 300
New York, NY 10013
Phone: (212) 941-8632
Fax: (212) 941-7148
www.sohorep.org
writerdirector@sohorep.org
Notes: Est. 1998. Five or six writer/director
pairs are selected to create plays from scratch.
From October–April, the Lab meets on alter-
nate weeks. Writers agree in advance to bring
in work three times during the six-month
cycle. At each meeting, Lab members read the
plays aloud, then discuss the work. At the end
of the cycle, the plays born from the Lab are
presented in a public reading series at Soho
Rep.
Submission Materials: application, full
script
Preferred Genre: Plays (No Musicals)
Preferred Length: Full-length
Submission Fee: No
Deadline(s): See website

Southern Writers Project (SWP)
1 Festival Dr.
Montgomery, AL 36117
Phone: (334) 271-5342
Fax: (334) 271-5348
www.southernwritersproject.net
swp@asf.net
Notes: Est. 1991. Prefer Southern or African American themed work or from a Southern writer. Develop unproduced scripts in week-long workshop with possible production. Response: 6 months.
Submission Materials: full script, S.A.S.E.
Preferred Genre: Plays (No Musicals)
Preferred Length: Full-length
Submission Fee: No

Sundance Institute Theatre Lab
180 Varick St.
Suite 1330
New York, NY 10014
Phone: (646) 822-9563
Fax: (310) 360-1975
www.sundance.org/programs/theatre-lab
theatre@sundance.org
Notes: The Sundance Institute Theatre Lab, the centerpiece of the Theatre Program, is a three-week play development retreat designed to support the creation of new work by playwrights, directors, composers and librettists, and to provide a place where that work can be effectively mentored and challenged. Operated under the umbrella of Sundance Institute, founded by Robert Redford, the Theatre Lab offers an independent-minded community for artists-both emerging and established -to engage with their work, ask questions, build text, and take risks.
Submission Materials: see website
Submission Fee: Yes
Deadline(s): September 15, 2013; 11/15/2013

The Kennedy Center New Visions/New Voices Festival (NVNV)
Kennedy Center
P.O. Box 101510
Arlington, VA 22210
Kim Peter Kovac, Director, KCTYA
Phone: (202) 416-8830
Fax: (202) 416-8297
www.kennedy-center.org/education/nvnv.html
kctya@kennedy-center.org
Notes: Est. 1991. Biennial (even years) weeklong developmental residency in May,

culminating in a national conference, to support new plays and musicals for young audiences.
Submission Materials: see website
Preferred Genre: Plays or Musicals
Preferred Length: One-Act
Special interest: Theatre for Young Audiences
Submission Fee: No
Deadline(s): See website

The New Harmony Project
Box 441062
Indianapolis, IN 46244
Joel Grynheim, Project Director
Phone: (317) 464-1103
Fax: (317) 464-1103
www.newharmonyproject.org
jgrynheim@newharmonyproject.org
Notes: Est. 1986. Development thru rehearsals and readings in 14 day conference of scripts that explore the human journey by offering hope and showing respect for the positive values of life.
Submission Materials: see website
Preferred Length: Full-length
Submission Fee: No
Deadline(s): See website

The PlayCrafters Group
11 Golf View Rd.
Doylestown, PA 18901
James Breckenridge, Creative Writing Consultant
Phone: (888) 399-2506
www.playcraftersgroup.com
hbcraft@att.net
Notes: We provide script analysis and private consultations to help writers better focus their creativity and present their work in compelling and commercially viable ways.
Submission Materials: see website
Preferred Genre: All genres
Submission Fee: No

The Scripteasers
3404 Hawk St.
San Diego, CA 92103
Jonathan Dunn-Rankin, Corresponding Secretary
Phone: (619) 295-4040
www.scripteasers.org
thescripteasers@msn.com
Notes: Est. 1948. Writers' development group with biweekly readings of original plays and

facilitated discussion. Staff: Jonathan Dunn-Rankin (Secretary).

Urban Retreat
Young Playwrights Inc
P.O. Box 5134
New York, NY 10185
Phone: (212) 594-5440
Fax: (212) 684-4902
www.youngplaywrights.org
admin@youngplaywrights.org
Notes: July workshop: authors age 14–21 collaborate with professional dramaturgs, directors, and actors on staged reading of a new play to be presented in an Off-Broadway theater.
Submission Materials: 10-pg sample, application
Preferred Genre: Plays (No Musicals)
Special interest: Theatre for Young Audiences
Submission Fee: Yes
Deadline(s): See website

Williamstown Theatre Festival
229 W. 42nd St., #801
New York, NY 10036
Phone: (212) 395-9090
Fax: (212) 395-9099
www.wtfestival.org
wtfinfo@wtfestival.org
Notes: Est. 1955. New Play Staged Reading Series offers 7 works/season. Agent Submission only.
Agent Only: Yes
Submission Materials: query letter, S.A.S.E.
Preferred Genre: Plays (No Musicals)
Preferred Length: Full-length
Submission Fee: No

Women of Color Productions, Inc.: Writers Development Lab
C/O The Field
161 Ave of the Americas, 14Floor
New York, NY 10013
Jacqueline Wade, Executive Producer
Phone: (646) 662-1808
www.womenofcolorpro.citymax.com
womenofcolorfilm@gmail.com

Women's Project Playwrights Lab
55 West End Ave.
New York, NY 10023
Megan Carter, Associate Artistic Director
Phone: (212) 765-1706
Fax: (212) 765-2024
www.womensproject.org
info@womensproject.org
Notes: 2-year program for playwrights, directors, and producers. Each Lab has 10 members who collaborate with guest artists, WP staff, industry professionals, and other Lab participants. Frequency: biennial

Write Now
900 S. Mitchell Drive
Tempe, AZ 85281
Jenny Millinger
Phone: (480) 921-5700
Fax: (480) 921-5777
www.writenow.co
jmillinger@childsplayaz.org
Notes: 1 week of development and staged readings for young audiences grades K–12. Work must be unpublished, unproduced (professionally).
Submission Materials: application, full script
Preferred Length: Any length
Special interest: Theatre for Young Audiences
Submission Fee: No
Deadline(s): See website

Young Playwrights Inc. Advanced Playwriting Workshop
PO Box 5134
New York, NY 10185
Phone: (212) 594-5440
Fax: (212) 684-4902
www.youngplaywrights.org
admin@youngplaywrights.org
Notes: Advanced Playwriting Workshop meets for 18 or younger in midtown Manhattan every Tue, 4:30–7:00pm, October–May. Exercises help members develop and revise new plays.
Submission Materials: see website
Preferred Genre: Plays (No Musicals)
Preferred Length: Any length
Submission Fee: Yes
Deadline(s): See website

Writer Resources

Emergency Funds

Authors League Fund—Emergency Funds
31 East 32nd Street, 7th Floor
New York, NY 10016
Phone: (212) 268-1208
Fax: (212) 564-5363
www.authorsleaguefund.org
staff@authorsleaguefund.org
Notes: The Authors League Fund was established by the Authors League of America, Inc., to help career authors and dramatists in the United States and in financial distress due to an urgent situation. The Fund makes interest-free loans to professional writers in need; for example, writers with health problems and inadequate health insurance, or older writers whose income has ceased. Loan-seekers must show need and documentation of their professional status. Method of contact: telephone, letter or email.
Agent Only: No
Submission Fee: No

Change Emergency Funds
Change, Inc.
P.O. Box 54
Captiva, FL 33924
Phone: (212) 473-3742
Notes: Awards of up to $1,000 for medical, living, or other emergencies. Open to artists of all disciplines, with no U.S. geographical restrictions; students are not eligible. Each applicant must submit a detailed letter describing the financial emergency, copies of outstanding bills, medical fee estimates, etc., and current financial statements, along with a career resume, exhibition or performance announcements, slides or photos of work and two letters of reference from someone in the affiliated field (no video tapes). Only complete applications will be accepted. Change, Inc does not issue more than one grant per person.
Agent Only: No
Submission Fee: No

Creative Resistance Fund
www.freedimensional.org
Notes: The Creative Resistance Fund (CRF) provides $1,500 distress grants to people in danger due to their use of creativity to fight injustice. The fund may be used to evacuate a dangerous situation or to cover living costs while weighing long-term options for safety.

Discipline(s) and media are: Visual arts, Sculpture, Performing arts, Textile art, Music, Literature, Educational programmes, New Media.
Agent Only: No
Submission Fee: No

Dramatists Guild Fund
1501 Broadway
Suite 701
New York, NY 10036
Rachel Routh, Executive Director
Phone: (212) 391-8384
Fax: (212) 944-0420
rrouth@dramatistsguild.com
Notes: The Dramatists Guild Fund awards one-time emergency grants to individual playwrights, lyricists and composers in need of temporary financial assistance due to unexpected illness or extreme hardship. To be considered for personal grant, you must have had a play or musical either presented for a paying audience anywhere in the United States or Canada, and/or published by a legitimate publishing/licensing company; or be an active member of The Dramatists Guild.
Agent Only: No
Submission Materials: see website
Submission Fee: No

El Pomar Foundation
Board of Trustees
10 Lake Circle
Colorado Springs, CO 80906
Phone: 1 (800) 554-7711
www.elpomar.org
Notes: The Foundation promotes the current and future well being of the people of Colorado through grantmaking and community stewardship. Funding interests include health, human services, education, arts and humanities, and civic and community initiatives. The Foundation's current focus is on assisting those most affected by the difficult economic situation. Application guidelines are available on the Web site. Grant: $50,000
Agent Only: No
Submission Fee: No

John Anson Kittredge Educational Fund
Key Trust Company of Maine
P.O. Box 1054
Augusta, ME 04332

Notes: Submit Applications to: P.O. Box 382203, Cambridge, MA 02238-2203 Grants awarded to artists in very special circumstances. $1,000–$10,000. Initial contact by letter stating purpose, amount requested, period of funding, supporting letter.
Agent Only: No
Submission Fee: No

Mary Mason Memorial Lemonade Fund
1663 Mission Street, #525
San Francisco, CA 94103
Dale Albright, Director of Field Services
Phone: (415) 430-1140
Fax: (415) 430-1145
www.theatrebayarea.org
dale@theatrebayarea.org
Notes: Mail application through US mail. Fund exists to support Bay Area theatre artists that are critically ill or facing a life threatening emergency.
Agent Only: No
Submission Materials: application
Submission Fee: No

PEN Writers Fund
588 Broadway, #303
New York, NY 10012
Phone: (212) 334-1660
Fax: (212) 334-2181
www.pen.org
lara@pen.org
Notes: Est. 1921. The PEN Writers Fund is an emergency fund for professionally published or produced-writers with serious financial difficulties. Depending on the situation, the fund gives grants or loans of up to $1,000. The maximum amount is given only under especially dire circumstances and when monies are available. The PEN Fund for Writers and Editors with HIV/AIDS, administered under the PEN Writers Fund, gives grants of up to $1,000 to professional writers and editors who face serious financial difficulties because of HIV or AIDS-related illness. The Writers Fund does not exist for research purposes, to enable the completion of writing projects, or to fund publications or organizations. The Writers Fund Committee meets approximately every two months to review applications.
Agent Only: No
Submission Materials: see website
Submission Fee: No

Santa Fe Arts Institute Emergency Funds
www.sfai.org/applications.html
Notes: As an outgrowth of our original Emergency Relief Residencies, SFAI has instituted an ongoing Emergency Relief Residency to provide residencies for artists and writers whose lives and work are compromised by domestic strife, political upheaval or natural disasters. Residencies are by application only. In response to the devastating effects of Hurricane Katrina, SFAI is ready to make available its facility to artists, writers and crafts people who lost homes, studios, art work or jobs.
Agent Only: No
Submission Fee: No

SFWA Legal Funds
www.sfwa.org/org/funds.htm
Notes: The SFWA Legal Fund makes loans available to authors who must take a writing-related dispute to court. Loans are made on a case-by-case basis, after review by the Grievance Committee and the SFWA attorney.
Agent Only: No
Submission Fee: No

Springboard Emergency Relief Fund
www.springboardforthearts.org/services/erf.asp
Notes: Springboard's Emergency Relief Fund exists to help meet the emergency needs of artists in need of immediate monies to cover an expense due to loss from fire, theft, health emergency, or other catastrophic, career-threatening event. The purpose of the Emergency Relief Fund is to expedite recovery from a specific economic crisis so that the artist applicant may continue their work. Artist applicants living in Minnesota, Iowa, North Dakota, South Dakota or Wisconsin may access up to $500 to meet or defray unexpected "emergency" expenses. Relief Fund payments are made directly to the business that the artist owes money, not to the artist applicant.
Agent Only: No
Submission Fee: No

TURN2US
www.turn2us.org.uk
Notes: Turn2us is a new independent charity that helps people access the money available to them—through welfare benefits, grants and other help. Their free, accessible website is a

comprehensive and invaluable resource that helps you find sources of financial support, quickly and easily, based on your particular needs and circumstances.
Agent Only: No
Submission Fee: No

Writer's Trust Woodcock Fund— Emergency Funds
90 Richmond Street East
Suite 200
Toronto, ON M5C 1P1, Canada
Phone: (416) 504-8222
Fax: (416) 504-9090
www.writerstrust.com
Notes: Provides emergency funding for established writers in mid-project who are facing financial crisis. Since its inception, the Woodcock Fund has supported 103 Canadian writers in financial difficulty. The total amount dispersed to date is $380,000.
Agent Only: No
Submission Fee: No

Membership & Service Organizations

Alliance of Artists Communities (AAC)
255 South Main St.
Providence, RI 02903
Phone: (401) 351-4320
Fax: (401) 351-4507
www.artistcommunities.org
aac@artistcommunities.org
Agent Only: No
Submission Fee: No

Alliance of Los Angeles Playwrights (ALAP)
7510 Sunset Blvd., #1050
Los Angeles, CA 90046
Dan Berkowitz, Jonathan Dorf, Co-Chairs
Phone: (323) 696-ALAP (2527)
www.laplaywrights.org
info@laplaywrights.org
Notes: Service and support organization for professional needs of Los Angeles playwrights.
Agent Only: No
Submission Materials: application
Submission Fee: Yes

Alternate ROOTS Inc.
1083 Austin Ave., NE
Atlanta, GA 30307
Shannon Turner, Manager of Programs & Services
Phone: (404) 577-1079
Fax: (404) 577-7991
www.alternateroots.org
shannon@alternateroots.org
Notes: Service organization for resident Southern playwrights, directors & choreographers creating original, community-based projects.
Agent Only: No
Submission Materials: application

Submission Fee: Yes

American Association of Community Theatre (AACT)
1300 Gendy St.
Fort Worth, TX 76107
Julie Crawford, Executive Director
Phone: (817) 732-3177
Fax: (817) 732-3178
www.aact.org
info@aact.org
Notes: Est. 1986. Non-producing company.
Agent Only: No
Submission Materials: see website
Submission Fee: Yes
Deadline(s): Beginning September 1, 2013; Ending November 1, 2013

Around the Block Urban Dramatic Literature Workgroup
5 E. 22nd St., #9-K
New York, NY 10010
Carlos Jerome, Workgroup Leader
Phone: (212) 673-9187
www.aroundtheblock.org
info@aroundtheblock.org
Notes: Est. 2001. Focusing on urban life. Special Interests: Urban life and dreams; Technology–community interface. Committed to color blind casting. Contact to participate. Response time: 2 weeks.
Agent Only: No
Submission Materials: see website
Preferred Genre: Plays (No Musicals)
Submission Fee: No

ASCAP (American Society of Composers, Authors & Publishers)
1 Lincoln Plaza
New York, NY 10023

Michael Kerker, Director of Musical Theatre
Phone: (212) 621-6234
www.ascap.com
mkerker@ascap.com
Notes: Est. 1914. Membership organization for composers, lyricists and publishers of musical works. Programs include winter and spring Musical Theater Workshops directed by Stephen Schwartz and Songwriters Showcases in NY and LA. Author must be published, recorded or performed.
Agent Only: No
Submission Materials: application
Preferred Genre: Musical theatre
Submission Fee: No

Association for Jewish Theatre (AJT)
2728 North Hampden Court, #1605
Chicago, IL 60614
Elayne LeTraunik, Coordinator
Phone: (773) 724-1554
www.afjt.com
virtualelayne@gmail.com
Notes: International network of Jewish theatre. Annual conference, newsletter, website, member pages. See submission guide on website.
Agent Only: No
Submission Materials: see website
Submission Fee: No

Association for Theatre in Higher Education (ATHE)
Box 1290
Boulder, CO 80306
Phone: (888) 284-3737
Fax: (303) 530-2168
www.athe.org
info@athe.org
Notes: Organization promoting excellence in theater education thru publications, conferences, advocacy, projects and collaborative efforts with other organizations.
Agent Only: No
Submission Materials: application
Preferred Genre: Educational
Submission Fee: Yes

Association of Authors' Representatives, Inc.
676A 9th Avenue, #312
New York, NY 10036
www.aar-online.org
administrator@aaronline.org
Agent Only: No
Submission Fee: Yes

Authors League Fund
31 E. 32nd St., Fl. 7
New York, NY 10016
Isabel Howe, Administrator
Phone: (212) 568-1208
Fax: (212) 564-5363
www.authorsleaguefund.org
staff@authorsleaguefund.org
Notes: Interest-free loans for personal emergencies of immediate need (rent, medical, etc.).
Agent Only: No
Submission Fee: No

Black Theatre Network
8306 Bluebird Way
Lorton, VA 22079
Artisia V. Green, President
Phone: (850) 656-9061
www.blacktheatrenetwork.org
avgreen@wm.edu
Agent Only: No
Submission Materials: see website
Special interest: African-American
Submission Fee: No

Black Women's Playwrights' Group
2229 Newton St, NE
Washington, DC 20018
Phone: (202) 635-2974
Fax: (202) 882-7239
www.blackwomenplaywrights.org
info@blackwomenplaywrights.org
Notes: The Black Women Playwrights' Group (BWPG) is a service and advocacy group for African American women playwrights writing for the professional theater. The mission of BWPG is to support and promote the work of our members as well advocate on critical issues within the theater world.
Agent Only: No
Submission Materials: see website
Special interest: Women's Interest
Submission Fee: No

Chicago Dramatists
1105 W. Chicago Ave.
Chicago, IL 60642
Russ Tutterow, Artistic Director
Phone: (312) 633-0630
www.chicagodramatists.org
newplays@chicagodramatists.org
Notes: Est. 1979. Developmental theater and playwright workshop. See "Programs" chapter on website for details.
Agent Only: No

Submission Materials: see website
Preferred Genre: All genres
Submission Fee: Yes

Dramatists Guild of America Inc.
1501 Broadway, Suite 701
New York, NY 10036
Rebecca Stump, Membership Associate
Phone: (212) 398-9366
Fax: (212) 944-0420
www.dramatistsguild.com
info@dramatistsguild.com
Notes: Est. 1920. Works for the professional rights of writers of stage works and the conditions under which those works are created and produced. Also fights to secure fair royalties and protect subsidiary rights, artistic control, and copyright ownership.
Agent Only: No
Submission Materials: application, full script
Preferred Genre: All genres
Preferred Length: Any length
Submission Fee: Yes

Educational Theatre Association
2343 Auburn Ave.
Cincinnati, OH 45219
Phone: (513) 421-3900
Fax: (513) 421-7077
www.edta.org
dlafleche@edta.org
Agent Only: No
Submission Materials: see website
Submission Fee: Yes

FirstStage [CA]
P.O. Box 38280
Los Angeles, CA 90038
Dennis Safren, Literary Manager
Phone: (323) 850-6271
Fax: (323) 850-6271
www.firststagela.org
firststagela@aol.com
Notes: Est. 1983. Develops new, unproduced work for stage and screen. Response: 6 months.
Agent Only: No
Submission Materials: full script
Preferred Genre: All genres
Submission Fee: No

Fractured Atlas
248 W. 35th St., 10th Floor
New York, NY 10001

Phone: (888) 692-7878
Fax: (212) 277-8025
www.fracturedatlas.org
support@fracturedatlas.org
Notes: Est. 2002. Microgrants for creative and organizational development.
Agent Only: No
Submission Materials: see website
Submission Fee: Yes
Deadline(s): See website

Greensboro Playwrights' Forum
200 N. Davie St., #2
Greensboro, NC 27401
Stephen D. Hyers, Managing Director
Phone: (336) 335-6426
Fax: (336) 373-2659
www.playwrightsforum.org
stephen@playwrightsforum.org
Notes: Est. 1993. Aids area dramatists in publishling, producing, and learning theater writing with monthly meetings & workshops, staged readings, newsletter, and studio space.
Agent Only: No
Submission Materials: application
Preferred Genre: All genres
Preferred Length: Any length
Submission Fee: Yes

Hispanic Organization of Latin Actors (HOLA)
107 Suffolk St., #302
New York, NY 10002
Manuel Alfaro, Executive Director
Phone: (212) 253-1015
Fax: (212) 253-9651
www.hellohola.org
holagram@hellohola.org
Agent Only: No
Submission Materials: see website
Special interest: Latino
Submission Fee: No

Inside Broadway
630 9th Ave., #802
New York, NY 10036
Phone: (212) 245-0710
Fax: (212) 245-3018
www.insidebroadway.org
mpresser@insidebroadway.org
Notes: Professional children's theater producing classic musicals in NYC public schools. Also offer hands-on, in-school residencies that enrich core curriculum through drama, dance, and music.

Agent Only: No
Submission Materials: see website
Preferred Genre: Musical theatre
Preferred Length: Any length
Special interest: Theatre for Young Audiences
Submission Fee: No

International Center for Women
www.womenplaywrights.org
admin@womenplaywrights.org
Notes: Dedicated to the Support of Female Dramatists around the world—through encouraging attention, production, translation, publication, and international distribution, providing means for communication, assisting development of their craft and setting critical standards, encouraging scholarly and critical examination, supporting efforts to gain equality, and freedom of expression without danger or harassment. Membership allows for access to listserv, members-only area of website, participation in online forums, contact information of fellow members, opportunity to catalogue/archive scripts at various places, apply for readings and grants.
Agent Only: No
Submission Materials: see website
Special interest: Women's Interest
Submission Fee: No

International Theatre Institute US Center (ITI/US)
520 8th Ave., Fl. 24
New York, NY 10018
Phone: (212) 609-5900
Fax: (212) 609-5901
www.tcg.org
iti@tcg.org
Notes: Founded in Prauge in 1948 by UNESCO and the international theatre community. Today, over 97 ITI Centers exist throughout the world to promote the international exchange of knowledge and practice in theatre arts and to deepen mutual understanding and creative cooperation between all people in the theatre arts. See website for further information.
Agent Only: No
Submission Fee: No

LA Stage Alliance
644 S. Figueroa St.
Los Angeles, CA 90017
Phone: (213) 614-0556

Fax: (213) 614-0561
www.lastagealliance.com
info@lastagealliance.com
Notes: Est. 1975. Nonprofit service organization of groups /individuals providing L.A. Stage magazine, networking opportunities, half-price tix, Ovation Awards, cooperative ads, info, referrals.
Agent Only: No
Submission Materials: application
Submission Fee: No

League of Chicago Theatres/League of Chicago Theatres Found
17 N. Wabash Ave., Suite 520
Chicago, IL 60602
Phone: (312) 554-9800
Fax: (312) 922-7202
www.chicagoplays.com
info@chicagoplays.com
Notes: Est. 1979.
Agent Only: No
Submission Materials: see website
Submission Fee: Yes

League of Professional Theatre Women
12 Stuyvesant Oval
apt 8-D
New York, NY 10009
Phone: (212) 414-8048
Fax: (212) 225-2378
www.theatrewomen.org
lindanyc@rcn.com
Notes: Nonprofit advocacy organization promoting visibility and increasing opportunities for women in the professional theater.
Agent Only: No
Submission Fee: Yes

Literary Managers & Dramaturgs of the Americas (LMDA)
P.O.Box 36.20985, P.A.C.C.
New York, NY 10129
Danielle Carroll, Admin Director
Phone: (800) 680-2148
www.lmda.org
lmdanyc@gmail.com
Notes: Est. 1985. Volunteer membership organization with conferences, quarterly journal, newsletter, advocacy caucuses, dramaturgy prize and more.
Agent Only: No
Submission Materials: application
Submission Fee: No

National Association of Women Artists
80 Fifth Ave
Suite 1405
New York, NY 10011
Phone: (212) 675-1616
Fax: (212) 675-1616
www.nawanet.org
office@nawanet.org
Notes: Promotes women artists of all backgrounds and traditions through exhibitions, programs, and its historic archive
Agent Only: No
Special interest: Women's Interest
Submission Fee: No

New Dramatists
424 W. 44th St.
New York, NY 10036
Emily Morse, Director of Artistic Development
Phone: (212) 757-6960
Fax: (212) 265-4738
www.newdramatists.org
newdramatists@newdramatists.org
Notes: Est. 1949. New Dramatists is dedicated to the playwright, and pursues a singular mission: To give playwrights time and space in the company of gifted peers to create work, realize their artistic potential, and make lasting contributions to the theatre.
Agent Only: No
Submission Materials: see website
Submission Fee: No
Deadline(s): between July 15 and September 15 annually

New Playwrights Foundation
P.O. Box 54
Santa Monica, CA 90406
Jeff Bergquist, Artistic Director
Phone: (310) 393-3682
www.newplaywrights.org
dialogue@newplaywrights.org
Notes: Est. 1969. A non-profit 501(c)3 corporation. The writers workshop meets every other Thursday, usually in Santa Monica. NPF has produced members' works for stage, film and video. Writers, actors, directors, producers, composers, and others are encouraged to attend workshop meetings free of charge.
Agent Only: No
Preferred Genre: All genres
Preferred Length: Any length
Submission Fee: Yes
Deadline(s): Ongoing

North Carolina Writers' Network (NCWN)
P.O. Box 21591
Winston-Salem, NC 27120
Ed Southern
Phone: (336) 293-8844
www.ncwriters.org
ed@ncwriters.org
Notes: Nonprofit to connect, promote and lead NC writers thru conferences, contests, newsletter, website, member pages, member book catalog, critique and consultation, etc.
Agent Only: No
Submission Materials: application
Preferred Genre: All genres
Submission Fee: Yes

OPERA America
330 7th Ave., Fl. 16
New York, NY 10001
Phone: (212) 796-8620
Fax: (212) 796-8631
www.operaamerica.org
frontdesk@operaamerica.org
Notes: National service organization promoting creation, presentation and enjoyment of opera. Provides professional development resources for composers, librettists, educators, etc.
Agent Only: No
Submission Materials: application
Preferred Genre: Opera
Submission Fee: Yes

Orange County Playwrights Alliance (OCPA)
21112 Indigo Circle
Huntington Beach, CA 92646
Eric Eberwein, Director
Phone: (714) 962-7686
www.ocplaywrights.org
firenbones@aol.com
Notes: Est. 1995. Member organization workshop of Orange County dramatists. Develops new works, staged readings, occasional productions.
Agent Only: No
Submission Materials: see website
Submission Fee: Yes

Pacific Northwest Writers Assn.
PMB 2717
1420 NW Gilman Blvd, St 2
Issaquah, WA 98027
Phone: (425) 673-2665
www.pnwa.org

pnwa@pnwa.org
Notes: Est. 1956.
Agent Only: No
Submission Materials: application
Submission Fee: No
Deadline(s): See website

Philadelphia Dramatists Center (PDC)
P.O. 22666
Philadelphia, PA 19110-2666
www.pdc1.org
director@pdc1.org
Notes: Membership organization for improving the craft, opportunities and conditions of dramatic writers. Members/non-members can sign up for e-mailing list.
Agent Only: No
Submission Materials: application
Submission Fee: Yes

Playformers
30 Waterside Plaza, #7D
New York, NY 10010
Phone: (917) 825-2663
playformers@earthlink.net
Notes: Est. 1987. Playwright Group. Monthly meetings (September–May) to read new work by members. Response: 2 months.
Agent Only: No
Submission Materials: full script, S.A.S.E.
Preferred Genre: All genres
Preferred Length: Any length
Submission Fee: Yes

Playwrights' Center (MN)
2301 Franklin Ave. E.
Minneapolis, MN 55406
Hayley Finn, Associate Producer
Phone: (612) 332-7481
Fax: (612) 332-6037
www.pwcenter.org
hayleyf@pwcenter.org
Notes: Provides services that support playwrights and playwriting. Programs include listed submission opportunities, fellowships, workshops, readings, classes and online member-to-member networking services.
Agent Only: No
Submission Materials: application
Submission Fee: Yes

Playwrights' Forum [MD]
Box 5322
Rockville, MD 20848
Phone: (301) 816-0569

www.playwrightsforum.org
pforum7@yahoo.com
Notes: Est. 1982. Author must be a Mid-Atlantic resident.
Agent Only: No
Submission Materials: application
Submission Fee: Yes
Deadline(s): January 15, 2013; May 15, 2013; Sept 15, 2013

Playwrights Guild of Canada (PGC)
215 Spadina Ave. Suite 210
Toronto, ON M5T-2C7, Canada
Phone: (416) 703-0201
Fax: (416) 703-0059
www.playwrightsguild.ca
info@playwrightsguild.ca
Notes: Est. 1972. National nonprofit offering triannual directory of Canadian plays/playwrights and quarterly magazine. Response: 3 weeks.
Agent Only: No
Submission Materials: application, resume
Submission Fee: Yes

Saskatchewan Writers Guild (SWG)
Box 3986
Regina, SK S4P 3R9, Canada
Phone: (306) 757-6310
www.skwriter.com
info@skwriter.com
Notes: Est. 1969. Membership is open to all writers, teachers, librarians, publishers, booksellers, students and others interested in Saskatchewan writing.
Agent Only: No
Submission Materials: see website
Submission Fee: Yes
Deadline(s): Last working day of June annually

The Actors Fund
729 7th Ave., Fl. 10
New York, NY 10019
Barbara Davis, Chief Operating Officer
Phone: (212) 221-7300
Fax: (212) 746-0238
www.actorsfund.org
info@actorsfund.org
Notes: The Actors Fund is a nationwide human services organization that helps all professionals in performing arts and entertainment (including writers). The Fund is a safety net, providing programs and services for those are in need, crisis or transition.

Agent Only: No
Submission Fee: No

The Field
161 6th Ave., Fl. 14
New York, NY 10013
Chongsi Chang, Program Associate,
Membership
Phone: (212) 691-6969
Fax: (212) 255-2053
www.thefield.org
chongsi@thefield.org
Notes: Est. 1986. Founded by artists for artists. The Field is dedicated to providing strate-
gic services to thousands of performing artists
and companies in New York City and beyond.
We foster creative exploration, steward innova-
tive management strategies, and are delighted
to help artists reach their fullest potential. The
Field offers Membership, Fiscal Sponsorship,
arts management workshops, creative opportunities, and residencies to artists working in any
performing arts discipline.
Agent Only: No
Preferred Genre: All genres
Preferred Length: Any length
Submission Fee: Yes

The New American Theatre
Hayworth Theatre Center, 2511 Wilsh
Los Angeles, CA 90057
Phone: (310) 701-0788
www.circustheatricals.com
jeannine@NewAmericanTheatre.com
Notes: Est. 1983. Membership company of
actors, directors and writers.
Agent Only: No
Submission Materials: see website
Preferred Genre: All genres
Preferred Length: Any length
Submission Fee: Yes

The Purple Circuit
921 N. Naomi St.
Burbank, CA 91505
Bill Kaiser, Co-founder/Editor
Phone: (818) 953-5096
www.buddybuddy.com/pc.html
purplecir@aol.com
Notes: Service group to promote Lesbian,
Gay, Bisexual, & Transgender (LGBT)
performing arts worldwide. Maintains
California show listings hotline (818-953-
5072), directory of Lesbian, Gay, Bisexual, &

Transgender -friendly venues, and freelisting
of playwrights.
Agent Only: No
Special interest: LGBT
Submission Fee: No

The Theatre Museum
40 Worth Street
Suite 824
New York, NY 10013
Phone: (212) 764-4112
information@thetheatremuseum.org
Notes: Est. 2003. The only non profit museum
in America with the mission to preserve, per-
petuate and protect the legacy of the theatre.
Agent Only: No
Submission Fee: No

The Writers' Guild of Great Britain
40 Rosebery Avenue
London, United Kingdom
Phone: (442) 078-3307 Ext 77
Fax: (442) 078-3347 Ext 77
www.writersguild.org.uk
anne@writersguild.org.uk
Notes: Trades Union Commission (TUC)-
affiliated union for professional writers living
or working in United Kingdom.
Agent Only: No
Submission Materials: see website
Submission Fee: Yes

The Writers Room
740 Broadway, Fl. 12
New York, NY 10003
Donna Brodie, Executive Director
Phone: (212) 254-6995
Fax: (212) 533-6059
www.writersroom.org
writersroom@writersroom.org
Notes: Est. 1978. Large loft with 44 work sta-
tions, library, storage area, kitchen/lounge and
phone room. Open 24/7. 1 month list for full-
time membership; no wait list for part-time.
Agent Only: No
Submission Materials: see website
Submission Fee: Yes

Theater Resources Unlimited (TRU)
Players Theater
115 MacDougal St.
New York, NY 10012
Bob Ost, Executive Director
Phone: (212) 714-7628
Fax: (212) 864-6301

www.truonline.org
trustaff1@gmail.com
Notes: Nonprofit created to help producers produce, emerging theater companies to emerge healthily and all theater professionals to understand and navigate the business of theater. Membership includes self-producing artists as well as career producers. Programs include monthly educational panels, producer boot camp workshops, a new plays and new musicals reading series, monthly programs for actor members, a producer mentorship program, a monthly community newsletter and much more.
Agent Only: No
Submission Materials: see website
Preferred Genre: Plays or Musicals
Preferred Length: Full-length
Submission Fee: Yes

Theatre Bay Area (TBA)
1663 Mission Street #525
San Francisco, CA 94103
Phone: (415) 430-1140
Fax: (415) 430-1145
www.theatrebayarea.org
tba@theatrebayarea.org
Notes: Nonprofit organization, individuals, and theater companies for Bay Area resident authors offering grants, publication and more.
Agent Only: No
Submission Materials: application
Submission Fee: Yes

Theatre Communications Group (TCG)
520 8th Ave., Fl. 24
New York, NY 10018
Phone: (212) 609-5900
Fax: (212) 609-5901
www.tcg.org
tcg@tcg.org
Notes: National service organization for nonprofit US professional theater. Services include grants, fellowships, workshops, conferences, advocacy, research, ticket discounts.
Agent Only: No
Submission Materials: application
Submission Fee: Yes

Theatre Development Fund (TDF)
520 8th Ave. #801
New York, NY 10018
David LeShay, Director of Communications
Phone: (212) 912-9770
Fax: (212) 768-1563

www.tdf.org
dleshay@tdf.org
Notes: Est. 1968. Enabling a diverse audience to attend live theatre and dance through discount ticket booths, memberships.
Agent Only: No
Submission Materials: application
Submission Fee: Yes

Theatre West
3333 Cahuenga Blvd. W.
Hollywood, CA 90068
John Gallogly, Executive Director
Phone: (323) 851-4839
Fax: (323) 851-5286
www.theatrewest.org
theatrewest@theatrewest.org
Notes: Est. 1962. Member organization. Author must be a resident of Southern California. Mandatory 6 hours/month volunterring in 1st year of membership. Scripts accepted for memebership only, not production. Theatre West is a memebership company and we select work based on member interest.
Agent Only: No
Submission Materials: full script
Preferred Genre: Plays or Musicals
Preferred Length: Full-length
Submission Fee: No

United States Copyright Office
101 Independence Ave., SE
Washington, DC 20003
Phone: (202) 707-3000
www.copyright.gov
Notes: Though registration isn't required for protection, copyright law provides several advantages to registration.
Agent Only: No
Submission Materials: see website
Submission Fee: Yes

Women In Theatre
11684 Ventura Blvd
Studio City, CA 91604
Phone: (818) 763-5222
www.womenintheatre.com
julia@lct2039.com
Notes: WIT's programming and activities evolved as a two-fold purpose: to both enlighten the power center in the Los Angeles theatre community of the contribution women can make, and to encourage women to explore opportunities for involvement. Activities include Quarterly Mixers, Luncheons with

special guest speakers, workshops, seminars and symposia on various topics are produced regularly. A weekly e-letter, monthly play readings, discounted theatre tickets and socials provide networking opportunities. WIT's membership uses its varied activities to educate and empower women in theatre, to bring various elements of theatre into the community though outreach programming and to develop works and audiences for theatre in the future.
Agent Only: No
Submission Materials: see website
Special interest: Women's Interest
Submission Fee: No

Women Playwrights' Initiative (WPI)
P.O. Box 1546
Orlando, FL 32802
Phone: (407) 380-1812
womenplaywrights.wordpress.com
womenplaywrights@gmail.com
Notes: Setting new stages for women's voices. Our mission is to foster the development and production of plays written by women, through educational outreach, workshops, readings and productions.
Agent Only: No
Submission Materials: see website
Special interest: Women's Interest
Submission Fee: No

Women Playwrights International
www.wpinternational.net
wpintl@wpinternational.net
Notes: The mission of Women Playwrights International is to further the work of women playwrights around the world by promoting their works, encouraging and assisting the development of their works and bringing international recognition to their works. "Women Playwrights" shall be understood to include all women working in the theater of all races, classes, ages, ethnic or religious background, sexual preferences, and women with disabilities.
Agent Only: No
Submission Materials: see website
Special interest: Women's Interest
Submission Fee: No

Women's Theatre Alliance
2936 N. Southport Ave.

Chicago, IL 60657
Brenda E. Kelly, President
Phone: (312) 408-9910
www.wtachicago.org
wtachicago@gmail.com
Notes: Membership organization devoted to supporting, promoting, and showcasing Chicago's female theatre artists.
Agent Only: No
Submission Materials: see website
Special interest: Women's Interest
Submission Fee: No

Writers Guild of America, East (WGAE)
555 W. 57th St., #1230
New York, NY 10019
Phone: (212) 767-7800
Fax: (212) 582-1909
www.wgae.org
strell@sunshinesachs.com
Notes: Est. 1954.
Agent Only: No
Submission Materials: see website
Submission Fee: Yes

Writers Guild of America, West (WGAW)
7000 W. 3rd St.
Los Angeles, CA 90048
Phone: (323) 951-4000
Fax: (323) 782-4800
www.wga.org
Agent Only: No
Submission Materials: see website
Submission Fee: Yes

Young Playwrights Inc.
P.O. Box 5134
New York, NY 10185
Sheri Goldhirsch, Artistic Director
Phone: (212) 594-5440
Fax: (212) 684-4902
www.youngplaywrights.org
admin@youngplaywrights.org
Notes: Est. 1981. Young Playwrights Inc. identifies and develops young (18 and younger) US playwrights by involving them as active participants in the highest quality professional productions of their plays.
Agent Only: No
Submission Materials: see website
Preferred Genre: Plays (No Musicals)
Submission Fee: Yes
Deadline(s): See website

Grant Writing

Without funding, your play or musical will never impact society the way you always dreamed. But have no fear, grant writing resources are here (literally, a few inches down)! With the help of these eager professionals, you can learn the ins and outs of crafting the perfect grant-seeking proposal. You have the creativity and drive; now you need the inside knowledge on how to find the right market for your project, speak the language of grant organizations, and focus your proposal to give it maximum strength. Once you have this invaluable skill set, you can even pay it forward and help other people make their dreams come true (not to mention get paid yourself).

—Hallie Steiner

Deborah Kluge
www.proposalwriter.com/contact.html
Notes: Personal advice website/blog from Deborah Kluge, Proposal Development Consultant/International Development Consultant.

ECS Grants, Inc.
Dr. Bruce Sliger
Phone: (770) 714-3336
dr.sliger@gmail.com
www.grantwriting.com/home.html
Fee?: Yes
Notes: ECS Grants works with various organizations and can help your school, non-profit, or community group learn the grant writing skills your team needs so you can continue offering the level of service you provide.

Education to Go:
Instructor-Facilitated Online Courses
Student Support: PO Box 760
Temecula, CA 92593-0760
ed2go.classes@cengage.com
www.ed2go.com/online-courses/grant-writing-a-to-z.html
Fee?: Yes
Notes: *A to Z Grant Writing* is an invigorating and informative course that will equip you with the skills and tools you need; online course on grant writing.

Federal Grants
www.federalgrants.com/grant-writing.html
Notes: Advice, resources, articles etc. relating to researching and writing grants, particularly federally funded grants.

Foundation Center
Phone: (800) 634-2953
onlinelibrarian@foundationcenter.org
foundationcenter.org
Notes: Established in 1956 and today supported by close to 550 foundations, the Foundation Center is the leading source of information about philanthropy worldwide. Through data, analysis, and training, it connects people who want to change the world to the resources they need to succeed.

Fundraiser Help
708 Lanham Place
Raleigh, NC 27615
Phone: (919) 870-8889
Fax: (919) 870-6466
www.fundraiserhelp.com/grant-writing.htm
Notes: Fundraiser Help is a web-based business that provides free fundraising information to site visitors. The website also provides an e-book (electronic book) for sale that contains all of the information on the website.

Government Grants
18340 Yorba Linda Blvd
Suite # 107-326
Yorba Linda, CA 92886
Phone: (714) 577-5386
Fax: (714) 961-1412
customersupport@grantseekerpro.us
www.grants.biz/grant_writing.htm
Fee?: Yes
Notes: Tips and strategies on writing grants.

Government Grant Money.Net
governmentgrantmoney.net
Notes: Grants offered, as well as advice on applying and obtaining grants.

GrantLinks
2151 Consulate Dr. Unit 13
Orlando, FL 32837
Phone: (877)-857-9002
grantlinks.net
Notes: Our mission is to help non profit
organizations, churches, small businesses
and individuals with grant writing services.
Whether you need a grant to fund new
nonprofit programs, start your business or
further your education, we have you covered!

Grant Training Center
P.O Box 2223
Arlington, VA 22202
Phone: (866) 704-7268
Fax: (571) 257-8865
granttrainingcenter.com
Fee?: Yes
Notes: The Grant Training Center's mission
is to train educators, researchers, non-profit
professionals, and public sector administrators
to advance their knowledge of federal,
foundation, corporate and individual giving,
and to submit winning proposals.

Grant Writing Training
Phone: (480) 768-7400
grantsconsulting@aol.com
www.grantwritingbootcamp.us
Notes: The mission of the Grant Writing
Training Foundation (GWTF) is to provide
affordable and relevant training in grant
seeking and proposal writing. Classes, articles
and other resources available.

Grant Writing USA
Phone: (800) 814-8191
cs@grantwritingusa.com
www.grantwritingusa.com
Fee?: Yes
Notes: Grant Writing USA delivers training
programs across America that dramatically
enhance performance in the areas of grant
writing, grants management and grant maker
research.

Grantwriters
grantwriters.com
Notes: Free tips and hints to writing grants.
Books and other resources for sale.

Non-Profit Blog.com
www.nonprofitgrantblog.com
Notes: Everything about finding grants and
how to write grant proposals that are effective.

Non-Profit Expert.com
www.nonprofitexpert.com/grant.htm
Note: Advice and articles on the ins and outs
of non profit organizations.

Resource Associates
Phone: (505) 326-4245
www.grantwriters.net
Notes: Free grant writers/grant writing
opportunities.

U.S. Environmental Protection Agency
www.epa.gov/ogd/recipient/tips.htm
Notes: Tips on Grant Writing.

Books On Writing for the Stage

Art, Craft, Theory, and Business

The following list was designed to aid writers in selecting the scriptwriting, craft and business
books that best fit their individual needs. Readers can generally assume that playwriting craft
books will explore action, character and dialogue. Specific aspects of craft that are emphasized
by the author are listed under features. Chapter or section titles that suggest further distinguish-
ing features are listed in quotes.

*The 2011 Screenwriter's and
Playwright's Market*
By: Chuck Sambuchino
Publisher: Writers Digest Books
Publication date: 3rd ed, November 26, 2010
ISBN: 978-1-58297-957-1
Features: Business strategies, Business
resources

American Theatre Magazine
Online: www.tcg.org
Contact: Theatre Communications Group
520 8th Avenue, 24th floor
New York, NY 10018-4156
212-609-5900
custserv@tcg.org
Features: National monthly magazine
for American professional not-for-profit

theatre featuring articles on important issues, productions and developments in contemporary theatre.

The Art and Craft of Playwriting
By: Jeffrey Hatcher
Publisher: FW Publications
ISBN: 978-1-884910-46-3
Features: Aristotle's theories, Interviews, "Space, Time, and Causality," Structure

The Art of Dramatic Writing
By: Lajos Egri
Publisher: Simon and Schuster
Publication date: June 1, 1960
ISBN: 978-0-671-21332-9
Features: Character behavior, Dialectics, "Orchestration," Premise, "Unity of Opposites"

The Art of the Playwright: Creating the Magic of Theatre, Second edition
By: William Packard
Publisher: Thunder's Mouth Press
Publication date: May 5, 1997
ISBN: 978-1-56025-117-0
Features: Business resources, "Contemporary and Avant Garde Playwrights," "Dramatic Versus Narrative"

The art of playwriting: being a practical treatise on the elements of dramatic construction; intended for the playwright, the student, and the dramatic critic
By: Alfred Hennequin
Publisher: Nabu Press
Publication date: September 8, 2010
ISBN: 978-1-171-70855-1
Features: Reproduction of playwriting guide pre-1923

The Art of Writing Drama
By: Michelene Wandor
Publisher: A&C BLACK
Publication date: September 2008
ISBN: 978-0-413-77586-3

An Artist's Guide to the Law
By: Richard Amada
Publisher: Focus Publishing /R. Pullins Co., Inc.
Publication date: February 1, 2010
ISBN: 978-1-58510-356-0
Features: Copyright, intellectual property, contracts

A More Perfect Ten: Writing and Producing the Ten Minute Play
By: Gary Garrison
Publisher: Focus Publishing/R. Pullins Co., Inc.
Publication date: November 30, 2008
ISBN: 978-1-58510-327-0
Features: Formatting for submission, list of theatres and festivals

Backwards & Forwards: A Technical Manual for Reading Plays, First edition
By: David Ball
Publisher: Southern Illinois University Press
Publication date: July 7, 1983
ISBN: 978-0-8093-1110-1
Features: Literary analysis

Blunt Playwright: An Introduction to Playwriting
By: Clem Martini
Publisher: Consortium Book
Publication date: September 30, 2007
ISBN: 978-0-88754-894-9
Features: Exercises, Play analyses, Rewriting, Workshopping

Business and Legal Forms For Theater, Second edition
By: Charles Grippo
Publisher: Allworth Press
ISBN: 978-1-58115-323-1
Features: 40 fill in the blank contracts with guidelines of how to use (Simple Production License, Collaborations, Song Licensing and much more)

Characters in Action: Playwriting the Easy Way, First Edition
By: Marsh Cassady (Author), Theodore O Zapel (Editor), Tom Myers (Designer)
Publisher: Meriwether Publishing Ltd.
Publication date: September 1, 1995
ISBN: 978-1-56608-010-1
Features: Playwriting

Collaborative Playwright: Practical Advice for Getting Your Play Written
By: Bruce Graham, Michele Volansky
Publisher: Heinemann
Publication date: March 30, 2007
ISBN: 978-0-325-00995-7
Features: Collaboration, Interviews, "Prewriting and Outlines," Rewriting

The Crafty Art of Playmaking
By: Alan Ayckbourn
Publisher: Palgrave Macmillan
Publication date: September 30, 2008
ISBN: 978-0-230-61488-8
Features: Directorial perspectives

Creating Unforgettable Characters
By: Linda Seger
Publisher: Henry Holt
Publication date: July 1, 1990
ISBN: 978-0-8050-1171-5
Features: Character psychology, "Creating Nonrealistic Charcters," Research

Developing Story Ideas, Second edition
By: Michael Rabiger
Publisher: Focal Press
Publication date: November 4, 2005
ISBN: 978-0-240-80736-2
Features: Artistic identity, Exercises, Generating ideas

Dramatic Writer's Companion: Tools to Develop Characters, Cause Scenes and Build Stories
By: Will Dunne
Publisher: University of Chicago Press
Publication date: April 15, 2009
ISBN: 978-0-226-17253-8
Features: Character development, Structure

Dramatists Toolkit: The Craft of the Working Playwright
By: Jeffrey Sweet
Publisher: Heinemann
Publication date: November 1, 1993
ISBN: 978-0-435-08629-9
Features: "Negotiations," "Violating Rituals"

The Elements of Playwriting
By: Louis E. Catron
Publisher: Waveland Press
Publication date: November 1, 2001
ISBN: 978-1-57766-227-3
Features: Basic principles, Creating characters, Step-by-step advice

The Female Dramatist: Profiles of Women Playwrights from Around the World from the Middle Ages to the Present Day
By: Elaine T. Partnow, Lesley Anne Hyatt
Publisher: Facts on File
Publication date: June 1998
ISBN: 978-0-8160-3015-6
Features: Theatre history

How to Write a Play (Teach Yourself)
By: David Carter
Publisher: NTC Publishing Group
Publication date: January 11th, 1999
IBSN-13: 978-0-8442-0231-0
Features: Writing of Stage, Film, TV, Radio Plays, Self-production, Marketing and Financial Guidance

In Their Own Words: Contemporary American Playwrights
By: David Savran
Publisher: Theatre Communications Group
Publication date: January 1, 1993
ISBN: 978-0-930452-70-4
Features: Interviews, Essays

Insight for Playwrights Magazine
Online: www.insightforplaywrights.com
Contact: Insight for Playwrights
11309 E Petra Ave
Mesa, AZ 85212
Features: Monthly publication featuring submission guidelines on theatres seeking new works, grants, contests, festivals, etc.

Making Musicals: An Informal Introduction to the World of Musical Theater, First Limelight edition
By: Tom Jones
Publisher: Limelight Editions
Publication date: August 1, 2004
ISBN: 978-0-87910-095-7
Features: History, How-to, Memoir

The Making of a Musical, First Limelight edition
By: Lehman Engel
Publisher: Limelight Editions
Publication date: January 1986
ISBN: 978-0-87910-049-0
Features: History, Musical writing advice, Producing

Musical Theatre Writer's Survival Guide
By: David Spencer
Publisher: Heinemann
Publication date: July 1, 2005
ISBN: 978-0-325-00786-1
Features: Musical writing, Collaboration, Business strategies, "Presentation, Formatting and Packaging," "The Spirit of the Thing, or: Adaptation"

Naked Playwriting: The Art, the Craft, and the Life Laid Bare

By: Robin U. Russin and William M. Downs
Publisher: Silman-James Press
Publication date: December 15, 2004
ISBN: 978-1-879505-76-6
Features: Business strategies, Generating ideas, Rewriting

The New, Improved Playwright's Survival Guide: Keeping the Drama in Your Work and Out of Your Life
By: Gary Garrison
Publisher: Heinemann Drama
Publication date: October 14, 2005
ISBN:978-0-325-00816-5
Features: Dramatic structure, Synopsizing a play, Uncovering inspiration, Dealing with criticism

New Playwriting Strategies: A Language-Based Approach to Playwriting
By: Paul C. Castagno
Publisher: Theatre Arts Book
ISBN: 978-0-87830-136-2
Features: "On Multivocality and Speech Genres," Play analyses

New Tax Guide for Writers, Artists, Performers and Other Creative People, 2012
By: Peter Jason Riley
Publisher: Focus Publishing/R. Pullins Co., Inc.
Publication date: January 1, 2012
ISBN: 978-1-58510-469-7
Features: Record-keeping, deductions, sample tax forms

Notes from a Practicing Writer: The Craft, Career, and Aesthetic of Playwriting
By: Ed Shockley
Publisher: Lightning Source
Publication date: January 30, 2007
ISBN: 978-0-9726906-3-8
Features: Business strategies, "Compression," "The Magic What-If," "Projection," Play analyses, "Reduction"

Play-Making: A Manual of Craftsmanship
By: William Archer
Publisher: Nabu Press
Publication date: September 8, 2010
ISBN: 978-1-171-75598-2
Features: Historical text

Playwrights on Playwriting: From Ibsen to Ionesco
By: Toby Cole, John Gassner (Introduction)

Publisher: Rowman & Littlefield Publishers, Inc.
Publication date: May 2001
ISBN: 978-0-8154-1141-3
Features: Interviews, Essays

Playwright's Guidebook
By: Stuart Spencer
Publisher: Farrar Straus and Grioux
Publication date: April 1, 2002
ISBN: 978-0-571-19991-4
Features: Exercises, Generating ideas, Rewriting, Structure, "High Stakes and High Hopes," "Writing from an Image"

The Playwright's Handbook, Revised edition
By: Frank Pike, Thomas G. Dunn
Publisher: Plume
Publication date: April 1, 1996
ISBN: 978-0-452-27588-1
Features: Rewriting, Business strategies, Workshops, "Sight, Hearing, Touch, Taste, Smell," "Understanding the Relationship of Ritual and Dram"

The Playwright's Process: Learning the Craft from Today's Leading Dramatists
By: Buzz McLaughlin
Publisher: Back Stage Books
Publication date: May 1, 1997
ISBN: 978-0-8230-8833-1
Features: Interviews, Rewriting, Development, "The Play Idea Worksheet," "The Short-form Biography," "The Long-form Biography"

Playwrights Teach Playwriting
By: Joan Harrington (Editor) and Brian Crystal (Editor)
Publisher: Smith & Kraus
Publication date: September 30, 2006
ISBN: 978-1-57525-423-4
Features: Essays, Interviews, Teaching methods

Playwrights' Voice, First edition
By: David Savran (Editor)
Publisher: Theatre Communications Group
Publication date: April 15, 1999
ISBN: 978-1-55936-163-7
Features: Interviews, Essays

Playwrights at Work
By: Paris Review (Author), George Plimpton (Editor), John Lahr (Introduction)
Publisher: Modern Library

Publication date: May 30, 2000
ISBN: 978-0-679-64021-9
Features: Interviews, Essays

The Playwright's Workbook
By: Jean-Claude Van Itallie
Publisher: Applause
Publication date: 1997
ISBN: 978-1-55783-302-0
Features: Exercises, Play analyses, Images, Various forms and genres

The Playwright's Workout
By: Liz Engelman, Michael Bigelow Dixon
Publisher: Smith and Krause Publishers
ISBN: 978-1-57525-617-7
Features: Exercises

Playwriting: A Complete Guide to Creating Theatre
By: Shelly Frome
Publisher: Mcfarland & Co Inc Pub
Publication date: March 1990
ISBN: 978-0-89950-425-4
Features: Quotations, Interviews, Submissions, Grants, Contests, Festivals, Agents, Examples

Playwriting: A Practical Guide
By: Noel Greig
Publisher: Routledge
Publication date: February 28, 2005
ISBN: 978-0415310444
Features: Generating ideas, Rewriting

Playwriting: A Study in Choices and Challenges (Lillenas Drama Resource How to Book)
By: Paul McCusker
Publisher: Lillenas Publishing Company
Publication date: May 1995
ISBN: 978-0-415-31044-4
Specialty: Christian writing

Playwriting, Brief and Brilliant
By: Julie Jensen
Publisher: Smith & Kraus
Publication date: October 30, 2007
ISBN: 978-1-57525-570-5
Features: Beginning, Re-writing, Writer's block, Marketing

Playwriting for Dummies
by Angelo Parra
Publisher: Wiley Publishing, Inc.
ISBN: 978-1-118-01722-7

Features: Practical (and fun) step-by-step coaching from idea to script to production.

Playwriting: From Formula to Form, First edition
By: William M. Downs (Author), Wright (Author)
Publisher: Wadsworth Publishing
Publication date: August 14, 1997
ISBN: 978-0-15-503861-5
Features: Fundamentals of formula, Marketing

Playwriting in Process – Thinking and Working Theatrically, Second edition
By: Michael Wright
Publisher: Focus Publishing/R. Pullins Co., Inc.
Publication date: Sept. 1, 2010
ISBN: 978-1-58510-340-9
Features: Character, plot, collaboration, unblocking, exercises

Playwriting Master Class – The Personality of Process and the Art of Rewriting
By: Michael Wright
Publisher: Focus Publishing /R. Pullins Co., Inc.
Publication date: August 1, 2010
ISBN: 978-1-58510-342-3
Features: Case studies, individual approaches, post-creative self-analysis

Playwriting: The First Workshop
By: Kathleen George
Publisher: Allworth Press
Publication date: August 1, 2008
ISBN: 978-1-58115-658-4
Features: Basic principles, Alternative approaches, Using autobiographical materials, Play analysis

Playwriting: The Fundamentals
By: Effiong Johnson
Publisher: Xlibris, Corp.
Publication date: February 16, 2011
ISBN: 978-1-4535-8490-3
Features: Nigerian theatre

Playwriting: The Structure of Action
By: Norman A. Bert, Sam Smiley
Publisher: Yale University Press
Publication date: October 30, 2005
ISBN: 978-0-300-10724-1
Features: Aristotle's principles, Generating ideas

Playwriting: Writing, Producing and Selling Your Play
By: Louis E. Catron
Publisher: Waveland Press
Publication date: July 1990
ISBN: 978-0-88133-564-4
Features: Business strategies, Aristotle's principals, Workshops

Practical Playwriting
By: David Copelin
Publisher: Writer, Inc.
Publication date: September 1998
ISBN: 978-0-87116-185-7
Features: Play development

The Power of the Playwright's Vision: Blueprints for the Working Writer
By: Gordon Farrell
Publisher: Heinemann Drama
Publication date: September 6, 2001
ISBN: 978-0-325-00242-2
Features: Blueprints of various playwrights' techniques

Reminiscence Theatre : Making Theatre from Memories
By: Glenda Jackson, Pam Schweitzer
Publisher: Jessica Kingsley Publishers
Publication date: January 15, 2006
ISBN: 978-1-84310-430-8
Features: Community building, Documentary, Teaching methods, Therapy

Script is Finished, Now What Do I Do: The Scriptwriter's Resource Book and Agent Guide
By: K. Callan
Publisher: SCB Distributors
Publication date: January 15, 2007
ISBN: 978-1-878355-18-8
Features: Business resources, Business strategies

Solving Your Script : Tools and Techniques for the Playwright
By: Jeffrey Sweet
Publisher: Heinemann
Publication date: February 15, 2001
ISBN: 978-0-325-00053-4
Features: "Negotiation Over Objects," "Different Relationships, Different Roles," "Disruption of a Ritual"

So You Want to Be a Playwright? : How to Write a Play and Get It Produced
By: Tim Fountain
Publisher: Nick Hern Books
Publication date: April 1, 2008
ISBN: 978-1-85459-716-8
Features: Finding the story, Construction, Strategies for production

Spaces of Creation: The Creative Process of Playwriting
By: Suzan Zeder (Author), Jim Hancock (Author)
Publisher: Heinemann Drama
Publication date: July 1, 2005
ISBN: 978-0-325-00684-0
Features: Exercises, Movement-based mind-body disciples, Creative process

The Stage Producers Business and Legal Guide
By: Charles Grippo
Publisher: Allworth Press
ISBN: 978-1-58115-241-8
Features: Organizing a theater company, Renting spaces, Licensing plays and musicals, Taxes, Managing a Non Profit Theater Company, Joint Ventures and much more

Stage Writers Handbook: A Complete Business Guide for Playwrights, Composers, Lyricists and Librettists
By: Dana Singer
Publisher: Theatre Communications Group
Publication date: May 1, 1996
ISBN: 978-1-55936-116-3
Features: Business resources, Business strategies

Stage Writing
By: Val Taylor
Publisher: Crowood Press
Publication date: September 1, 2002
ISBN: 978-1-86126-452-7
Features: Building relationships, Understanding physical space, Developing story, Creating characters and dialogue, Building a strong structure, Writing effective stage directions, Textual analysis

Strategies for Playbuilding : Helping Groups Translate Issues into Theater
By: Will Weigler
Publisher: Heinemann
Publication date: March 15, 2001

ISBN: 978-0-325-00340-5
Features: Community building, Documentary, Teaching methods

Teaching Young Playwrights
By: Gerald Chapman, Lisa A Barnett
Publisher: Heinemann
Publication date: November 26, 1990
ISBN: 978-0-435-08212-3
Features: Exercises, Teaching methods

Teach Yourself Writing a Play
By: Ann Gawthorpe, Lesley Brown
Publisher: McGraw-Hill
Publication date: October 26, 2007
ISBN: 978-0-07-149697-1
Features: Business strategies, Generating ideas, Genres, Rewriting

Theory and Technique of Playwriting
By: John Howard Lawson
Publisher: Hill & Wang Pub
Publication date: 1961
ISBN: 978-0-8090-0525-3
Features: Historical text

To Be a Playwright, New edition
By: Janet Neipris
Publisher: Theatre Arts Book
Publication date: September 28, 2005
ISBN: 978-0-87830-188-1
Features: "Twelve Habits of Successful Playwrights," "Adapting from Fact and Fiction," "Critics"

The Way of Story: The Craft & Soul of Writing
By: Catherine Ann Jones
Publisher: Ingram Publisher Services
Publication date: August 1, 2007
ISBN: 978-1-932907-32-2
Features: Dialogue Structure, Rewriting, Generating ideas

Words with Music: Creating the Broadway Musical Libretto, Updated & revised edition
By: Lehman Engel
Publisher: Applause Books
Publication date: January 1, 2006
ISBN: 978-1-55783-554-3
Features: Musical theatre writing

Worlds in Words: Storytelling in Contemporary Theatre and Playwriting, New edition

By: Mateusz Borowski (Author, Editor), Malgorzata Sugiera (Editor)
Publisher: Cambridge Scholars Publishing
Publication date: October 1, 2010
ISBN: 978-1-4438-2109-4
Features: Essays on technique

Working on a New Play: A Play Development Handbook for Actors, Directors, Designers and Playwrights, Second edition
By: Edward M. Cohen
Publisher: Limelight Editions
Publication date: July 1, 2004
ISBN: 978-0-87910-190-9
Features: Play development

"Writer's Block" Busters : 101 Exercises to Clear the Deadwood and Make Room for Flights of Fancy
By: Velina Hasu Houston
Publisher: Smith & Kraus
Publication date: September 16, 2008
ISBN: 978-1-57525-597-2
Features: Exercises

Writing For The Stage: A Practical Playwriting Guide
By: Leroy Clark
Publisher: Allyn & Bacon
Publication date: September 23, 2005
ISBN: 978-0-205-41297-6

The Writer Got Screwed (but didn't have to): Guide to the Legal and Business Practices of Writing for the Entertainment Industry
By: Brooke A. Wharton
Publisher: Harper Paperbacks
Publication date: March 14, 1997
ISBN: 978-0-06-273236-1
Features: Business strategies

The Writer's Journey: Mythic Structure for Writers
By: Christopher Vogler
Publisher: Ingram Publisher Services
Publication date: November 1, 2007
ISBN: 978-1-932907-36-0
Features: Mythic structure, Mythic characters

Writing 45-minute One-act Plays, Skits, Monologues, & Animation Scripts for Drama Workshops : Adapting Current Events, Social Issues, Life Stories, News & Histories
By: Anne Hart

Publisher: ASJA Press
Publication date: March 14, 2005
ISBN: 978-0-595-34597-7
Features: One-act plays, Documentary

Writing Dialogue for Scripts: Effective Dialogue for Film, TV, Radio, and Stage, Third edition
By: Rib Davis
Publisher: A&C Black
Publication date: January 1, 2009
ISBN: 978-1-4081-0134-6
Features: Dialogue

Writing the Broadway Musical
By: Aaron Frankel
Publisher: Perseus Books Group
Publication date: August 17, 2000
ISBN: 978-0-306-80943-9
Features: Musical writing

Writing Musical Theatre
By: Allen Cohen, Steven L. Rosenhaus
Publisher: St. Martins Press
Publication date: February 7, 2006
ISBN: 978-1-4039-6395-6
Features: Musical writing, Adaptations, Business strategies

Writing Your First Play
By: Stephen Sossaman
Publisher: Prentice Hall
Publication date: August 11, 2000
ISBN: 978-0-13-027416-8
Features: Step-by-step, Critical revision, Exercises

Writing: Working in the Theatre
By: Robert Emmet Long (Editor), Paula Vogel (Foreword)
Publisher: Continuum
Publication date: January 15, 2008
ISBN: 978-0-8264-1807-4
Features: Production, Recent shows

You Can Write a Play!, Revised edition
By: Milton E. Polsky
Publisher: Applause Books
Publication date: February 1, 2002
ISBN: 978-1-55783-485-0
Features: Exercises

Young At Art : Classroom Playbuilding in Practice, First edition
By: Christine Hatton and Sarah Lovesy
Publisher: David Fulton Publish
Publication date: November 24, 2008
ISBN: 978-0-415-45478-0
Features: Exercises, Teaching methods

Index of Special Interests

African-American

American

Asian-American

Deaf

Disabled

Jewish

Latino

LGBT

Multi-Ethnic

Native American

Theatre for Young Audiences

Women's Interest

Submission Calendar

| April 15, 2013 | FUSION Theatre Company | 32 |
| April 15, 2013 | John Gassner Memorial Playwriting Award | 34 |

May

May 1, 2013	Artist Trust	45
May 1, 2013	Bellagio Center Creative Arts Residencies	14
May 1, 2013	Dorland Mountain Arts Colony	15
May 1, 2013	Page 73 Productions	51
May 1, 2013	Weathervane Playhouse	29
May 15, 2013	Community Theatre Association of Michigan	31
May 15, 2013	Playwrights' Forum [MD]	143
May 21, 2013	Charleston Stage	65

June

June 1, 2013	Charles M. Getchell Award, SETC	30
June 1, 2013	Children's Theatre of Cincinnati [OH]	65
June 1, 2013	Christopher Brian Wolk Award	31
June 1, 2013	Firehouse Theatre Project's Festival of New American Plays	22
June 1, 2013	Jackie White Memorial Nat'l. Children's Play Writing Contest	33
June 1, 2013	MetLife Foundation's Nuestras Voces National Playwriting Com	36
June 1, 2013	Saskatchewan Writers Guild (SWG)	143
June 15, 2013	Charleston Stage	65
June 30, 2013	Hawthornden Retreat for Writers	15
June 30, 2013	IATI Theatre (Instituto Arte Teatral Internacional)	76
June 30, 2013	Lanesboro Residency Program Fellowships	16

July

July 1, 2013	Playwrights Gallery	132
July 15, 2013	New Dramatists	142
July 15, 2013	Norfolk Southern Foundation	51
July 30, 2013	TriArts at the Sharon Playhouse	106

August

August 1, 2013	Academy for New Musical Theatre (ANMT)	128
August 1, 2013	BMI Lehman Engel Musical Theatre Workshop	128
August 1, 2013	Dayton Playhouse FutureFest	21
August 1, 2013	Jewish Ensemble Theater Festival of New Plays	23
August 1, 2013	Looking Glass Theatre [NY]	81
August 15, 2013	Altos de Chavon	14
August 31, 2013	Marin Theater Company (MTC)	82
August 31, 2013	Ten Minute Musicals Project	42

September

| September 1, 2013 | Actors Collective | 57 |
| September 1, 2013 | American Association of Community Theatre (AACT) | 138 |

Submission Calendar

October

November

December

Index of Unsolicited Opportunities

Index of No Fee Opportunities

Index of Listings

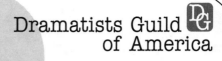

Dramatists Guild of America

Membership Application

I am a. . . (please check all that apply)

☐ Playwright　　☐ Composer　　☐ Lyricist　　☐ Librettist

Mr/Ms Dr/Mrs　First Name　　Middle　　Last Name

Pseudonym or Alternate Professional Name

Address (Street)

City/State/Zip or Postal Code

Country

Home Phone

Cell Phone

E-mail Address

Social Security Number　　Date of Birth

Agent/Agency Name

Agent/Agency Phone & Address

I have enclosed the appropriate support materials with my application

☐ **MEMBER:**
any one of the following:
1. a copy of a **review** or a **program** from a production of my work before a paying audience.
-or-
2. a copy of a published **script** by a legitimate widely-recognized publisher.

☐ **ASSOCIATE:**
any one of the following:
1. a copy of a **script**
-or-
2. a **program** from a reading or workshop of my work

☐ **FULL-TIME STUDENT DISCOUNT**
please submit the following:

a **letter** from my professor on Univ. letterhead.

GRADUATION DATE:

MO / DAY / YEAR

I qualify for the following level of membership (please check only one)

☐ Member $130/yr.　☐ Associate $90/yr.　☐ Student Discount
50% off either Associate or Member dues, depending on eligibility

RESIDENTS OF CANADA PLEASE ADD $10 TO MEMBERSHIP FEE. RESIDENTS OUTSIDE THE U.S. AND CANADA, PLEASE ADD $20 TO MEMBERSHIP FEE.

☐ Enclosed is my check made payable to Dramatists Guild of America, Inc.

☐ Please bill my credit card　☐ VISA　☐ MasterCard　☐ Discover Card　☐ AMEX

Account Number　　＿＿ / ＿＿＿ Exp. Date

Signature

Mail to: The Dramatists Guild of America; Attn: Membership Dept.; 1501 Broadway, suite 701; New York, NY 10036